The Application of Expert Systems in Libraries and Information Centres

The Application of Expert Systems in Libraries and Information Centres

Editor
Anne Morris

Bowker-Saur
London • Melbourne • Munich • New York

British Library Cataloguing in Publication Data
Application of expert systems in libraries and information centres.
I. Morris, Anne, *1950-*
025.00285633

ISBN 0 86291 276 8

Library of Congress Cataloguing-in-Publication Data
Application of expert systems in libraries and information centres / edited by Anne Morris.
p. cm.
Includes index.
ISBN 0-86291-276-8
1. Expert systems (Computer science) — Library applications. 2. Information technology. 3. Libraries — Automation. I. Morris, Anne, 1950- .
Z678.93.E93A66 1992
025.3'0285 — dc20

91-38751
CIP

Bowker-Saur is part of the Professional Division of Reed International Books

Cover design by Calverts Press
Typeset by SunSetters
Printed on acid free paper
Printed and bound in Great Britain by Antony Rowe Ltd, Chippenham, Wiltshire

About the contributors

Ralph Alberico

Ralph Alberico is currently head of the Undergraduate Library at the University of Texas at Austin. In addition to numerous articles, he is the author of *Microcomputers for the online searcher* (Meckler, 1987) and co-author of *Expert systems for reference and information retrieval* (Meckler, 1990). He is a contributing editor of the journal *Computers in Libraries* and serves on the editorial board of the electronic journal *PACS Review* (Public Access Computer Systems Review). Previous positions include serving as Head of Reference at James Madison University in Virginia and at Loyola University in New Orleans. He was educated at the State University of New York at Buffalo and at the University of Alabama.

Bill Black

Bill Black is Brother International Lecturer in Machine Translation at the Centre for Computational Linguistics, UMIST, Manchester. He studied Philosophy and Sociology, then Linguistics, at Leeds University, and before taking up his present post, he taught and researched in Computer Science at Teeside Polytechnic and UMIST. His current research includes work on robust human-machine dialogue in natural language and on automatic abstracting, supported by the CEC and the British Library.

Roy Davies

Roy Davies is the subject librarian for mathematics, computer science, operational research, and earth sciences at the University of Exeter. Previously he held professional posts at the Ministry of Defence and the Polytechnic of Wales. He has a BSc in chemistry and a postgraduate diploma in librarianship, both from the University of Strathclyde, and a postgraduate diploma in computer science from the Polytechnic of Wales. His publications include papers on the implications of AI for librarianship, qualitative data analysis, and the inference of novel hypotheses from the results of information retrieval.

Forbes Gibb

Forbes Gibb is currently Head of Department of Information Science at Strathclyde University. He is founding Editor of *Expert Systems for Information Management* and European Editor of *Online Review*. His research interests are concentrated on advanced techniques for text analysis, storage and retrieval, and the impact of telecommunications on business.

Anne Morris

Anne Morris is a lecturer in Information Processing in the Department of Information and Library Studies at Loughborough University. She has postgraduate degrees in ergonomics, information technology and mathematics and has written numerous articles on expert systems. Anne Morris is also co-author of *Human aspects of library automation* and co-editor of the *Directory of expert system tools.*

Alastair G. Smith

Alastair G. Smith is a lecturer in the Department of Library and Information Studies, Victoria University of Wellington, New Zealand where he specializes in information retrieval and in scientific and technical information work. He has a BSc in physics from the University of Auckland, gained a Diploma of the New Zealand Library School, and is an Associate member of the New Zealand Library Association. He has experience in patent information work, and held positions as a reference librarian and special librarian before helping establish two New Zealand online information services.

Gwyneth Tseng

Gwyneth Tseng is a Lecturer in the Department of Information and Library Studies at Loughborough University. After graduating in Physics she moved into academic library work and obtained a masters degree in Information Studies in 1976. Now her main teaching specialism is information retrieval. She has been professionally active and has published on a range of topics within the discipline of information and library studies, including a number of articles on online business database selection and use of expert systems.

Preface

The last decade has seen expert systems develop into one of the most successful fields of artificial intelligence. Commercial organiaztions on both sides of the Atlantic, have recognized he enormous potential of such systems and have forced the frontier of knowledge forward at a rapid pace. Expert systems, no longer confined to the research laboratory although still in an early evolutionary stage, have added a new dimension to information processing. In addition to executing complex computation, computers are now able to offer users advice and solve problems that would normally require human expertise.

Expert systems have been used very successfully in both industry and commerce, reputedly saving some companies millions of dollars a year. Against this background, it is not surprising that the library and information services (LIS) sector, traditionally at the forefront of computer technologies, has been researching, assessing and debating the likely impact of expert systems on the information professions in recent years.

The purpose of this book is to review the progress made so far in applying expert systems technology to library and information work. It is aimed at students, researchers and practitioners in the information or computing field who are keen to explore the potential of using expert systems in this area. No previous knowledge is assumed; a glossary of terms is provided for readers unfamiliar with expert systems jargon. Chapter 1 provides an overview of expert systems technology covering historical aspects and the link to its parent discipline – Artificial Intelligence, the characteristics and application of expert systems, and detailed guidance on the anatomy and development of such systems. Chapter 2 examines the use of expert systems technology to simplify online information retrieval. In particular, it looks at the functionality of intermediary systems, software which mediates between the searcher and remote online information retrieval systems, and gives selected examples which illustrate how expert systems technology has been used in their development. Chapter 3 focuses on the use of expert systems in reference work, describing models of the reference process and research that has been undertaken in this area. Chapter 4 looks at knowledge-based indexing and the need for new approaches to information storage and retrieval. The next Chapter examines the links between rule-based systems, natural language processing and abstracting. It is concerned with the linguistic aspects of the process of accessing sources of information, and with how rule-based techniques, such as those used in expert systems, can be used to facilitate the process. Chapter 6 reviews the progress made in applying expert systems technology to cataloguing. The final Chapter attempts to predict the impact of expert systems and AI on libraries over the next ten years. Five areas are considered: knowledge media, knowledge industries, knowledge institutions, modes of discourse and implications.

The editor and the publisher are pleased to receive suggestions and observations regarding this book's contents and usage.

Anne Morris

Contents

Chapter 1

Overview of expert systems

Anne Morris

1 Introduction

Expert systems are computer-based systems that use knowledge and reasoning techniques to solve problems that would normally require human expertise. Knowledge obtained from experts and from other sources such as textbooks, journal articles, manuals and databases is entered into the system in a coded form, which is then used by the system's inferencing and reasoning processes to offer advice on request. Expert systems belong to the broader discipline of artificial intelligence (AI) which has been defined by Barr and Feigenbaum (1981) as: 'the part of computer science that is concerned with designing intelligent computer systems, that is, systems that exhibit the characteristics we associate with intelligence in human behaviour – understanding language, learning, reasoning, solving problems, and so on'.

AI, as a separate discipline, started in the 1950s when it was recognized that computers were not just giant calculators, dealing with numbers, but logic machines that could process symbols, expressed as numbers, letters of the alphabet, or words in a language (Borko, 1985). Since then AI has grown rapidly and today encompasses not only expert systems but many different areas of research including natural language understanding, machine vision, robotics, automatic programming and intelligent computer-aided instruction.

The first expert systems, described in more detail later, were developed by researchers from the Heuristic Programming Project at Stanford University, California, led by Professor Feigenbaum. The success of these systems combined with the increase in computer processing power gave encouragement to other researchers and created a steady interest in the commercial sector. Most of this early work occurred in the USA. The Lighthill report of 1969, which was sceptical about the value of AI, effectively stopped all UK and government funding for work in this field during this period (Barrett and Beerel, 1988).

The turning point came in 1981, when the Japanese announced their plan to build a so-called 'fifth generation' computer having intelligence approaching that of a human being. It can be seen from Table 1.1 that such a computer would be a huge step forward, having natural language capabilities, and processing and reasoning capabilities far greater than machines available either then or now. To meet these objectives, the Japanese outlined an ambitious programme involving four main areas of investigation: man–machine interfaces; software engineering; very large-scale integrated circuits; and knowledge-based systems.

Overnight, AI and expert systems became of national importance. The US and European governments reacted defensively to prevent the Japanese dominating the information industries of the 1990s and beyond. Research programmes aimed at stimulating collaboration between industry and academic organizations and forcing technological pace were set up with great haste. The next year, 1982, saw the start of the Alvey programme administered by the UK Department of Industry, the ESPRIT programme (European Strategic Program for Research in Information Technology) funded by the European Community, and a major programme of research coordinated by the

Generation	*Dates*	*Component*	*Description*
1st	1945 – mid 1950s	Vacuum tubes	Big, slow unreliable computers
2nd	mid 1950s – 1965	Transistors	More reliable but still slow; used machine-level instructions
3rd	1965 – early 1970s	Integrated circuits	Quicker, smaller, more reliable; used 'high-level' languages
4th	early 1970s – present	Large/very large scale integrated circuits (LSI/VLSI)	Systems used today, speed, reliability & 'high-level' language facility much improved.
5th	?	Even larger scale integrated circuits? New materials?	Systems having natural language intelligent interfaces, based on new parallel architectures (known as non-Van Newman architectures) new memory organizations, new programming languages and new

Table 1.1 *Computer generations*

Microelectronics and Computer Technology Corporation (MCC) in the United States.

In the rush to gain advantage, many corporations invested huge sums of money in research and development projects. Expert system tools quickly became available and the number of courses and journals in expert systems mushroomed. Unfortunately the rapid growth fuelled exaggerated claims about the capabilities of expert systems. Not surprisingly, many of the projects in the early 1980s fell short of expectations. This led to a period of disillusionment and a sharp fall in the popularity of expert systems in about 1986, particularly in the USA. Fortunately, today a more realistic view of expert systems prevails. Most people now accept that an expert system cannot completely replace a human expert and that it is not a panacea for an organization's loss of human expertise or lack of investment in training.

1.1 Characteristic features of expert systems

Expert systems are different from conventional programs in many respects, for example:

1. Expert systems contain practical knowledge (facts and heuristics) obtained from at least one human expert and should perform at an expert's level of competence within a specialized area. Conventional programs do not try to emulate human experts.

2. The knowledge is coded and kept separate from the rest of the program in a part called the *knowledge base*. This permits easy refinement of the knowledge without recompilation of the control part of the program, which is often known as the inference engine. This arrangement also enables expert systems to be more easily updated, and thus improved, at a later date. It also means that the control and interface mechanisms of some systems can be used with different knowledge bases. Systems of this type are called expert system shells. With conventional programs, knowledge about the problem and control information would be intermixed, making improvement and later development more complicated.

3. Knowledge is represented with the use of symbols using techniques known as production rules, frames, semantic nets, logic, and more. This natural form of representation means that the knowledge base is easy to examine and modify. Conventional programs can only manipulate numerical or alphabetical (string) data, not symbols.

4. Expert systems attempt to generate the 'best' possible answer by exploring many solution paths. They do this using heuristic searching techniques which will be discussed later. Conventional programs are executed according to a predefined algorithm and have only one solution path.

5. Expert systems are able to offer explanations or justifications on demand. Since expert systems are typically interactive, they are capable of explaining how or why information is needed and how particular conclusions are reached. This can be provided in the middle or at the end of consultations. Information of this type is provided to boost the user's confidence in the system and is not generally provided with conventional programs.

6. Expert systems can occasionally make mistakes. This is not surprising, because the systems have to rely on human expertise and are designed to behave like human experts. However, they do have an advantage over conventional systems in that program code can be more easily changed when mistakes occur, and some expert systems have the ability to 'learn' from their errors.

7. Expert systems are able to handle incomplete information. When an expert system fails to find a fact from the knowledge base that is needed to derive a conclusion, it first asks the user for the information. If the information cannot be supplied then the system will try another line of reasoning. Obviously if too much information is missing, the system will be unable to solve the problem. Conventional programs would crash immediately if the data needed were unavailable.

8. Some expert systems are also able to handle uncertain information. Expert systems offering this facility require certainty factors, confidence factors, or probabilities to be associated with information. These are used to indicate the extent to which the expert believes the information is true. They are used during the inferencing process to express a degree of confidence in the conclusion reached. This type of approach is rarely, if ever, used in conventional programming.

1.2 Why are expert systems important?

The motivation for building expert systems must lie in the benefits obtained. This is particularly true in the commercial and industrial sectors, where the return from an expert system development would be expected to far exceed the costs incurred. What then are the possible benefits? These would depend on individual situations but the more general advantages are listed below:

1. Experts can be freed from routine tasks and made available for more exciting, creative and demanding work.

2. Expertise can be pooled when more than one expert contributes to the system development. The pooling exercise can assist in the refinement of procedures and help to make them more consistent.

3. Knowledge can be safeguarded, developed and distributed. Enormous sums of money are spent on training individuals, yet all their knowledge and expertise is lost when they die or leave the company. Expert systems offer a way of capturing this expertise and knowledge whilst at the same time making it available to other people.

4. Expertise can be available 24 hours a day. Since expert systems provide explanations for advice given, they can be used without the presence of the expert.

5. Expert systems can be used for training purposes. The problem-solving and explanation capabilities of expert systems are particularly useful in training situations. Training can also be distributed throughout a company and done on an individual basis at times suited to the employee.

6. Expert systems can provide a standardized approach to problem solving.

7. The development of an expert system offers the expert an opportunity to critically assess and improve his problem-solving behaviour.

8. The performance of non-experts can be improved over a period of time and may eventually even reach expert status.

9. In many situations, expert systems can provide solutions to problems far more quickly than a human expert.

10. Expert systems have the potential for saving companies a vast amount of money, thus increasing profits.

1.3 Applications of expert systems

The huge potential of expert systems has not gone unrecognized in academia, industry or commerce. The early systems, developed in the research environment, prepared the ground well for much bigger and better systems. Today the technology can boast a wide range of application areas, several of which are discussed below.

1.3.1 EARLY SYSTEMS

The first expert system to be developed was DENDRAL at Stanford University in the late 1960s (Lindsay *et al.*, 1980). DENDRAL is capable of determining the chemical structure of unknown compounds by analysing mass spectrometry data. DENDRAL has been successfully used by many chemists and has even resulted in the discovery of new chemical structures.

Following the success of DENDRAL, the same research team produced MYCIN. MYCIN is an expert system designed to deal with problems in the diagnosis and treatment of infectious blood diseases (Shortliffe, 1976). Work on the system continued until the 1980s, when tests showed that its performance compared favourably with that of physicians (Lenat and Brown, 1984). Several projects related to MYCIN were also completed at Stanford; these included a knowledge acquisition component called THEIRESIUS (Davis, 1982), NEOMYCIN and GUIDON tutorial type versions of MYCIN (Clancey, 1981; Bramer, 1982), PUFF (an aid to diagnosing pulmonary disease) and EMYCIN, an expert system shell.

Other notable early systems in the medical field include PIP (Pauker *et al.*, 1976) used to record the medical history of patients with oedema; INTERNIST-1/CADUCEUS (Pople, 1982) that attempts to diagnose internal diseases; and CASNET (Weiss *et al.*, 1978) developed to assist in the diagnosis and treatment of glaucoma.

Early commercial expert system projects include PROSPECTOR, (Gaschnig, 1982) a system that assists geologists in the discovery of mineral deposits, and RI, now enhanced and called X/CON, that is used by the Digital Equipment Corporation to configure VAX computers to customer specifications.

1.3.2 SOCIAL AND PUBLIC SECTOR APPLICATIONS

In recent years a number of researchers have applied expert systems technology to social applications. The systems produced have attempted to 'improve both the quality and quantity of advice and expertise available to the man in the street' (Smith, 1988). Examples include systems designed to:

- provide advice for expectant mothers about maternity rights
- offer advice on an employee's rights regarding dismissal

- provide information and advice about the maze of local authority housing grants and planning procedures
- provide guidance on the legislation and practice relating to social security benefits
- assist with car maintenance
- provide assistance with travel planning

A few of these types of expert systems are already available to the general public via local authority viewdata systems. One can imagine that in the near future such programs might also be available in public libraries, citizens advice bureaux and the like.

1.3.3 FINANCIAL APPLICATIONS

Many financial organizations, such as banks, insurance companies and finance houses, are now using expert systems to try to give them a competitive edge. Expert systems have been used for a wide variety of applications in this field including systems designed to:

- assess customer credit risk
- assess insurance premiums and risks involved
- give advice on investment, stock exchange regulations, tax and mortgages
- assess business insolvency
- assess insurance claims

Big stakes are involved in such systems. For example, it is estimated by the developers of the UNDERWRITING ADVISOR that the use of this system could save insurance companies whose annual commercial premiums average $250 million, a total of $35 million over a 5-year period (Wolfgram, Dear and Galbraith, 1987, p26).

1.3.4 INDUSTRIAL APPLICATIONS

A survey in 1988 showed that most large industrial and manufacturing companies in the UK had either introduced expert systems into their daily operations or were experimenting with the technology (O'Neill and Morris, 1989). Applications in this area include:

- fault diagnosis (e.g. from computer circuits to whole plants)
- control (trouble-shooting, air traffic control, production control etc.)
- design (machines, plants, circuits, etc.)
- military operations
- quality assurance

- design/construction planning
- software design
- planning of complex administrative procedures

Numerous applications can also be found in education. For a fuller account of applications the reader is referred to the numerous texts available on the topic (e.g. Waterman, 1986; Lindsey, 1988; Wolfgram, Dear and Galbraith, 1987; and Feigenbaum, McCorduck and Nii, 1988).

2 Components of an expert system

Conceptually expert systems have four basic components (Figure 1.1): the knowledge base, the interface, the inference mechanism or inference engine, and the global database.

2.1 Knowledge base

A knowledge base is the part of the program that contains the knowledge associated with a specific domain. It includes facts about objects (physical or conceptual entities), together with information about the relationships between them and a set of rules for solving problems in a given domain. The latter is derived from the heuristics, which com-

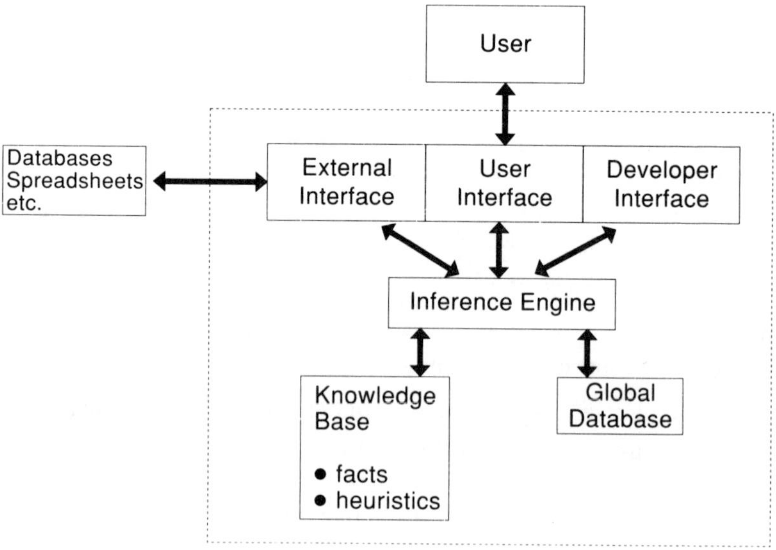

Figure 1.1 *Architecture of an idealized expert system*

prise judgements, intuition and experience, obtained from the expert(s). Sometimes the knowledge base also contains metarules, which are rules about rules, and other types of knowledge such as definitions, explanations, constraints and descriptions. Precisely what is incorporated, and the way the knowledge is represented will depend on the nature of the expert system. The techniques used are described in a later section.

2.2 Interface

The interface can be considered as having three main parts: the user interface, the developer's interface and an external interface.

The user interface is the section of the program which enables the user to communicate with the expert system. Most expert systems are interactive; they need users to input information about a particular situation before they can offer advice. The exceptions are where expert systems are used in closed-loop process control applications. In these cases the input and output of the expert system is via other machines. Such systems will not be considered in this book. Most of the existing user interfaces of expert systems are menu-driven, accepting single words or short phrases from the human user. A few have limited natural language capabilities, but much work still remains to be done in this area. A good user interface to an expert system will allow the user:

- to ask questions, such as why advice has been given, how a conclusion has been reached or why certain information is needed
- to volunteer information before being asked
- to change a previous answer
- to ask for context-sensitive help on demand
- to examine the state of reasoning at any time
- to save a session to disk for later perusal
- to resume a session previously abandoned mid-way

In addition to these characteristics, expert systems need to be easy to learn and use, and involve a minimal amount of typing by the user.

Most of today's integrated expert system tools will provide a developer's interface. This enables a knowledge engineer (the name for the developer), to build the knowledge base, test it and make modifications. Since this process is iterative and can involve many cycles, it is essential that the program offers user-friendly editing facilities and good diagnostic capabilities. Easy access to the user's interface for testing the system is also important. Morris (1987) discusses both the developer's and the user interface requirements in some detail.

The external interface is concerned with the exchange of data from sources other than the user, for example spreadsheet and database packages, data files, special programs, CD-ROM products or even online hosts. Early expert systems had very poor or non-existent external interfaces. The situation is now changing, however, as the demand for integrated computer systems becomes ever more important (O'Neill and Morris, 1989).

2.3 Inference mechanism

The inference mechanism is responsible for actually solving the problem posed by the user. It does this by using a set of algorithms or decision-making strategies to generate inferences from the facts and heuristics held in the knowledge base and/or information obtained from the user (Lachman, 1989). The algorithms also control the sequence in which inferences are generated, add newly inferred facts to the global database and, in some cases, process confidence levels when dealing with incomplete or uncertain data.

The main purpose of using algorithms is to find a solution to the problem posed as efficiently as possible. Problem-solving algorithms used in expert systems can be divided into three layers (Wolfgram, Dear and Galbraith, 1987):

1. General methods which are regarded as the building blocks of problem-solving techniques.
2. Control strategies which guide the direction and execution of the search.
3. Additional reasoning techniques which assist with modelling and searching for the solution path.

General search methods can be divided into two categories: blind searches and heuristic searches. Blind searches do not employ intelligent decision making in the search; the paths chosen are arbitrary. Examples of blind search techniques include *exhaustive*, where every possible path through a decision tree or network is analysed; *breadth-first*, where all the paths at the top of the hierarchy are examined before going on to the next level; and *depth-first*, where the search continues down through the levels along one path until either a solution has been found or it meets a dead end, in which case it has to backtrack to find the next possible path. Heuristic searches are more efficient than blind searches because they attempt to identify the pathways which will most likely lead to a solution. Examples of heuristic searches include hill-climbing, best-first, branch-and-bound, A^* algorithm and generate-and-test, details of which can be found in most books on AI (see, for example, Rich, 1983).

Control strategies, or reasoning strategies as they are sometimes called, are used to decide what operators to apply at each stage of the search. The most common control strategies used in expert systems are forward chaining, backward chaining and bi-directional. Forward chaining strategies start with the data and work forward to find a solution. In rule-based systems, the facts are matched with the antecedent, or the 'IF', part of the rules. If a match occurs the rule is fired and the consequent, or the 'THEN', part of the rules becomes the new fact. Chaining continues with user interaction, where necessary, until the solution is found. Backward chaining works in the opposite direction. In this case the process starts by identifying possible solutions. It then searches the knowledge base for relevant facts or requests information from users to either verify or disprove them in turn. In rule-based systems using backward chaining, facts are matched with the consequent part of the rules. Forward chaining and backward chaining strategies are also known as data-driven and goal-directed searching techniques, respectively, for obvious reasons. Bi-directional strategies use a combination of both forward and backward chaining to try to arrive at a solution more quickly.

Additional reasoning techniques are often incorporated into the inference engine to deal with uncertainty and anomalies between the facts and relationships in the knowledge base. The commonly used techniques are: Bayesian probabilities, the use of certainty factors, degrees of belief and measures based on fuzzy logic. All attempt to give the user some idea of the confidence he can place on the advice given. Another technique, which is becoming more popular, is blackboarding. This is often used when the knowledge required to solve a problem is segmented into several independent knowledge bases and/or databases. The blackboard acts as a global knowledge base, receiving and storing problem-solving knowledge from any of the independent sources. Further information on these and other control strategies can be found in Hayes-Roth (1984); Keller (1987); Graham (1989); and Harmon and Sawyer (1990).

2.4 Global database

The global database is the section of the program that keeps track of the problem by storing data such as the user's answers to questions, facts obtained from external sources, intermediate results of reasoning and any conclusions reached so far (Barrett and Beerel, 1988). It is really just a working store and is wiped clean after each session.

3 Knowledge acquisition and representation

One of the most difficult tasks facing expert system developers is 'knowledge acquisition' (Sowizral, 1985). Knowledge acquisition can be defined as the process which 'involves eliciting, analysing and interpreting the knowledge which a human expert uses when solving a particular problem, and then transforming this knowledge into a suitable machine representation' (Kidd, 1987). Knowledge acquisition can be extremely slow and costly as well as difficult, and justly earns the reputation of being the main bottleneck in the development of an expert system. To reduce the tedium and improve the effectiveness of knowledge acquisition, a variety of techniques has been developed. This section outlines these techniques and the common knowledge representation formalisms.

3.1 Knowledge acquisition techniques

Before using any of the techniques described below it is essential that knowledge engineers have thoroughly familiarized themselves with the problem or domain area. Grover (1983) suggests that knowledge engineers would be advised to produce something like a Domain Definition Handbook which might contain:

- a general description of the problem
- a bibliography of principal references
- a glossary of terminology
- identification of experts
- characterization of users
- definition of suitable measures of performance
- description of example reasoning scenarios

Armed with this background knowledge the developer can start the process of acquiring the expertise or private knowledge of the domain expert that stems from the accumulation of years, and sometimes decades, of practical experience. This includes:

- knowledge of concepts in the domain and the relationships between them
- the relative importance and validity of the concepts and relationships
- knowledge about routine procedures
- strategies for dealing with unexpected cases
- facts and heuristics (little known rules-of-thumb) used to make educated guesses when necessary and to deal with inconsistent or incomplete data
- classificatory knowledge which allows the expert to make fine distinctions among a number of similar items

Obviously this process can be omitted if the domain expert is also the knowledge engineer. There are pros and cons, however, to the expert being the knowledge engineer (O'Neill and Morris, 1989). The majority of books about knowledge acquisition warn against being 'one's own expert' because systems produced in this way can be provincial in effect and can contain idiosyncrasies.

The main techniques used in knowledge acquisition are: interviewing, protocol analysis, observation, and multidimensional techniques. These are discussed briefly below. For more detailed information, readers are referred to Hart (1986); Kidd (1988) Neale (1988); Diaper (1989); Neale and Morris (1989); and Boose and Gaines (1990).

3.1.1 INTERVIEWING

Interviewing is by far the most common method of knowledge acquisition (O'Neill and Morris, 1989). Interviews are particularly useful for acquiring basic knowledge about the problem domain such as concepts, general rules and control strategies. Apart from the first meeting with the expert, which is likely to be unstructured since the primary objective is to establish rapport, interviews should be focused with specific aims and objectives in mind. In focused interviews the knowledge engineer controls the direction of the interview by asking questions about selected topics. To help this process a number of questioning strategies have been developed. These include:

1. Distinction of goals. Experts are asked what evidence is necessary to distinguish between one goal (conclusion) and another.
2. Reclassification. Experts are asked to work backwards from goals and sub-goals by elaborating on the actions or decisions on which they are supported.
3. Dividing the domain. After dividing the domain into manageable chunks, the expert is given a set of facts (e.g. symptoms) and forward chains through successive sub-goals to reach the final goal (solution).
4. Systematic symptom-to-fault links. Here a list of all possible faults in a system and all possible symptoms are presented to the expert, who is asked which faults would produce which symptoms.
5. Critical incident. This involves the expert being asked to recall particularly memorable cases.
6. Forward scenario simulation. In this the expert describes in detail how he would solve hypothetical problems posed by the interviewer.

3.1.2 PROTOCOL ANALYSIS

Protocol analysis is a technique which attempts to record and analyse an expert's step-by step information processing and decision-making behaviour. It basically involves asking the expert to think aloud while solving a problem. All the verbalizations, which are tape recorded, are then transcribed into protocols and analysed for meaningful relationships. In some cases, where video tape has been used, a skilful knowledge engineer can also take into account body language and eye movement when analysing the importance of such relationships.

Protocol analysis has been successfully used in a number of domains but it does have a few shortcomings. Its major drawback is that it is extremely time consuming – this is particularly true of the transcription phase. Experts can also think faster than they talk, therefore any analysis will only be partial. For these reasons, protocol analysis is best followed up with other techniques such as interviewing.

3.1.3 OBSERVATION

Observation is similar to protocol analysis except that experts are not required to think aloud. Recordings consist of natural dialogue and, if video images have been taken, the expert in action. Some researchers have found it more effective than protocol analysis in the field of medical diagnosis (Cookson, Holman and Thompson, 1985; Fenn *et al.*, 1986), but it still has the same drawbacks: lengthy, time-consuming transcriptions containing repetitions, contradictions and inaudible mutterings. Observing an expert at work, however, can be a useful familiarization exercise at the beginning of a project. Rarely, if ever, can the technique be used alone.

3.1.4 MULTIDIMENSIONAL TECHNIQUES

The purpose of these techniques is to elicit structural criteria which are used by the expert to organize his concepts, and thus to form a representational 'map' of the domain, which is often difficult to put into words (Gammack, 1987). The most common technique used, particularly by academics, is card sorting. With card sorting, experts are asked to sort cards, each bearing the name of one concept, into groups according to any criteria they choose. This is repeated until the expert runs out of criteria. When analysed, the knowledge engineer should be able to formulate a conceptual map of the domain. This technique was successfully used by researchers when identifying how librarians chose between different sources of online information (Morris, Tseng and Newham, 1988). Two other techniques, multidimensional scaling and repertory grid, are similar in that they involve the experts comparing concepts to identify any differences between them. For discussion of these techniques, see, for example, Neale (1988).

3.2 Knowledge representation

Knowledge representation is concerned with how knowledge is organized and represented in the knowledge base. There are several methodologies available in AI but the five most common methods used in expert systems are as follows:

- production rules
- semantic networks
- frames
- predicate calculus
- hybrid of the above

By far the most popular method is production rules. This is particularly true in the case of microcomputer systems where, up until recently, lack of power has prevented the use of more complex and demanding representation techniques. The dependence on production rules is likely to change, however, as microcomputers become more powerful.

3.2.1 PRODUCTION RULES

Production rules are used to represent relationships in terms of English-like conditional statements. The basic conditional statement is of the form If-Then:

IF (condition)
THEN (action or conclusion)

which reads 'IF the condition is true THEN either the action should be taken or a conclusion has been reached'.

Production rules can be much more complicated, incorporating the operators 'and', 'or' and 'not' for example. To illustrate this, examine the rule below, which might feature in an expert system to advise library staff on whether to fine a member of staff for an overdue book.

IF user is staff
AND overdue letters>2
AND excuse is not plausible
AND staff member is not on library finance committee
AND staff member is not the librarian's spouse
THEN fine = days_overdue x 25p

AND advice is 'make them pay!'

The condition part of the rule, (before the THEN part), is also referred to as the antecedent, premise or left-hand side (LHS). Similarly the action part of the rule, (the THEN part) is also referred to as the consequent, conclusion, or right-hand side (RHS). Uncertainties can also be expressed in rules by attaching certainty factors to either the antecedent or the consequent part of the rule. Take for example the following simple rule:

IF distance in miles>2

AND weather is rainy CONFIDENCE 75

OR weather is windy CONFIDENCE 90

THEN transportation is car

In this case, if the user has to go more than two miles and he is at least 75% confident that it is raining, or at least 90% sure that it is windy, he is recommended to travel by car.

There are several advantages to rule-based systems:

1. Rules are easy to express and to understand.
2. The system is modular in design, in that rules can be added, deleted or changed without affecting the others.
3. Rules can represent procedural as well as descriptive knowledge.
4. Small rule-based systems are generally quick to develop.

The two main disadvantages of rule-based systems are:

1. They impose a very rigid structure, which makes it difficult to follow the flow of reasoning and to identify hierarchical levels within the problem area.
2. They are generally inefficient in execution because they are unable to make use of the more sophisticated reasoning strategies detailed in an earlier section.

3.2.2 SEMANTIC NETS

A semantic net, or semantic network, is a general structure used for representing descriptive knowledge. It is a graphical representation of the concepts and relationships existing in a particular domain. Concepts (or objects or events) are represented by nodes, and the relationships between them are represented by the links which span the nodes. The links are more commonly referred to as arcs, and have an arrow at one end to show the direction of the relationship (Figure 1.2).

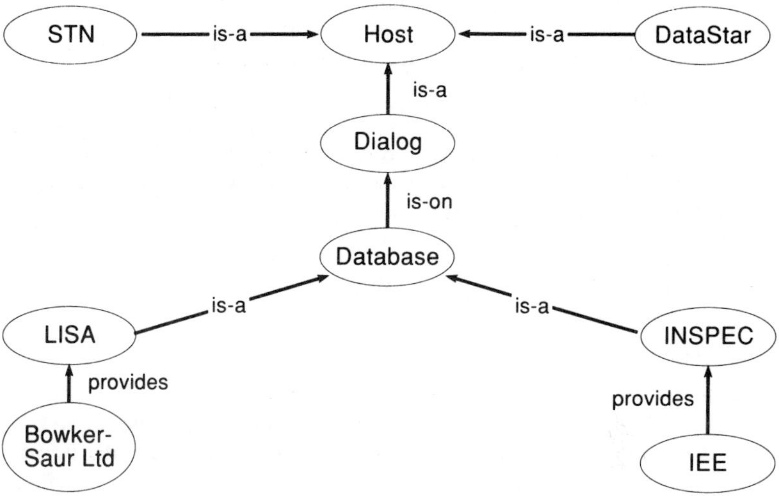

Figure 1.2 *A simple semantic network*

Many different types of relationships can be expressed in a semantic net, for example 'is-a', which means 'is an example of'; 'has' or 'has-a-value'; and 'is-used-by'. One concept may be linked to several other concepts, and two concepts may have several relationships. The relationships between objects may also be used to create inheritance hierarchies in the network. In these cases objects can inherit properties from other objects.

The main value of a semantic net is to provide the developer with a structural representation of a complex set of relationships. It is of little direct use to computers, however, since they cannot handle diagrams. To be of value, the semantic net has to be translated into 'triples', which represent links in the network. One triple, obtained from Figure 1.2 would be:

(Dialog) (is-a) (host)

Once in the computer, it may be possible to obtain a network form again, depending on the type of machine and the availability of graphics software.

The advantages of semantic nets are:

1. They provide a powerful representation of relationships between objects.

2. They are flexible – nodes and arcs can be easily added, deleted or modified.

3. They provide inheritance facilities which enable assertions to be made about the relationship between two objects, even when no arc exists between the two nodes.

The disadvantages of semantic nets include:

1. Procedural knowledge cannot be represented, therefore they invariably have to be used with some other representation method, usually production rules.

2. It is difficult to distinguish between an individual inheritance and a class of inheritance.

3.2.3 FRAMES

Frames were devised by Marvin Minsky (1975) as a way of representing both descriptive and procedural knowledge. Each frame represents an idea or object and contains data associated with it. The data, sometimes referred to as attributes, are held in 'slots' within each frame. Slots, which can be abstractly regarded as 'fields' in database terminology, may contain a variety of information such as default values, rules, value options, certainty values or pointers to other frames. The pointers give rise to inheritance capabilities. Frames can be linked together in this way to form a hierarchy, or even several interlinked hierarchies.

The reasoning process for frame representation involves trying to 'fill in the slots' and selecting the most likely frames that will result in a conclusion. Figure 1.3 shows what a hypothetical frame might look like in an expert system to advise users about which online database would meet their particular needs. In this case, 'Mega online database' would be offered to the user as a possibility, if he wanted up-to-date UK coverage on computing or electrical engineering. He could also be told that it was available on Dialog.

Mega online database	
Slots	Values
Hosts	Dialog, +
Information	Computing, Electrical engineering
Coverage	U.K.
Update frequency	Everyday
Sources covered	If needed, get from database-1

Figure 1.3 *An example of a frame*

The main advantages of frame representation are:

1. It is efficient, since the structure facilitates economical inferencing.
2. The knowledge base is concise.
3. Hierarchical relationships can be represented.

The disadvantages include:

1. The knowledge must be capable of being represented in 'chunks' to fit the frame format.
2. Few expert system tools for microcomputers provide frame facilities.

3.2.4 FIRST ORDER LOGIC

Logic has been used to represent knowledge and thought for centuries. It is also one of the most developed problem-solving techniques, having its own syntax and concise vocabulary. It is not surprising, therefore, that it has found a niche in expert systems development.

Over the years, different types of logic systems have been devised: propositional calculus, predicate calculus, first-order predicate calculus, and Horn clause logic. Propositional calculus can be used to verify whether a given proposition is true or false. Predicate calculus, which is an extension of propositional calculus, can also be used to represent relationships and general statements about objects or people. First-order predicate calculus is the logic system most often used in AI work and is described in more detail below. Horn clause logic is the logic system supported by PROLOG, an AI language which will be discussed later.

First-order predicate calculus comprises variables, predicates, connectives, qualifiers and functions. Variables represent objects, whereas predicates describe relationships between objects or make statements about them. Connectives, such as AND ($\wedge$ or &), OR ($\vee$), NOT ($\neg$), IMPLIES ($\rightarrow$) or EQUIVALENT ($\equiv$), are used when complex sentences are needed. Qualifiers are attached to variables and functions are used to determine values of objects, rather than just true or false. Below is a simple example to illustrate the logic.

$$\text{IS-A(x,author)} \equiv \text{writes(x,books)} \wedge \text{has-published (x,books)}$$

This is interpreted as x is an author if x writes books and x has had a book or books published. In this case 'x' is the variable and 'IS-A', 'writes', and 'has-published' are predicates. The logic will either return true or false.

The major advantages of first-order predicate logic are that it is easy to follow the statements once the rudiments of the system have been learnt, it is very precise, and it is modular, in that statements can be added, modified or deleted easily. The precise nature of the logic system can also be a disadvantage, since it is difficult to represent special cases or heuristic knowledge.

3.2.5 HYBRIDS

Hybrid representation schemes attempt to incorporate the best features of all the other methods. Typically the knowledge is represented by frames and production rules, with first-order predicate logic embedded to provide additional information about relationships. Expert system environments (see next section) usually have hybrid representation schemes.

In conclusion, it must be said that each of the methods have advantages and disadvantages and these have to be weighed up during the selection phase. Undoubtedly, the main consideration should be whether the knowledge representation scheme is capable of mimicking the real world application. Some knowledge is best expressed by a diagram or a drawing, whereas other knowledge may be better represented using general descriptive techniques. Either way, system development will be much faster if the knowledge representation method selected matches the expert's viewpoint.

4 Expert system tools

Three distinct types of software tools are available to aid ES development. These are:

- AI programming languages
- expert system shells
- knowledge engineering environments

4.1 AI programming languages

AI programming languages differ from conventional programming language such as BASIC, FORTRAN, C and COBOL in that they have facilities for symbol handling and dealing with dynamic data structures. The two most common AI languages are LISP and PROLOG.

LISP is a complicated language developed in 1958 by John McCarthy and much favoured by AI researchers in the USA (Barret and Beerel, 1988). A LISP program basically consists of a series of commands that manipulate symbols. The data structure is represented by lists (ordered sets of data items) which can be manipulated by mathematical functions, predicate logic and logical connectives.

Specialized features of LISP include powerful debugging facilities, the availability of both a compiler and an interpreter for program development, runtime checking, dynamic storage allocation enabling programs to be larger than they would otherwise be, and a macro capability allowing for easy extensions of the language (Wolfgram, Dear and Galbraith, 1987; Myers, 1986). Partly due to the macro capability and partly because of the need to accommodate different hardware, many versions of LISP are now available.

PROLOG, which stands for PROgramming in LOGic, was invented by Alain Colmerauer and colleagues in France in about 1970. Based on the concepts of formal predicate logic, PROLOG uses symbolic representations in the form of clauses to specify known facts about objects and the relationship between them. A PROLOG program thus consists of clauses or statements of facts and rules (Myers, 1986).

A fact can be of the form:

works (robert, anne)

which translated means Robert works for Anne. Note that this fact indicates the relationship between Robert and Anne.

A rule can be expressed in the form:

manager (x,y):- works (y,x)

where the expression ':-' substitutes for 'if'. In English this reads as follows: 'someone is the manager of an employee if the employee works for that someone'.

To interrogate a PROLOG program directly involves asking questions in a specific format. The question 'who is the manager of Robert?' would look as follows:

? - manager (x,robert)

The reply given by the system would be:

x = anne

Since it would be unrealistic to expect users of expert systems to interact in this way, expert systems written in PROLOG are usually front-ended, with a more user-friendly interface.

PROLOG is popular in Europe and Japan and its adherents believe it is easier to learn and use than LISP. Other advantages include its compactness (uses much less memory than LISP) and the fact that it can be more easily moved from one machine to another. LISP supporters, however, maintain that it is hard to write efficient programs in PROLOG because of the lack of supporting tools and utilities. Like LISP, PROLOG has many language derivations.

Two other AI languages are becoming more popular: OPS-S and POPLOG. OPS-S, which is used by DEC for their X/CON system, is a rule-based programming language which includes a complex forward-chaining inference engine, whereas POPLOG is a language which combines the features of both LISP and PROLOG.

4.2 Expert-system shells

Since learning AI languages can take months, many developers prefer to use expert-system shells. These are 'off the shelf' expert systems without a knowledge base. Once purchasers insert the knowledge of their choice, the shell responds as a complete expert system. Shells provide as a minimum the following:

- facilities for constructing the knowledge base (an English-like language far easier to learn than the AI languages, an editor, display and browsing facilities, rule validator and a debugging component)
- an inference engine
- an interface
- a global database

Some also provide graphic windowing facilities, spelling checkers and interfaces to traditional software tools such as word processing, spreadsheets and communication programs designed for use on personal computers.

Shells have been widely and successfully used in industry in the UK (O'Neill and Morris, 1989), their main advantage being that systems can be built quickly. Sometimes shells are used only to develop early prototypes to test out ideas. In other cases they form part of the delivery platform. Their popularity is in part due to their simplicity. Most of the commercial shells rely on the use of production rules to represent knowledge. A few do, however, also offer features such as frames and object-orientated programming. The inferencing techniques used vary from shell to shell; some offer forward chaining, others backward chaining and a few can do either. In the majority of cases, though, the inferencing facilities are rather unsophisticated in comparison to knowledge engineering environments (see below). Popular shells in the UK include CRYSTAL and LEONARDO.

CRYSTAL is a rule-based expert-system shell which also provides interfaces to other software and file formats, for example ASCII files, Lotus 1-2-3, and Symphony 2. CRYSTAL incorporates a screen painter, rule animator, rule interpreter, rule editor, query handling routines and approximately 100 functions. It is mainly menu-driven and very easy to use.

LEONARDO is a shell that provides both a rule-based and a frame-based knowledge representation scheme. It supports forward and backward chaining and a default mechanism which employs both. Also provided are a set of productivity toolkits – graphics, screen designer, interfaces to other software including Lotus, dBases, DataEase, Btrieve, and statistics and mathematics libraries. An extended version of LEONARDO also includes facilities for the management of uncertainty using either Bayesian or certainty factor models.

4.3 Knowledge engineering environments

Environments, also known as toolkits or hybrid tools, are much more sophisticated than expert-system shells. Until recently, environments were available only in LISP and ran only on LISP-configured machines. In practice this meant the need for large, expensive hardware, often workstations dedicated to symbolic processing. However, the market is now seeing the introduction of mid-size environments capable of running on PCs (Harmon, Maus and Morrissey, 1988).

Environments use object-orientated programming techniques. Such techniques require elements of each problem under investigation to be classified as objects which can then contain facts, if–then rules or pointers to other objects. Using this approach, systems containing several thousand rules can be built.

Environments are not for beginners, as a thorough knowledge of LISP is usually required. Once learnt, though, they can be extremely powerful. One of the main advantages is that they facilitate the development of complex, graphically orientated user interfaces. Two of the best known environments are KEE and Knowledge Craft.

KEE, which stands for Knowledge Engineering Environment, was developed by Intellicorp in the USA. It is an object-orientated environment which provides knowledge-representation tools, various reasoning strategies, and graphical interface facilities for both users and developers. Frames, called units, form the basis for the knowledge representation. Slots within the units contain the actual data, and facets associated with each slot describe the inheritance, value class, and any developer-defined attributes. Rules and procedures are also supported. Inference is carried out through inheritance, forward chaining, backward chaining, or a mixture of these three methods. A hypothetical reasoning capability called KEEworlds and an interactive graphics system called KEEpictures are also provided. KEE has been used for the development of a number of successful systems, but Intellicorp suggest that the most appropriate applications area is in manufacturing (Morris and Reed, 1989). KEE users need to be experienced LISP programmers.

Knowledge Craft is a product of the Carnegie Group, Pittsburgh, Pennsylvania, but is available through Carnegie (UK) Ltd. It provides an integrated set of tools for knowledge representation, reasoning and interfacing with end-users. It consists of a ‘set of integrated tools, including a schema-based representation language called CRL, functions for manipulating CRL knowledge bases, special-purpose languages for implementing reasoning and inferencing strategies, and a number of workbenches and interface tools to assist in the development of user applications' (Morris and Reed, 1989). Knowledge Craft has been used for a wide variety of applications.

4.4 Selection of expert system tools

Barrett and Beerel (1988) suggest that the following motto be adopted when selecting expert system tools: 'Use a shell if you can, an environment where you should, and an AI language when you must.'

Shells are the most cost-effective choice where applications can be developed by such tools. If finance is not a problem and an extensive expert system is required, then environments can provide the best support. AI languages can be used, if they must, for specialized developments where only limited funds are available. However, a large investment in time should be expected when programming from scratch.

Considerations when buying expert system tools include:

1. Hardware requirements. Can the tool run on existing computers or will special hardware be required?

2. Software requirements. Does the tool require additional software to run? Some environments, for example, require LISP to be resident.

3. Cost. Although cost should not be a primary factor for software consideration in many cases it is! When estimating total costs it is important to consider training and development support, maintenance and possible runtime-only system requirements.

4. Vendor suitability. Questions that need to be asked here are: Is the software supplier reliable, established and financially sound? Does he provide maintenance and good support? Are upgrades supplied free of charge? Can he supply a list of past applications and happy customers?

5. Power and capacity. Many expert system shells have imposed limits on the number of rules they can accommodate. It is important, therefore, to check this and the response time for large systems.

6. Interface capabilities. User-friendly interfaces are a must for both the developer and the eventual users of the system. Facilities to look for include editing flexibility and ease of use, consistency and appropriate use of menus and

pop-up windows, adequate message and prompt facilities, graphics capabilities, user-friendly help, how and why facilities, easy-to-use debugging facilities, and the ability to customize format screens.

7. Knowledge representation methods. Shells use a variety of different methods: rules, semantic networks, frames, object-orientated approaches etc. all with or without uncertainty facilities. Some representation methods suit some types of knowledge better than others. Consequently, this aspect will need to be addressed thoroughly before a tool is selected.

8. Inference and control methods. A number of inference and control methods exist. Again the preferred method depends on the application. Tools supporting forward chaining are generally better for applications involving forecasting and prediction, whereas for diagnosis-type applications, tools offering backward chaining are to be preferred.

There is no doubt that the selection of an expert system tool is a major task. The wrong selection can jeopardize the successful outcome of a project. Expert system developers faced with this task would find the *Directory of expert system tools* (Morris and Reed, 1989) helpful and some of the textbooks in the field, for example Barrett and Beerel, 1988 (Chapter 9); Harmon, Maus and Morrissey, 1988: Guida and Tasso, 1989, part 4; Patterson, 1990, Section 15.6 and Savory, 1990, Section 1.1. Software reviews in AI magazines and conference exhibitions can also yield useful information.

5 The development of expert systems

Early investigative expert systems work was characterized by the iterative prototyping approach, so much so that it has now been adopted as the norm. The prototyping approach is discussed by Luger and Stubblefield (1989) as a process in which 'expert systems are built by progressive approximations, with the program's mistakes leading to corrections or additions to the knowledge base.' Not all researchers agree with this type of approach, Bader *et al.*, (1988), for example, said 'development to date has been unstructured and sympathetically called incremental development or prototyping'. They argue for a more structured approach, which is gaining ground amongst developers. They believe that whilst the nature of expert systems work does require a degree of informality and a flexibility of approach, this can be achieved in a structured and coherent manner. Structured development techniques are reported to have several advantages:

1. They enable boundaries to be set, and prevent systems from 'growing like Topsy' and falling over under the weight of an amorphous mass of confused information.
2. They ensure cohesion and understanding between team members, and provide a framework for discussion between developers, funders, experts and users.
3. They enforce documentation. A great deal of experimental work is lost because it is not written down.
4. Documentation ensures that input from users, experts etc., can be formally recorded and used either in system development or for other valuable purposes.
5. Mistakes and errors are more easily identified and can be repaired as the system develops.
6. Maintenance and extension of the system at a later date is easier if a structured and documented methodology has been followed.
7. Transference of information and knowledge across sites in multisite teams is more coherent and effective.

Above all, a structured design methodology, which incorporates a general overview of the system development cycle and a separate schedule of each stage in that cycle, should ensure that the overall aims of the system are not lost in the minutiae of the constituent parts. Equally important is good overall management, the recognition that users should be involved throughout the project, and that human factors should be considered as an integral part of the system development cycle.

Several development methodologies have been described in the literature, many of which have been reviewed and analysed by Guida and Tasso (1989). All the expert systems methodologies reported are and divided into distinct phases, and the one described below, which is based on a method advocated by Guida and Tasso (1989) is no exception:

- Phase 1 – Feasibility study
- Phase 2 – Early prototype development
- Phase 3 – Full prototype development
- Phase 4 – Installation of the expert system
- Phase 5 – Operation and maintenance

5.1 Phase 1: Feasibility study

This phase, is, as the title suggests, concerned with establishing whether expert systems development is possible, appropriate and justified. Unfortunately, this stage is often rushed through in the hurry to get to grips with the 'real' work, or worse, completely omitted. Feasibility studies should precede any development work and should provide a forum for all those involved – experts, users, developers, funders – to get together to discuss their needs and interests, and decide how these can best be addressed.

Communication at this stage is vital, because misunderstandings here reverberate throughout the system development cycle. Discussions, therefore, should include analysis of the nature and scope of the problem and an assessment the various technologies which might be helpful in its solution – of which the expert systems is just one alternative. The five main aspects which the feasibility study should cover are:

1. The technical feasibility of the expert systems application. Obviously the current state of the art in expert systems technology is a factor here, but it should be borne in mind that expert systems development is only possible if the tasks are cognitive, easily understood and do not require common sense, and if genuine experts, who can articulate their methods and agree on solutions, actually exist. Waterman (1986) and Prerau (1989) also suggest that expert systems development is appropriate only when the task requires human expertise, has practical value, is of manageable size, and requires symbol manipulation and heuristic solutions.

2. The organizational impact. Of importance here are the organizational requirements associated with the introduction of the expert systems into the working environment.

3. The practical implementability. This aspect should focus on the availability of needed resources such as personnel, hardware, software and experts. Of vital importance is the availability of experts who have credibility and authority, time to offer to the project and good communication skills and who are cooperative and easy to work with.

4. The cost benefits. Expert systems development is only justified when the task solution has a high payoff or when human expertise is scarce, needed in many locations or in a hostile environment, or is being lost (Waterman, 1986). A thorough analysis, therefore, of both direct and indirect costs and benefits over time is required.

5. The environmental opportunity. The factors to consider here

are managerial support, user attitudes and involvement, funding availability, marketability, global corporate trends etc.

The outcome of this phase should be a detailed report covering all five aspects, the precise goals of the expert system, and a project plan. This report can then provide the basis for a managerial decision about whether to proceed with the system development.

5.2 Phase 2: Early prototype development

Developing and demonstrating a prototype early in the project life cycle has several advantages:

- it can assist with validating or refining some of the technical decisions made in Phase 1
- it can help in the knowledge acquisition process
- it can help stimulate experts
- it can help motivate and secure the support of managers
- it can be used to elicit users' needs and requirements and to obtain valuable feedback from potential users on the system's usefulness and general design, particularly with respect to interface specifications
- it can assist with decisions about the choice of software

Essentially, creating a prototype involves selecting a subsection of the problem domain; eliciting knowledge from the experts; selecting a suitable tool; coding and loading the knowledge into the system; and verifying and refining it. This is an iterative process and the cycle (apart from the selection of the subproblem area and possibly the tool) may be repeated several times before a satisfactory prototype is completed. The products of this phase should include documentation and a prototype which is large enough to be able to function convincingly.

5.3 Phase 3: Full prototype development

The main goal of this phase is to construct a laboratory-tested, fully operational, prototype expert system which meets the specifications as detailed in Phase 1 and revised in the light of Phase 2. Basically the building of this system follows the same iterative process as described in Phase 2, but on a much larger scale and degree of complexity. This system may, however, be completely different from the early prototype developed in Phase 2. In many cases it will not be possible to incrementally develop it from the early prototype. The development of this system will necessitate formal testing with realistic data samples obtained from users and experts to assess its validity and acceptability.

5.4 Phase 4: Installation of the expert system

This phase is concerned with installing the expert system in its new operational environment. Ideally the development and target (real) environment should be similar, or at least compatible in terms of hardware and software, so that the target system can be obtained through minimal incremental development of the full prototype. However, where this is not the case, some reimplementation of the full prototype may have to take place. This situation is likely if the expert system has to be installed in several sites each having different hardware and software. As soon as it is installed in the real operational environment, field testing and a complete evaluation should be carried out. Throughout this phase it should be remembered that users need to be supported. In addition to the provision of good manuals, they need moral encouragement and adequate training.

5.5 Phase 5: Operation and maintenance

This phase is concerned with the operation, maintenance and possible extension of the system in the target environment, and is therefore concerned with supporting its use, monitoring performance and correcting bugs and faults. Obviously all these functions should be maintained for the entire operational life of the expert system. Important criteria in assessing whether the expert system is successful include:

- correctness of conclusions
- user-friendliness of the interface
- quality of advice and applications
- speed of response
- user acceptance
- cost/benefits

6 Conclusions

The field of expert systems has come a long way since the late 1960s. Once the sole prerogative of academics, expert systems technology has now matured and entered the arena of industry and commerce, where it is receiving much acclaim (Feigenbaum, McCorduck and Nii, 1988). The last decade has seen many advances, not least in the development of more adequate expert systems tools; better interfaces for end-users, developers and to external programs; more efficient structured development procedures; improved knowledge-acquisition techniques; better knowledge-representation methods; and better system architectures and inference procedures. Improvements in hardware have also contributed to the advancement of the field. Such advancements are encouraging and are likely to continue in the foreseeable future, as much still remains to be done. The next decade will see yet further development in the areas mentioned above, as well as more emphasis on the provision of better explantation facilities; improved maintenance and validation procedures; improved natural language capabilities; the introduction of more non-rule-based systems and systems that have the ability to learn from themselves; and on more integrated expert systems, (expert systems embedded in other programs). These are undoubtedly exciting times for expert systems development and research. The future holds much promise and is discussed in considerably more detail in the last chapter of the book.

References

Bader, J.E. *et al.*, (1988) Practical engineering of knowledge-based systems. *Information and Software Technology*, 30 June 1988, 266-277

Barr, A. and Feigenbaum, E.A. (1981) *The handbook of artificial intelligence*, Vol. 1. Los Altos, California: Morgan Kaufmann

Barrett, M.L. and Beerel, A.C. (1988) *Expert systems in business, a practical approach.* Chichester: Ellis Horwood

Boose, J.M. and Gaines, B.R. (1990) *The foundations of knowledge acquisition.* London: Academic Press

Borko, H. (1985) Artificial intelligence and expert systems research, and their possible impact on information science education. *Education for Information*, **3**,(2), 103-144

Bramer, M.A. (1982) A survey and critical review of expert systems research. In *Introductory readings in expert systems*, D. Michie, ed. pp. 3-27. London: Gordon and Breach

Clancey, W.J. (1981) *Methodology for building an intelligent tutoring system.* Computer Science Department Report No. STAN-CS_81_894, Palo Alto, CA: Stanford University

Cookson, M.J., Holman, J.G. and Thompson, D.G. (1985) Knowledge acquisition for medical expert systems: a system for eliciting diagnostic decision-making histories. In: *Research and development in expert systems*, M.A. Bramer, ed. pp. 113-116. Cambridge: Cambridge University Press

Davis, R. (1982) Expert systems: where are we? and where do we go from here? *AI Magazine*, **3**,(2), 3-22

Diaper, D. (1989) ed. *Knowledge elicitation: principles, techniques and applications.* Chichester: Ellis Horwood

Feigenbaum, E., McCorduck, P. and Nii, H.P. (1988) *The rise of the expert company.* London: MacMillan

Fenn, J.A. *et al.*, (1986) An expert assistant for electromyography. *Biomedical Measurement Infomatics and Control*, **1**,(4), 210-214

Gammack, J.G. (1987) Formalising implicit domain structure. In: *Knowledge acquisition for engineering applications.* C.J. Pavelin and M.D. Wilson, eds. Rutherford Appleton Labroratory Report, 26-35, Didcot: Rutherford Appleton Laboratory

Gaschnig, J. (1982) Prospector: an expert system for mineral exploration. In *Introductory readings in expert systems*, D. Michie, ed. pp. 47-64. London: Gordon and Breach

Graham, I. (1989) Inside the inference engine. In: *Expert systems, principles and case studies*, 2nd edn, ed. R. Forsyth, pp. 57-82, London: Chapman and Hall

Grover, M.D. (1983) A pragmatic knowledge acquisition methodology. In *Proceedings of the Eighth International Joint Conference on Artificial Intelligence (IJCAI-83)*, Karlsruhe, West Germany, 1983, 436-438

Guida, G. and Tasso, C. (1989) Building expert systems: from lifecycle to development. In *Topics in expert system design*. G. Guida and C. Tasso eds. pp. 3-24, Oxford: North-Holland

Harmon, P., Maus, R., and Morrissey, W. (1988) *Expert systems, tools and applications.* Chichester: John Wiley and Sons

Harmon, P. and Sawyer, B. (1990) *Creating expert systems for business and industry.* London: John Wiley and Sons

Hart, A. (1986) *Knowledge acquisition for expert systems.* London: Kogan Page

Hayes-Roth, F. (1984) The knowledged-based expert system: a tutorial. *Computer*, **17**,(9), 11-28

Keller, R. (1987) *Expert system technology.* Englewood Cliffs, NJ: Yourdon Press

Kidd, A.L. (1987) *Knowledge acquisition for expert systems: a practical handbook.* New York: Plenum Press

Lachman, R. (1989) Expert systems: a cognitive science perspective. *Behaviour Research Methods, Instruments, & Computers*, **21**(2), 195-204

Lenat, D.B. and Brown, J.S. (1984) Why AM and Eurisko appear to work. *Artificial Intelligence*, **23**(3), 269-294.

Lindsay, R.K. *et al.*, (1980) *Applications of artificial intelligence for organic chemistry; the DENDRAL Project.* New York: McGraw Hill

Lindsay, S. (1988) *Practical applications of expert systems.* Wellesley, Massachusetts: QED Information Sciences.

Luger, G.F. and Stubblefield, W.A. (1989) *Artificial intelligence and the design of expert systems.* Redwood City, CA: The Benjamin/Cummings Publishing Company

Martin, J. and Oxman, S. (1988) *Building expert systems: a tutorial.* Englewood Cliffs, NJ: Prentice Hall

Minsky, M. (1975) A framework for representing knowledge. In: *The psychology of computer vision.* P.H. Winston ed. pp. 211-277 London: McGraw-Hill

Morris, A. (1987) Expert systems – interface insight. In: *People and Computers III*, D. Diaper and R. Winder eds. pp. 307-324, Cambridge: Cambridge University Press

Morris, A and Reed, A. (1989) *Directory of expert systems tools.* Oxford: Learned Information (Europe) Ltd

Morris, A., Tseng, G.M. and Newham, G. (1988) The selection of online databases and hosts – an expert approach. In: *Proceedings of 12th International Online Conference*, pp. 139-148. Oxford: Learned Information (Europe) Ltd

Myers, W. (1986) Introduction to expert systems. *IEEE Expert*, Spring, 100-109.

Neale, I.M. (1988) First generation expert systems: a review of knowledge acquisitions methodologies. *Knowledge Engineering Review*, **3**,(2), 105-145.

Neale, I.M. and Morris, A. (1989) Knowledge acquisition for expert systems: a brief review. *Expert Systems for Information Management*, **1**,(3), 178-192.

O'Neill, M and Morris A. (1989) Expert systems in the United Kingdom: an evaluation of development methodologies. *Expert Systems*, **6**,(2), 90-99

Patterson, D.W. (1990) *Introduction to artificial intelligence and expert systems.* Englewood Cliffs, NJ: Prentice-Hall

Pauker, S.G. *et al.*, (1976) Towards the simulation of clinical cognition. Taking a present illness by computer. *American Journal of Medicine*, **60**,(7), 981-986

Pople, H. (1982) Heuristic methods for imposing structure on ill-structured problems: the structuring of medical diagnostics. In *Proceedings of the 5th International Joint Conference on Artificial Intelligence (IJCAI)*, pp.1030-1037. Cambridge, MA: William Kaufmann

Prerau, D.S. (1989) Choosing an expert system domain. In *Topics in expert systems design*, G. Guida, and C. Tasso, eds. pp. 27-43. Oxford: North-Holland

Rich, E. (1983) *Artificial intelligence.* New York: McGraw Hill

Savory, S.E. (1990) *Expert systems for the professional.* Chichester: Ellis Horwood

Shortcliffe, E.H. (1976) *Computer-based medical consultations: MYCIN.* New York: Elsevier/North-Holland

Smith, P. (1988) *Expert system development in Prolog and Turbo-Prolog.* Wilmslow: Sigma Press

Sowizral, M.A. (1985) Expert systems. *Annual Review of Information Sciences and Technology (ARIST)*, **20**, 179-199

Waterman, D.A. (1986) *A guide to expert systems.* Wokingham: Addison-Wesley

Weiss, S.M. *et al.*, (1978) A model-based method for computer-aided medical decision making. *Artificial Intelligence*, **11**, 145-172

Wolfgram, D.D., Dear, T.J. and Galbraith, C.S. (1987) *Expert systems for the technical professional.* Chichester: John Wiley and Sons

Chapter 2

Knowledge-based indexing

Forbes Gibb

1 Introduction

The analysis of text in order to identify its essential subject matter is a fundamental component of the information science curriculum and of practitioners' day-to-day activities. The ability to match information needs with relevant information resources assumes that there are reliable and consistent mechanisms for representing, storing and retrieving the concepts expressed in a document. These representations (or document surrogates) have traditionally taken one of three forms:

- derived indexing terms
- assigned indexing terms
- abstracts

A *derived indexing term* is a subject representation which is based purely upon information which is manifest in the document (Foskett, 1982). No attempt is made to use external knowledge sources, such as authority lists of terms, or to introduce or collocate synonymous terms. The literary warrant is, therefore, document- and – by implication – collection-specific. Access to a document is achieved by matching the word types which are contained in a query statement with the stored indexing terms (though perhaps making allowances for variant forms). Derived indexing is extensively used in computerized information retrieval systems in the form of file inversion. In such systems, the indexing terms associated with a document tend to be atomic (i.e. single uncoordinated words) and occur in very large numbers.

An *assigned indexing term* is a subject representation based upon an analysis of the concepts contained within a document. Significant use is therefore made of knowledge sources outside the document, including subject specialism and authority lists of terms, in order to introduce or collocate synonymous terms and to ensure that a standard representation of the relevant subject matter is used. In addition, relationships between terms such as broader, narrower and related, may be exploited. The literary warrant is therefore much more extensive and is based upon consensus knowledge derived from many subject specialists and document collections. Retrieval can then be based upon matching the specific concepts (as opposed to the same word tokens) which appear in the query presented to the system with the stored indexing terms. This semantic linking assumes a much higher level of intellectual effort and domain knowledge, and has been predominantly the province of human indexers. In such systems the terms tend to be molecular (i.e. precoordinated) and occur in much smaller numbers. In practice, many information retrieval systems make use of both derived and assigned indexing terms to provide sufficient (though not necessarily efficient) retrieval routes.

Assigned indexing terms can also take the form of *classificators*, which represent a much higher conceptual level analysis of the 'aboutness' of a document. Although classification can be viewed as a special form of indexing, it is primarily used to arrange or collocate documents in a helpful order on the basis of similarity of subject matter, rather than to provide access points to specific texts. Classification is therefore concerned with the *grouping* of documents while other forms of indexing are principally involved with *describing* documents. To this extent classification can be viewed more conveniently as a process of assigning a document to a conceptual slot in a network of related subjects.

Abstracts (dealt with elsewhere within this volume) are also based on an analysis of the concepts contained in a document. They may, for example, be derived by identifying significant sentences, or created *de novo*. Although abstracts will not be considered specifically in this chapter, it is clear that some researchers view abstracting as a more general process of text condensation, in which the output may vary in form 'from a single concept... to selected parts of the original text' (Kuhlen, 1983).

The skills used to produce document surrogates based on the analysis of text clearly involve tasks which are recognized to be suitable for conversion to a knowledge-based approach:

- they involve considerable human expertise (i.e. it is a non-trivial task)
- they can use facts about, for instance, indexing systems
- they can use facts about how other documents have been analysed
- they can use rules on how, for instance, specific indexing systems should be used (e.g. synonym control, word order, form of entry etc.)

- they can use rules on how indexing of documents in general should proceed (identifying the focus of document, exhaustivity and specificity etc.)

These skills are an intriguing mix of public, proprietary, personal and common-sense knowledge (Boisot, 1987), each of which is characterized by differing degrees of codification and diffusion. Public knowledge, which is highly codified and diffused, is principally encountered within the indexing domain in the form of consensus-based publications such as classification schema, thesauri and subject heading lists. In addition, public knowledge includes indexing principles, such as degree of specificity, and conventions for arranging index entries. Proprietary knowledge, while showing similar degrees of codification, is normally restricted to a specific organization or other closed community. Examples include local indexing systems and subject heading lists; local conventions for the implementation of a general indexing system; local enhancements of a general indexing system; and precedent, in the form of existing index entries. The codification of local indexing principles does, of course, make them inherently diffusible, and several schema which have been developed to meet internal needs (Thesaurofacet, MeSH etc.) have subsequently moved into the public arena.

Personal knowledge, which has relatively low levels of codification and diffusion, is an important component of the indexing process, and one that is extremely difficult to capture in a knowledge-based system. It includes subject familiarity and related models of the problem domain; understanding of information-seeking behaviour; experience of using indexing tools; and knowledge of users and the needs of the community which is being served. While some of these aspects may be supported by limited documentation (for instance user profiles or aide-memoires), personal knowledge is essentially an internal, unarticulated resource which makes a major contribution to the differing performance characteristics of individual indexers. Common-sense knowledge is also largely uncodified, but has a shared social context which differentiates it from personal knowledge. A particular convention for arranging index entries may have to be made explicit; that an arrangement is needed in the first place is taken for granted.

Much of the knowledge used by indexers is therefore likely to be extremely difficult to capture, codify or generalize as it is often based on local conventions and precedent, perceptions of target audiences, interpretation of codes of practice, familiarity with the subject domain, and perceptions of the world in general. The problems of inter-indexer inconsistency would seem to support this view. It should be emphasized, therefore, that much of the research that is described in this chapter has drawn extensively on linguistic theories, rather than indexing theories, in an attempt to produce general purpose, domain-independent indexing tools.

2 The need for new approaches to information storage and retrieval

2.1 Limitations of current systems

Most current information storage and retrieval systems have been developed around core technologies that have altered little since the 1960s. Although there are a limited number of products which have incorporated novel features (for instance Status/IQ, TOPIC and Construe) the market consists primarily of systems which rely upon a marriage of convenience between Boolean search techniques and the inverted file. Such systems suffer from a number of well documented problems.

Boolean operators can be used to retrieve documents on the basis of logical relationships between sought terms, but are recognized to be poor at retrieving on the basis of syntactic or semantic relationships (see for instance Schwarz 1990; Mauldin *et al.*, 1987). Although the use of distance constraints (e.g. positional operators) can preserve some of the contextual information inherent in running text, there is still considerable potential for ambiguity and noise to affect the effectiveness of the retrieval process.

Inverted files, particularly in full-text systems, carry significant mass storage overheads and are expensive to maintain and update. Further, the indexes required to support retrieval are built from the original text with minimal editing: a stopword list containing high-frequency general-purpose or function words is the most sophisticated technique in general use. Although the elimination of stopwords can compress the text by 40-50% (Salton and McGill, 1983), the indexes will occupy typically a further 50-100% of the space needed to store the original text (Maller, 1980). In practice many of the terms stored in these indexes will never be used for retrieval purposes.

Post-coordination of uncontrolled vocabulary in full-text retrieval systems tends to result in much lower precision measures, a direct consequence of the limitations of Boolean operators. The use of pre-coordinated phrases, on the other hand, is a precision-oriented device (Salton, 1986; Fagan, 1987) which, when combined with the recall-oriented methodologies discussed below, should offer significant improvements in overall IR performance (Gibb and Smart, 1990a).

In a free text environment, the user must be able to identify every form of a word which is being sought (processing, processor, processes, processed etc.) in order to improve recall. More problematically, they are also faced with unexpected variants of word form – misspellings – which can form a significant percentage of index entries in databases where expediency has replaced quality control. The traditional approach has been to use suffix and prefix stripping or, more generally, truncation of word stems in order to retrieve as many words with a common root as possible. However, it is clear that the shorter and more common the stem is, the worse are the retrieval results (Ruge and Schwartz, 1988), and that suffixing need not lead to improved retrieval performance (Harman, 1987). The user must also anticipate all of the synonyms and abbreviations for each topic of interest (Krawczak *et al.*, 1987), resolve homonymic ambiguities (bear = an animal, a broker, a star, barley, an ill-bred fellow, or a pillow case) and must cater for multiple variations of word order (processing of text, text processor, a word processor for scientific text applications, etc).

Browsing is restricted to scrolling linearly through the index(es), retrieved records, or, in a limited number of cases, thesaural relationships. The user is therefore unable to navigate from one text to another on the basis of intellectual, logical, structural, functional, procedural or semantic links. Each text is viewed as an autonomous unit of information which should be evaluated and treated entirely separately from any other text.

Database developers who wish to enhance access through the use of controlled vocabulary find that the costs of maintaining such a vocabulary are high: ten full-time experts are required to maintain the National Library of Medicine's Medical Subject Headings list up to date. In addition, manual indexing of documents is recognized to be prone to inter-indexer inconsistency, and introduces an unnecessary delay in the communication process.

Users are expected to learn a synthetic retrieval language for each information retrieval system that they use and to be able to translate their information need into this language. As a result, up to five models of the problem domain may be in competition with each other, each of which employs (or is required to employ) one or more languages in order to express its view of the domain:

- the author's description (natural language)
- the indexing language (controlled language)
- the indexer's interpretation of document and indexing language (natural and controlled language)
- the intermediary's interpretation of the user's problem and expectations of how the solutions will be represented in the database (natural, controlled and artificial language)
- the end-user's information need (natural language)

The degree of overlap between these models will largely dictate the retrieval performance of the system. However, the degree to which these models actually overlap unassisted may be worryingly low. Indexers are trained to impose a degree of control and structure on the literature of a domain, yet inter-indexing inconsistency is known to be a problem (Sievert and Andrews, 1991). Outside this area of expertise, the lack of precision with which humans name objects is even more manifest: it has been found that random pairs of people use the same word for an object only 10-20% of the time (Furnas *et al.*, 1983). Vocabulary mismatch is therefore viewed as one of the major causes of low recall performance in information storage and retrieval systems (Furnas *et al.*, 1988). Increasing the overlap between these models and ensuring a closer fit between the conceptual elements of queries and documents, therefore, must be a prime objective of any information retrieval system.

From the perspective of the database manager, conventional information storage and retrieval systems can be seen to make significant demands on expensive resources (mass storage, processing, manpower etc.); from a user perspective they make significant demands on the user's ability to predict the structure of the domain within which he or she is trying to operate. These factors combine to produce systems which are less efficient and effective than desired.

2.2 Possible solutions to the information storage and retrieval problem

Approaches which have been advocated to solve the problems discussed above include the use of specialized computer architectures, hypertext, automatic indexing (based on statistical and/or probabilistic techniques), and expert system and related knowledge-based technologies. With increased reliance on the electronic generation and dissemination of documents it is likely that gigabytes, and even terabytes, of text will need to be analysed by organizations, making traditional database applications pale into insignificance. The scale of the problem has therefore brought information retrieval research out of the academic laboratory and into the commercial sector.

The raw processing power offered by parallel and related specialized computer architectures makes them an extremely attractive delivery platform for large-scale applications. A number of these specialized computer architectures (e.g. MPP, HSTS, DAP, CAFS, Memex and the Connection Machine) have already been successfully applied to text retrieval problems and have been shown to offer improved precision/recall performance. In the case of the Connection Machine (Waltz, 1987), it has also been shown that a retrieval system can have a flexible and responsive retrieval mechanism, so much so that the Connection Machine has been implemented by at least one major commercial database host. However, such systems currently suffer from a number of practical disadvantages which make them less attractive to system developers:

- they are still extremely expensive
- they require specialized technical skills for development purposes
- they are designed to be back-end processors for mainframes
- they are not off-the-shelf solutions
- software is limited

However, as the cost/performance ratio improves, it can be expected that specialist architectures will increasingly move into the mainstream of information retrieval systems development.

Hypertext is a technology which has caught the imagination of information scientists and authors alike. However, as with the first phase of expert systems, it has probably been oversold as a solution to all information production and retrieval problems. It has been shown to be effective in assisting users who have ill-defined information needs, or wish to discover information, but is generally less successful for goal-oriented searches. This is a direct result of the fact that hypertext research has concentrated on the preservation and creation of the explicit intellectual and structural links between text units which facilitate browsing. Despite observations concerning the potential of document surrogates for creating hypertext links (Reimer and Hahn, 1988), the indexing of text units has been generally ignored or conveniently overlooked by hypertext developers. In addition, hypertext poses major challenges for the authors of hyperdocuments: the cognitive style of users will vary significantly from one to the next, and studies of styles of reading indicate that the retrieval of information from a text is a poorly understood process (McKnight *et al.*, 1989). On its own, therefore, hypertext is unlikely to be an instant panacea to information handling problems.

The search for reliable methods of automatic indexing has occupied the hearts and minds of information scientists for almost 40 years. The start of this quest can be traced to the late 1950s, when Luhn began to apply computing power to text, as opposed to data, processing. Luhn proposed that 'the frequency of word occurrence in an article furnishes a useful measurement of word significance' (Luhn, 1957), and in so doing established the use of statistical information for the automatic analysis of text and set information science off on a multi-million dollar trail of research effort.

Luhn conjectured that words which appeared very frequently were likely to be function words and therefore unsuitable for representing the subject matter of a document. This hypothesis was based on earlier work carried out by Zipf (Zipf, 1949) which identified a 'principle of least effort' in the use of language: a writer will tend to repeat words rather than employ new ones, and the most frequent words will tend to be short, function words (such as 'in', 'the', 'it' etc.) which cost the least effort to use. He further conjectured that words which appeared very infrequently indicated concepts which were dealt with in a superficial fashion and were therefore unlikely to represent the core subject matter of a document. The remaining middle-frequency words were then deemed to be suitable as index terms for the document.

Luhn's work was arguably crude but highlighted two important issues which underpin current research. Firstly, he demonstrated that it is possible to express indexing procedures in the form of rules (albeit derived empirically rather than from a human expert):

IF frequency of word <= upper threshold

AND frequency of word >= lower threshold

THEN use word as index term

Secondly, he recognized that rules employing raw statistical information are unlikely to be domain-independent: for instance, the thresholds used in the above rule have to be re-established empirically when the indexing system is moved from one problem or subject domain to another.

Automatic indexing, based on statistical or probabilistic techniques, has been a focus of research interest since the 1950s but has still to find wide-scale commercial acceptance; the window of improvement appears to have been too small to justify the shift from a proven (if limited) method for information storage and retrieval. Moreover, it is now generally recognized that statistical techniques of text analysis have reached their limit of effectiveness and that new approaches must be adopted if significant improvements in retrieval performance are to be achieved (Salton and Smith, 1989).

If specialized architectures, hypertext and statistical techniques do not individually offer salvation, what then is the solution? This author would argue that the road to improving information storage and retrieval lies in the integration of several technologies, and that the most important of these are those which exploit knowledge-based techniques. If the quality of indexing can be improved by adopting knowledge-based techniques, and the same tools are used to analyse the text *and* queries, then it will be possible to increase the overlap between the models which currently compete – but which should cooperate – in the storage and retrieval process (Gibb and Smart, 1990b). As technology costs drop, the raw processing power offered by specialized architectures, combined with sophisticated knowledge-based indexing systems and hypertext/hypermedia technologies, should hold the key to many document and record management problems.

The review that follows concentrates on the state of research into the automatic knowledge-based indexing of documents, but it should be noted that research is also being undertaken into computer-assisted indexing. The MedIndex system (Humphrey, 1987; 1989) assists indexers to select the most appropriate indexing terms from MeSH, the National Library of Medicine's computerized thesaurus. The system provides prescriptive aids, such as enforcing the rule of specificity which is common to most manual indexing systems, as well as suggestive aids, such as prompting users to fill slots in the frame structures.

3 A generalized architecture for knowledge-based indexing

While an analysis of the literature on research into knowledge-based indexing techniques reveals considerable differences in implementation methodologies, there appears to be wide consensus on the knowledge sources, rule sets and processes that are necessary to build effective systems. This section therefore discusses the generalized architecture for knowledge-based indexing shown in Figure 2.1, and highlights some of the different approaches adopted by specific system designers. The architecture is shown as a phased, or hierarchic, system as this is the predominant structure adopted by research teams. This is primarily a reflection of the fact that there has been only limited implementation of operational systems beyond the morphosyntactic analysis phases. However, cascaded structures, with greater facility for interaction between the separate phases, have also been proposed (Hahn, 1987) and may become more widely used as semantic and pragmatic knowledge is exploited to a greater extent. It should also be noted that the principles discussed below for the analysis of full text can be applied to bibliographic databases as well as those containing the full text of documents (see for instance Chafetz and Mikolajuk, 1989; Mikolajuk and Chafetz, 1989).

3.1 System goals

Within the mainstream indexing community there has been a well established practice of expressing concepts as nouns wherever possible, and rules have been developed to assist in the choice of singular or plural forms (Foskett, 1982). PRECIS, arguably the most advanced intellectually applied indexing system, '...consistently chooses nouns or noun phrases as indexing terms' (Austin, 1984).

Equally, within the automated indexing community there is wide

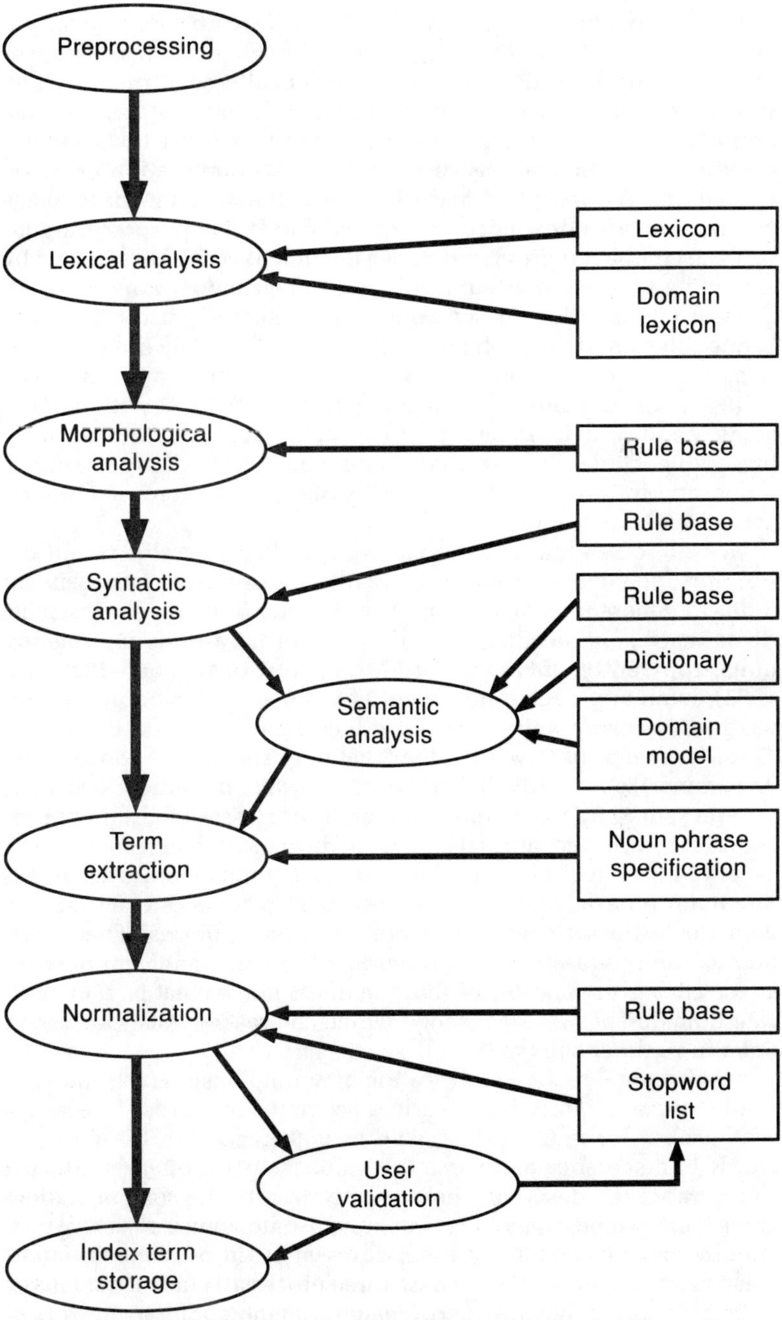

Figure 2.1 *Generalized architecture for knowledge-based indexing*

consensus that the noun phrase should be the main source of output for a knowledge-based indexing system, though there are differences of opinion on how this output should be filtered, structured and stored. The noun phrase has been consistently proposed as the most important text unit for generating descriptors for a text, and for avoiding the problems associated with post-coordination of single word terms. A description of FASIT, one of the first systems to incorporate syntactic knowledge for automatic indexing purposes, argues that '...a compact representation of a document could be achieved by extracting and grouping subject indicators, primarily noun phrases, using a combination of semantic and syntactic criteria' and that '...one solution to the problem of ambiguity of single word combinations is the use of longer units of text' (Dillon and Gray, 1983). The ability to identify and uniquely interpret noun phrases within documents should, it is argued, improve both precision and recall by preserving context, recognizing and conflating different surface forms, and introducing the possibility of synonym control (Gay and Croft, 1990).

Not all noun phrases, however, may in themselves be useful descriptors for a text: they may require filtering or further processing in order to generate suitable subject indicators. Rouault, for instance, states that '...one needn't take all the noun phrases as information units; apparently, only main THEMES...must be retained' (Rouault, 1985), in an approach reminiscent of Luhn's discussion of the conventions used by authors to introduce new topics (Luhn, 1957). These conventions can include verbal cues such as 'in conclusion', 'to summarize', etc. (Black and Johnson, 1988); document structure, as represented by paragraph boundaries; or classes of noun phrases. For example, a recent analysis of medical texts confirms that the generally used technique for introducing a topic is to use an indefinite noun phrase (Hein, 1989). Subsequent references to a topic are then made through definite anaphoric noun phrases. These anaphoric noun phrases are also important clues to what Hein refers to as the *background profile* of the area of discourse: that is, they indicate domain-specific knowledge which the reader must possess in order to comprehend the text.

Fundamental to the identification of noun phrases is the ability to resolve the ambiguity inherent in a sequence of words (typically a sentence). A system must be able to both recognize the forms of words in a sentence and parse the sequence of words to produce a structure which describes their organization in the sentence. More ambitious systems may even attempt to understand that sentence (and hence any constituent noun phrases) based on some notion of meaning (Winograd, 1983). These three processes require the system to be able to resolve any, and ideally all, ambiguous features contained within a sequence of words. Ambiguity is generally divided into two main classes – lexical and structural (Winograd, 1983; Copestake and Jones, 1990) – but many subclasses of specific types of ambiguity (ellipsis, conjoined forms etc.) can also be defined. The discussion that follows concentrates on the problems associated with four of these subclasses and how they impact on the functionality that may be demanded of a knowledge-based indexing system:

- morphological ambiguity (e.g. is the word 'bear' a verb or a noun?)
- syntactic ambiguity (e.g. is the word 'bear' an object or a subject?)
- semantic ambiguity (e.g. is the word 'bear' an animal or a form of barley?)
- unresolvable ambiguity (e.g. 'he shot the man with the gun' – did the man who was shot have a gun?)

3.2 Preprocessing of text

The input to the system must, by implication, be in electronic form. Although this part of the system lies outside of the indexing processes proper, it should be noted that knowledge-based principles may need to be developed in order to ensure that this input is in an acceptable form for processing. Documents will either be in machine-readable form or will need to be converted.

Machine-readable documents are likely to fall into one of three main types: simple ASCII files; application-specific files using a proprietary mark-up language; and files conforming to a standardized mark-up language such as SGML, FORMEX or ODA. It should prove relatively easy to translate proprietary mark-up languages to standard ones and thus ensure that non-lexical information can be exploited. ASCII files, on the other hand, will form the output from scanners and exported documents from applications and will have no marked-up document structure, which may result in problems of interpretation of running text. It will be necessary to develop an interpreter which has the ability to identify implicit document structure and automatically tag logical units of text. Typographical conventions such as italics will also be lost, making it impossible to differentiate, for instance, between exemplars in a sentence and the text referring to those exemplars. This will cause problems for the indexing engine and – unless developers can translate and preserve the codes used to indicate typographical element – will introduce an undesirable element of noise into the system.

If the document is not in electronic form it will need to be either keyed or scanned into the system. Although scanning technologies have improved substantially they may require considerable human intervention to resolve problems, to teach the relevant software to recognize new fonts or difficult characters, or to differentiate between text and non-text components. Where gigabytes of text are concerned, the level of human intervention can easily become non-justifiable. Ongoing research into knowledge-based techniques for recognizing text and non-text components should ensure that integrated, end-to-end document management systems can be built.

The result of these manual or automated processes should be a clean (i.e. without non-text items) file containing mark-up codes indicating its logical structure, its relationship to graphical, tabular or other non-text material extracted from the source file, and its relationship to other files of text in the database. The need for mark-up codes is becoming increasingly important: there is widespread agreement that text analysis should be carried out at the level of paragraphs and sections in order to take context, conceptual/logical structure (Fox, 1987) and text coherence (Hahn, 1989) into account. This is based on the assumption that a document consists of logical and/or semantic chunks which have been chosen by the author in order to facilitate communications and provide contextual links. More specifically, it is known that changes of topic or focus occur predominantly at paragraph or section boundaries (Reimer and Hahn, 1988). The conventional view of a whole document as the working unit for indexing purposes should therefore be abandoned. Instead, analysis should take place at a much lower level of document structure. SIMPR, for example, manipulates a document in units referred to as texts (Gibb and Smart, 1990c). Each text is defined as a heading and the paragraphs that follow it up to, but not including, the next heading. A group of related texts forms a textset. By dealing with documents in smaller units which generally focus on more specific topics, there can be a higher confidence that features such as anaphoras and semantic ambiguity can be controlled, and that descriptors can be built into complex thematic units (Reimer and Hahn, 1988).

The relationships between texts have been normally restricted to membership of a parent document. For instance, heading hierarchies (Gibb and Smart, 1990d) can be generated which organize the texts in a document into a tree structure which corresponds to the contents table of a book. At retrieval time the user can use the heading hierarchy as a browsing tool or as a search refiner. However, the lure of hypertext has prompted several investigations into the generation of automatic links based not only on explicit hierarchic document structure but also on similarity of content (e.g. Bernstein, 1990). The use of automatically derived indexing terms to provide bridges between texts which are semantically close should help to eliminate a major bottleneck in the production of large-scale hypertexts.

3.3 Lexical analysis

The preprocessed text must then be matched against a lexicon(s) in order to identify those words which are not recognized by the system. Early research into natural language processing tended to use lexicons which were extremely small and generally quite specialized (Slator, 1989). However, more recent research has focused on the building of large, general-purpose lexicons. This is a non-trivial task but is essential if reliable parsing of text is to be achieved. The lexicon will usually be built from two resources: machine-readable dictionaries and corpora of natural language texts (Amsler, 1989; Karlsson *et al.*, 1990). As an example, the RUCL ENGTWOL master lexicon was built using the Brown Corpus, the Lancaster Oslo Bergen corpus, the Longman Dictionary of Contemporary English (LDOCE) and the Grolier Encyclopaedia. These electronic sources contained approximately 3 million word forms from which a lexicon of 52 000 entries was built. The entries can be divided into word forms which belong to closed and open classes. Closed word classes contain a fixed set of members and additions are either very rare or non-existent. Closed classes include prepositions, conjunctions and pronouns, and all their members will be included in the lexicon. Open classes, on the other hand, are constantly being added to as language evolves to cater for new concepts. The open classes include adjectives, verbs, adverbs and nouns. Some of these classes (e.g. verbs) are more stable than others and it is relatively easy to specify a general-purpose list of members. Others, such as nouns, grow very rapidly and are often domain-specific in their usage. As a consequence they are much more difficult to list comprehensively.

A general-purpose lexicon, therefore, will need to be augmented when it is used within a specific subject domain. This can be achieved by simply adding new words to the master lexicon or, more flexibly, complementing the master lexicon with domain-specific lexicons. This is partly a result of the fact that dictionaries and lexicons are inherently historic knowledge bases and that language develops faster than consensus can be achieved on the role and meaning of particular words. This genesis and gradual acceptance of terminology is, of course, even more problematic for systems which depend upon controlled vocabularies for document descriptors. It is also a consequence of the high incidence of proper names, abbreviations and usages which are specific to a particular literature. Amsler's work on newswires revealed that 64% of the words encountered were not in the Merriam-Webster Seventh Collegiate dictionary. Of these, 25% were proper names, 25% were inflected forms, 16% were hyphenated forms, 8% were misspellings, and 25% were new words (Amsler, 1989). Any lexicon, therefore, must be supported by tools for manually or automatically acquiring new knowledge.

Manual updating of lexicons is the most common method of dealing with new words and this can be achieved using a relatively simple decision tree. Fortunately, the number of irregular forms is a stable closed class and any new words will have regular, predictable, and hence easily generated, endings. In addition most of these words will be nouns and related forms (abbreviations and proper names). However, in the early stages of processing a large body of texts within a domain, when the novelty ratio will be high, this dialogue between the system and the user can be extremely time-consuming. The number of new words encountered can then be expected to decrease as the number of texts processed and lexical entries generated grow. Recent research (Zernik, 1989; Jacob and Zernik, 1981) has demonstrated that it is also possible to automatically classify a new word using a corpus of syntactically analysed sentences and a set of existing lexical categories, and that predictions can also be made about syntactic and semantic features.

The recognition of new lexical entries need not be restricted to a single continuous sequence of alphabetical characters: it is equally important to be able to recognize nominal compounds within particular domains. Lexinet, a lexicon management tool for large textual databases (Chartron, 1989), uses statistical and combinatorial algorithms to identify and generate compound terms which are presented to experts developing a controlled vocabulary for that domain. The approach is entirely corpus-based and has a reported success rate of 45% for compound terms and 38% for uniterms. Work at the Research Unit for Computational Linguistics at Helsinki (Vitoulainen, 1990 pers. comm.) and at Bellcore (Amsler, 1989) has also shown that domain-specific compounds can be generated for inclusion in a domain lexicon once morphosyntactic ambiguity has been resolved. The identification of compound terms is of particular relevance to the editors of controlled vocabularies, such as thesauri, where precoordination is a significant factor in improving retrieval precision.

3.4 Morphosyntactic analysis

Once the words in a text have been recognized in, or added to, the system lexicon(s) they can be passed to the modules responsible for parsing. Parsing consists of two main functions:

- morphological analysis (including clause boundary determination and morphological disambiguation)
- syntactic analysis (including syntactic function assignment and disambiguation)

Some systems collapse the activities of morphological and syntactic analysis into a single integrated process, but for the purposes of this review they will be considered as discrete, interrelated phases.

3.4.1 MORPHOLOGICAL ANALYSIS

The information input to a morphological analyser will vary from system to system, but will normally consist of all the possible morphological (and possibly syntactic) forms stored in the lexicon for a particular word. For instance, the word *train* could have any of the following interpretations:

Noun – singular

Verb – first/second person present tense (I/we/you train)
– first/second person future tense (I/we/you will train)
– first/second person present subjunctive tense (I/we/you might train)
– infinitive (to train)
– imperative (train the dog)

The objective of the system must now be to disambiguate these analyses by either directly selecting a correct interpretation or by eliminating the incorrect one(s). The selection of a unique interpretation may, of course, be impossible due to ambiguity in either the word sequence or the grammar itself. Some systems therefore force a word into a class using statistical and probabilistic methods, while others may generate more than one interpretation.

The use of a constraint grammar (CG) to eliminate unwanted interpretations has been shown to be highly successful (Karlsson *et al.*, 1990). This is based on the maxim that 'having eliminated the impossible, whatever remains, however improbable, must be the truth' (Doyle, 1890) and does not carry the risks associated with conventional statistical or probabilistic approaches. The constraints are expressed as quadruples consisting of domain, operator, target and context conditions (Karetnyk *et al.*, 1991). The *domain* indicates an element to be disambiguated, for example, the reading(s) of a particular word form, while the *target* defines the reading that the constraint is about. The target may refer to a single reading, such as 'V PRES', or to all of the members of a declared set of grammatical features, such as VFIN. These sets consist of a set name followed by the elements in that set, e.g.:

(DET 'DET')
(VFIN 'V PRES' 'V PAST' 'V IMP' 'V SUBJUNCTIVE')

The *operator* defines the operation to be performed on the reading(s). There are three disambiguation operators which will discard or retain target or non-target readings, depending on whether the context conditions are met. The *context* conditions are expressed as triples consisting of polarity (which may be either negative or positive), position (which allows the context conditions to be defined relative to the position of the target reading), and set (which is a set name as described above). For example, the quadruple:

(@w=0 "PREP" (-1 DET))

states that if a word (@w) has a reading with the feature "PREP" then the reading is discarded (=0) iff the preceding word (i.e. the word in position -1) has a reading with feature "DET".

The CG shows a number of advantages over existing parsers. Firstly, the constraints have been developed from an extensive analysis of large text corpora and each constraint therefore embodies a true statement about the rules of grammar. Secondly, an interpretation is *always* produced for a word. Thirdly, if the interpretation is ambiguous there is a near certainty that the correct interpretation is contained in the analysis. Fourthly, a developer can control the degree of risk that is embodied in the constraints in order to respond to specific system goals and objectives. Finally, as a result of the corpus-based approach taken during development, the CG is domain-independent and highly robust; it can, for example, interpret units of text which are not at the sentence level, such as section headings.

3.4.2 SYNTACTIC ANALYSIS

The input to the syntactic analysis phase will be text which has been partially or completely disambiguated at a morphological level. Systems which preserve unresolvable ambiguities rather than forcing words into a single category will inevitably exacerbate the processing problems associated with syntactic analysis, but may be more reliable. Although acceptable results can be achieved purely on the basis of morphological analysis, there is considerable scope for inaccurate candidate indexing terms to be extracted from the system (Gibb *et al.*, 1990e). Syntactic information provides a mechanism for resolving many of the problems associated with pattern matching based purely on word forms.

More than one syntactic structure might, of course, fit any particular sequence of morphologically analysed text, and procedures must be available to eliminate any inherent ambiguity. Not surprisingly, many different approaches have been adopted when assigning syntactic labels to words, including statistical techniques (Rouault, 1985), probabilistic precedence matrices (Berrut and Palmer, 1986) and elimination techniques (Karlsson *et al.*, 1990).

Syntactic analysis may not necessarily be carried out on the whole of the input text. As well as being subjected to full parsing, text may be processed selectively, using partial parsing or text skimming. An example of a system which relies on a complete parse is SIMPR, which uses the novel constraint grammar discussed above to produce a correct morphosyntactic interpretation of a piece of running text. Two central ideas behind the development of the Constraint Grammar Parser (CGP) are the maximal use made of morphological information for parsing purposes, and the use of constraints to gradually reduce the possible syntactic labels associated with a morphologically analysed word to a cohort of size one (Karlsson *et al.*, 1990). As has been noted above, the CGP has been developed on the basis of large-scale corpus studies and incorporates both deterministic and probabilistic constraints. Unresolved ambiguities are preserved in the output from the CGP which differs from most conventional parsing systems in that it is an annotated, linear flat string of word forms rather than a parse tree.

Partial parsing of texts has a number of attractions, not least of which is the reduction in processing time. TOPIC, for example only recognizes in detail words which are significant to its performance (e.g. nouns, adjectives, quantifiers) and discards the others from further analysis (Hahn, 1990). COP adopts a similar strategy through its use of a minimal specification principle to limit the detail incorporated in the grammar and parser by including no more than is necessary to make the distinctions needed by their structural descriptions (Metzler and Haas, 1989; Metzler *et al.*, 1990a; 1990b). Alternatively, the resolution of morphosyntactic ambiguity can be limited to only those words of importance which form part of a noun group (Berrut and Palmer, 1986). Text skimming (or selective parsing) involves restricting the parse to areas of text which contain certain words which might be of interest. This implies the existence of domain-specific semantic knowledge which is used as an initial filter. The text is then subjected to either a partial or full parse. SCISOR, for instance, employs a bottom-up full parser with a top-down skimming parser (Jacobs and Rau, 1988). There is clearly a trade-off between full and partial parsing. Full parsing will be computationally intensive, but will ensure maximum information is available for later stages of the indexing process. Partial parsing will be computationally cheaper but limits the information that is extracted to features which have been preselected on a pragmatic basis. Partial parsing arguably compromises the potential effectiveness of the indexing system.

3.5 Term extraction

The output from the syntactic analysis phase will be text which has been partially or completely disambiguated, depending on the parsing strategy adopted. As with morphological analysis, preserving residual ambiguity ensures that no potential information is lost. However it must be recognized that this carries an extra processing overhead and can lead to the introduction of noise through false matches against desired syntactic structures.

The extraction of terms from syntactically analysed text, as has been noted in Section 3.1, is based primarily on the recognition of noun phrases, although simpler systems do exist which simply extract nouns (Kimoto *et al.*, 1989). Extraction can be based on a general grammar for noun phrases or on specific noun phrase structures. The specification of such structures may well be domain-dependent: it has been shown that there are marked differences in syntactic patterns between the sublanguages which represent subject disciplines (Bonzi, 1990). For example, in technical discourse the present tense tends to be used to express central ideas, while the past tense forms are used for information which is supplied to support these core concepts. The function for which a document has been written will also affect syntactic patterns. Technical documentation (operating manuals, etc.) makes significant use of imperatives and directive statements (Slocum, 1986; Gibb *et al.*, 1990f). It may also be possible to recognize conventions for introducing important concepts: for example families of *indicator phrases* have been identified which signal that the rest of the sentence will contain an important statement (Paice, 1981). In addition to the evidence provided by syntactic features, dominant concepts may be identified using statistical information. Reimer argues that 'A major criterion for determining the salience of a concept is the frequency of its explicit and implicit mention in the text as recognized by the text parsing process' (Reimer and Hahn, 1988) TOPIC uses a conceptual parser which concentrates on the interaction of nominals (e.g. nouns and adjectives) in text, including features such as anaphoras and ellipses. Because the parser ignores the role of verbs, its understanding capabilities are limited to the recognition of semantic and thematic relationships within a taxonomic and terminological schema. Each concept in this schema is represented as a frame whose slots represents specific property classes. For example a frame could be created for database management systems which would have slots for properties such as operating system, manufacturer, programming language etc. These properties, in turn, may also be represented as concept frames within the knowledge base. Each occurrence of a word token (within the class of nominals) is matched against the concept frames in order to build up a picture of the 'aboutness' of the text being analysed. In addition to direct, or explicit, matches, the system is able to identify implicit references to concepts through features such as anaphoras and ellipses. Both explicit and implicit references to concepts are then recorded by incrementing the activation weights of frames and their slots in the domain knowledge base. This emphasis on implicit references ensures that semantic, rather than lexical, repetition can be identified.

FASIT (Dillon and Gray, 1983) uses 161 predefined concept forms built around desired combinations of syntactic categories. These concept forms are specified in such a way as to be able to accommodate any unresolved ambiguities present in the text once it has passed through the syntactic categorizer. For example, the word 'academic' in 'academic libraries' could be interpreted as an adjective (JJ) or as a noun (NN). The phrase 'academic libraries' would be extracted by the concept form JJ-NN NN (indicating a noun preceded by a word which might be either an adjective or a noun). A total of 11 ambiguous tags is built into the concept forms, of which only three (adjective-noun, noun-verb, and past-tense–past participle) occur with any great frequency. Dillon found that of these only the latter two caused serious selection problems, a feature confirmed by more recent work on the SIMPR project. Similar approaches have been adopted by Antoniadis, (Antoniadis *et al.*, 1988), Salton (Salton, 1989) and researchers on SIMPR (Gibb *et al.*, 1990a). Antoniadis uses a library of *generators* which recognize simple sequences of premodified nouns or a limited number of more complex noun phrases, which are connected by *'de'* or *'a'* . Salton uses a phrase generation system which contains components to recognize simple pre- and post-modified noun sequences, phrases linked by *of*, and conjunctive constructions using 'and' or a comma. There is also a component which provides special treatment for words which occur in titles and section headings (which may not have sentence-level text sequences), and capitalized words.

SIMPR uses a series of augmented transition networks (ATNs) to process morphosyntactically analysed texts. A transition network consists of a number of nodes, each of which represents a state, linked by a number of arcs, each of which represents the transition of a system from one state to another after the occurrence of a specified event. An ATN incorporates recursive functions (essential for natural language processing) and memory (in the form of counters and registers) which can control traversal of arcs (Noble, 1988). The SIMPR ATNs currently recognise simple pre- and post-modified noun groups, phrases linked by *'in'*, *'of'*, variants of the word *'its'*, variants of the verb *'to be'*, selected conjunctive constructions, and action–object phrases. For example the SIMPR PARWOS module can extract the following sequences:

boiler plates

reinforced steel plates

vent hole in the fuel tank filler cap

engine from its mountings

engine is clean

blocked or fractured pipes

blocked pipes and drains

removing the engine

A wider range of prepositional phrase attachments and '*is-a*' and '*has-a*' links are currently being implemented in order to preserve and indicate much richer relationships between individual noun groups. The output from the SIMPR text segment extraction module is viewed as being either atomic (*plates*), molecular (*steel plates*) or macromolecular (*bending of steel plates by lateral loads*).

An alternative, but domain-dependent, approach to term extraction is to use semantic parsing techniques. Semantic parsing exploits conceptual, factual and pragmatic knowledge to select only those elements which match predetermined topics, and has been successfully applied in TOPIC (Hahn, 1989; 1990) and REST (Croft and Lewis, 1987). These topics characterize a particular domain of discourse and must be supplied to the indexing system by a human expert, typically in the form of a frame-based taxonomy. The system matches extracted concepts against these frames to build, in turn, a frame-based representation of the document.

Controlled vocabulary can be used not only to identify relevant topics in a text, but also to classify texts by associating them with a node in an organized conceptual schema. This schema could be a classification scheme, a thesaurus, or a more complex semantic net-like structure. Project-Advisor (Beutler, 1988) makes use of a faceted classification system to provide descriptors for projects in order to identify reusable project results. A concept in the classification scheme may have taxonomic links and associative links. The associative links are expressed as confidence factors (between 0 and 1) which show the strength of association between terms. A collection of associated terms is stored as a hierarchical grouping called a context. A project description is linked to the facet designated by that context if a threshold value is exceeded. A very similar approach is taken by TOPIC (née RUBRIC) where taxonomic and attribute relationships can be expressed between concepts (Tong *et al.*, 1987).

MULTOS (Eirun and Krieplin, 1988) makes use of a predefined hierarchy of types which is used to generate conceptual structure definitions for a specific document. A conceptual structure is interpreted as being an aggregate of a number of conceptual components, each of which represents an attribute of a document which has some commonly understood meaning within an organization. Interestingly, the tasks of text analysis and document classification are considered to be distinct and autonomous.

FACT (Fenn, 1987) also makes a firm separation between the two tasks on the basis that 'the requirements [for indexing] may change according to the needs of individual users or due to other factors'. FACT is designed to work initially within the field of electromyography, where it has been used to analyse and classify the diagnostic comment at the end of an EMG report. It takes parse trees from a syntactic analyser and passes them for semantic processing using a semantic grammar and a knowledge base which contains frame-based hierarchies of domain-specific concept entities. The semantic grammar looks for certain statement types (disorders, findings, symptoms etc.) which represent the way that EMG concepts can be combined within and between sentences. Once a statement type has been instantiated, the grammar seeks a match for associated lexical items with the concept hierarchies. Once a pointer to an element in the concept hierarchy has been found, the system will seek to establish the most specific entity below that point, based on any modifiers present in the relevant noun phrase. The hierarchies cover topics such as:

disorders

anatomical structures

pathophysiological states

EMG tests

EMG findings

Each concept entity has a set of relevant attributes (synonyms, parent–child, location etc.) associated with it which can be used to express complex relationships with other entities, as well as pointers to additional sources of information such as case reports and pictures.

Researchers on SIMPR have also investigated the potential of frame-based classification schema (Revie, 1990; Revie and Smart 1990) backed by classification and machine-learning algorithms to automatically assign documents to concept frames (Ward *et al.*, 1990). A novel feature of this research is its use of faceted classification techniques which avoid many of the problems associated with conventional taxonomic or hierarchical classification systems. The intrinsic multidimensional aspects of a faceted approach mean that a document can be classified in several different ways, and its relationship to other document and document groups can be viewed from different perspectives. Three types of facets have been identified: generic, transportable and domain-specific. Generic facets are those which have universal applicability, such as space and time concepts, while transportable facets can be used across some, but not all, subject domains. Important groups within these two types might, therefore, be available as part of a starter kit which could be used by the developer of a new classification schema. Domain-specific facets, on the other hand will, by definition, be of a highly specialist nature and generally developed for a specific application.

IOTA (Bruandet, 1987) extracts atomic (i.e. single term) concepts from a text and groups them together into cliques (maximal complete subgraphs). The candidate concepts are restricted to adjectives, nouns and connectors between nouns (i.e. conjunctions and prepositions). These are then formed into cliques using cooccurrence data and distance functions between lexical classes. These cliques can then be used to generate noun phrases (based on permutations of the constituent elements of the cliques) for indexing purposes. In addition, individual terms within a clique can have a strength of association computed (equivalent to the attribute links and confidence factors discussed above). Finally, contextual synonyms can also be computed between terms which belong to different cliques. The results of this indexing process are then automatically integrated with existing domain knowledge produced from previous analyses.

The automatic recognition and classification of concepts have also been investigated using a model of how humans use schemas stored in long-term memory to understand text, and how they acquire and incorporate new schemas (Gomez and Segami, 1989). Concepts are represented using frame-type structures which are linked through is-a and classes-of slots to produce a hierarchical schema called an LTM (long-term memory). At the topmost level the hierarchy is divided into physical things and ideas. Sentences are syntactically analysed and the system then identifies concepts and relations, using three type of representations which can be added to the LTM: object structures, action structures and event structures. As concepts are extracted from the text they are then matched against the LTM to see whether they already exist. New concepts are then integrated with the LTM and existing concepts augmented to show new relationships etc.

A further feature that can contribute to the enhancement of syntactic pattern matching in order to extract noun phrases is anaphoric resolution, a particularly difficult area of language analysis. An anaphora is a reference to a concept which has been mentioned previously in a text, as for instance:

> Remove the brake lining and replace it with a new one.

These constructs require the reader to infer the complete reference which may be between phrases or sentences. Studies have shown that anaphoras tend to refer to integral, rather than peripheral, concepts in a text (Bonzi and Liddy, 1989; Hein, 1989). There are several classifications of anaphora, of which the most predominant are pronouns and subject, or truncated, references. It has been shown, however, that not all classes of anaphora contribute positively to system performance (Bonzi and Liddy, 1988; Liddy, 1990): four out of ten of Bonzi's classes were shown to replace less integral concepts in abstracts. The use of anaphoras may also vary according to the domain or function of the texts being analysed. In technical documentation, for example, Badenoch has suggested that truncated anaphoric references provide a more useful mechanism for preserving the context of specific terms than pronominal anaphoras, producing more standard analytics, and eliminating redundancy in any generated index (Gibb *et al.*, 1990b). For example, given the text:

> Remove the fuel pump filter. Clean the filter and replace it.

there is a high confidence factor that the second sentence should be linked to the most recent occurrence of a noun phrase containing the word 'filter' and that it can be interpreted as:

> Clean the fuel pump filter and replace it.

This type of binding has been found to be most common where a diatomic analytic (such as fuel pump) is subsequently referred to by only the latter, and hence unspecified, word of the pair.

Although the retrieval process proper lies outside the scope of this chapter, it should be noted that the linguistic analysis tools developed on several projects have been successfully applied to query statements as well. However new noun phrase constructions and normalization rules (see next section) may have to be defined in order to ensure that matches can be made between query and documents. For example, the query: 'How do I remove the engine?' will have to be recognized as an isomerism and isomorphism of: 'Removing the engine'.

Lessons may also be learned from commercial products such as Q&A (Hendrix and Walter, 1987) which have developed query grammars for conventional database applications. Q&A's Intelligent Assistant searches for syntactic patterns which centre on the vocabulary used in the retrieval process (find, show, record, document, etc), e.g.:

> *find* all *records* on marketing department personnel
> *show* any *document* on annual rates of return

3.6 Normalization

The output from the generation process consists of a set of phrases which can be considered as candidates for document descriptors (Amsler, 1989; Gibb and Smart, 1990b). This is a natural outcome of the objective of domain-independency that characterizes the parsing strategies that have been discussed above. Syntactic structures will often match text sequences that contribute very little to a description of the subject matter of a text, and therefore they may not be reliable enough to be used in an unprocessed or unedited form.

The most common form of processing of phrases is normalization. Normalization ensures that phrases are stored in a standardized fashion, thereby removing the need for users to have to make allowances for different word forms (isomeric normalization) or word order (isomorphic normalization) at retrieval time (Gibb and Smart, 1990a). For example, the phrases 'removing the engine' and 'engine removal' are semantically equivalent and (ideally) should both be matched to a request for information on 'how the engine is removed.' Consistent word order is important for several reasons. It ensures a consistent representation of topics as well as a consistent presentation of these topics to the user. It also plays the key role in identifying which are the *specifying* and which are the *specified* elements in a noun phrase. A sequence of words making up a noun phrase which does not contain a preposition generally specifies from left to right, while word sequences with an interposed preposition specify in the opposite direction (e.g. engine removal; removal of the engine).

Isomeric normalization ensures that different forms of a word (*processing, processes, processed* etc.) can be reduced to a canonical base form (*process*). This form of normalization is based upon linguistic principles that have universal applicability (although it can be tailored for particular domains), and in some systems is applied before the extraction of noun phrases takes place. Isomorphic normalization, on the other hand, is not necessarily based upon universally applicable rules and often requires the presence of semantic knowledge to ensure that structural transformations result in sensible output. For instance, while most phrases linked by *'of'*, e.g.: *processing of text*; *removal of engine*; can be transformed to: *text processing*; *engine removal*; the phrase: *centre of the earth*, does not produce an acceptable sequence when transformed using the same rule.

A third form of normalization is the removal of stopwords. Stopword removal has been widely implemented in automatic indexing systems and general-purpose lists have been developed by various research groups. These contain commonly occurring function words *'in'*, *'at'*, etc.) supplemented by weak adjectives and nouns, (*'some'*, *'various'*, etc.), pronouns, adverbs, determiners, and other high-frequency and general-application words. However, these can also be supplemented by domain-dependent stopword lists. SIMPR, for example, utilizes a document structure stopword list to eliminate phrases such as *appendix eight* while ensuring that certain phrases containing the word *appendix* are not excluded in the medical field (Gibb *et al.*, 1990a). A variation on this type of normalization consists of using a combination of startword lists and exclusion classes, e.g. remove all comparative adjectives except those in a domain list.

One way to improve the quality of the candidate analytics which are generated by the indexing engine would be to incorporate a user validation module. Validation of analytics by a human expert has not been widely implemented because of the delays that it would introduce in the processing of documents. However, the exclusion of any human intervention will inevitably limit the information that is available concerning system performance and the ability of the system to be tailored to a particular domain. A feedback loop from a validation module could be used to automatically generate a domain- or user-specific stopword list. Given the limited vocabulary used within a particular domain (5000 words is typical), it is possible that extensive user validation would only be necessary in the initial development phase of a database. Once a representative sample of documents has been added to the database, the domain--specific stopword list should be relatively stable. A stopword list of this type would also provide a form of semantic parsing by excluding concepts which have been judged to be non-relevant to a particular community of users. A second and more ambitious form of feedback control would be to use a learning mechanism (such as a neural network) to adjust the specifications which are used to select noun phrases as candidates.

3.7 Some observations on semantic ambiguity

Ambiguity is present at a number of levels in natural language; the problems of morphological and syntactic ambiguity have been discussed above in terms of the classes of words and syntactic structures that can be identified in a particular text sequence. The analysis that takes place is based on a closed class of labels which can be assigned to a particular word, and it must be recognized that the choice of initial labels will dictate in part the types of ambiguity that can be recognized and resolved. Within a particular formalism, for instance, it may be impossible to decide whether the phrase: 'fuel tank filler cap' should be interpreted as: 'a cap on the fuel tank filler', or: 'a filler cap on the fuel tank'.

Equally, the inherent ambiguity in conjunctions makes it impossible to decide whether: 'information and computer science' should be interpreted as: 'information science and computer science', or: 'information *and* computer science'.

In fact it is unlikely whether these types of ambiguity can be dealt with using syntactic methods alone: they require the use of deep semantic and/or pragmatic knowledge for a specific domain before an attempt can be made at resolving the ambiguity. Even then the ambiguity may be unresolvable without reference to the originator of the text.

A second form of semantic ambiguity is related to the homonymic or context-specific nature of certain words. For example in the phrase: 'he photographed the bank', it is not clear whether this refers to a financial institution, part of a river, an array of objects, etc. Equally, the phrase: 'passing out parade' has a very particular meaning other than that which its separate constituents might suggest. A number of researchers are currently investigating word sense disambiguation using machine-readable dictionaries, effectively extending the role of the lexicon (Krovetz and Croft, 1989; Velardi and Pazienza, 1989). The availability of dictionaries and the effort that is being expended to enhance their content and structure should mean that they will be an increasingly important element in system development. The Longmans Dictionary of Common English, for example, includes a number of features which have been incorporated to assist general users. However, these can also be used to produce specialist dictionaries and could be exploited by index system developers. These features include sets of primitives organized into a type hierarchy; a set of subject codes, and a controlled vocabulary for definitions (Slator, 1989).

4 Conclusions

Knowledge-based indexing has reached the point where it works at least as well as other automatic indexing techniques. Although earlier comparisons between syntactic and non-syntactic methods (Fagan, 1987) showed that retrieval results for syntactic systems were generally poorer, considerable advances have been made in the design of general purpose indexing engines. The contributions from linguistics have been particularly noticeable. There are now a number of electronic lexicons and dictionaries, and powerful morphosyntactic analysers available to the system developer. In addition, these tools have been largely corpus-based, which has ensured that they reflect real-world applications.

A second important development has been the appearance of techniques for semantic parsing. These have provided an opportunity to tailor general-purpose indexing engines (which are based on morphosyntactic analysis) to specific applications. The combination of information science theory and artificial intelligence technologies has produced a number of powerful techniques for capturing the aboutness of a document as well as identifying descriptors which would provide access points to specific sections of text. One drawback with semantic parsing is that it requires the system developer to provide a knowledge base for the domain which is being analysed.

Given the highly specialized areas that most of these systems will be designed to service, it is unlikely that off-the-shelf knowledge bases will be available, and that considerable resources will have to be dedicated to the building of a reliable representation of the domain. One area of research that needs to be investigated, therefore, concerns the development of tools to assist in the building of appropriate knowledge bases, including thesauri, classification schemes and case frames. It is evident that LIS professionals should have an important contribution to make to this area of knowledge engineering (Morris and O'Neill, 1990).

Knowledge-based indexing has clearly reached an important stage in its development: commercial systems are starting to appear (e.g. TOPIC and Construe) and several pre-commercial products are waiting in the wings. The next phase of development should see its integration with a number of information processing technologies: high-performance computer architectures, hypermedia engines, optical scanning devices, and ultra storage devices.

References

Amsler, R.A. (1989) Research toward the development of a lexical knowledge base for natural language processing. In *Proceedings of the Twelfth Annual International ACM SIGIR Conference on Research and Development in Information Retrieval* (Cambridge MA, 1989), eds. N.J. Belkin and C.J. Van Rijsbergen, pp. 242-249. New York: Association for Computing Machinery

Antoniadis, G. *et al.* (1988) A French text recognition model for information retrieval. In *Proceedings of the Eleventh ACM SIGIR Conference on Research and Development in Information Retrieval* (Grenoble, 1988), ed. Y. Chiaramella, pp. 67-83. Grenoble: Presses Universitaires

Austin, D. (1984) *PRECIS: a manual of concept analysis and indexing*, 2nd edn. London: British Library

Bernstein, M. (1990) An apprentice that discovers hypertext links. In *Proceedings of the First European Conference on Hypertext* (INRIA, France, 1990) pp. 212-222. Cambridge. Cambridge University Press

Berrut, C. and Palmer, P. (1986) Solving grammatical ambiguities within a surface syntactical parser for automatic indexing. In *Proceedings of the Ninth ACM SIGIR Conference on Research and Development in Information Retrieval* (Pisa, Italy, 1986), ed F. Rabitti, pp. 123-130. New York: Association for Computing Machinery

Beutler, K.P. (1988) The 'descriptive search' to realize a knowledge-based retrieval of reusable project results. In *Artificial intelligence in real-time control* (Swansea, UK, 1988), pp. 109-112 London: IFAC

Black, W.J. and Johnson, F.C. (1988) A practical evaluation of two rule-based automatic abstracting techniques. *Expert Systems for Information Management*, **1**,(3),159-177

Boisot, M. (1987) *Information and organizations: the manager as anthropolologist*. London: Fontana

Bonzi, S. and Liddy, E. (1988) The use of anaphoric resolution for document description in information retrieval. In *Proceedings of the Eleventh ACM SIGIR Conference on Research and Development in Information Retrieval* (Grenoble, 1988), ed Y. Chiaramella, pp. 53-66. Grenoble: Presses Universitaires

Bonzi, S. (1990) Syntactic patterns in scientific sublanguages: a study of four disciplines. *Journal of the American Society for Information Science*, **41**,(2), 121-131.

Bruandet, M-F. (1987) Outline of a knowledge-based model for intelligent information retrieval system. In *Proceedings of the Tenth Annual International ACM SIGIR Conference on Research and Development in Information Retrieval* (Cambridge MA, 1987), eds. C.T. Yu and C.J. Van Rijsbergen, pp. 33-43. New York: Association for Computing Machinery

Chafetz, B. and Mikolajuk, Z. (1989) *Bibliography retrieval based on title understanding*. Presented at ASIS Annual Meeting (San Diego, CA, 1989)

Chartron, G. (1989) Lexicon management tools for large textual databases: the Lexinet system. *Journal of Information Science*, **15**, (6), 339-344

Copestake, A. and Jones, K.S. (1990) Natural language interfaces to databases. *Knowledge Engineering Review*, **5**,(4), 225-250

Croft, W.B. and Lewis, D.D. (1987) An approach to natural language processing for document retrieval. In *Proceedings of the Tenth Annual International ACM SIGIR Conference on Research and Development in Information Retrieval* (Cambridge MA, 1987), ed. C.T. Yu and C.J. Van Rijsbergen, pp. 26-32. New York: Association for Computing Machinery

Dillon, M. and Gray, A.S. (1983) FASIT: a fully automatic syntactically based indexing system. *Journal of the American Society for Information Science*, **34**,(2), 99-108

Doyle, A.C. (1890) *The sign of four*. London: Ward Lock

Eirund, H. and Kreplin, K. (1988) Knowledge-based document classification supporting integrated document handling. In *Proceedings of the Eleventh ACM SIGIR Conference on Research and Development in Information Retrieval* (Grenoble, 1988), ed Y. Chiaramella, pp. 189-196. Grenoble: Presses Universitaries

Fagan, J.L. (1987) Automatic phrase indexing for document retrieval: an examination of syntactic and non-syntactic methods. In *Proceedings of the Tenth Annual International ACM SIGIR Conference on Research and Development in Information Retrieval* (Cambridge MA, 1987), ed C.T. Yu and C.J. Van Rijsbergen pp. 99-101. New York: Association for Computing Machinery

Fenn, J.A. (1987) Using a knowledge base for automatic text classification. In *Recent Developments and Applications of Natural Language Understanding* (London, 1987), pp. 99-101. Uxbridge: Unicom Seminars

Foskett, A.C. (1982) *The subject approach to information*, 4th edn. London: Clive Bingley

Fox, E.A. (1987) Development of the CODER system: a testbed for artificial intelligence methods in information retrieval. *Information Processing and Management,* **23**,(4), 341-366

Furnas, G.W. *et al.* (1983) Statistical semantics: analysis of the potential performance of keyword information systems. *Bell System Technical Journal*, **62**,(6), 1753-1806

Furnas, G.W. *et al.* (1988) Information retrieval using a singular value decomposition model of latent semantic structure. In *Proceedings of the Eleventh ACM SIGIR Conference on Research and Development in Information Retrieval* (Grenoble, 1988), Y. Chiaramella, pp. 465-480. Grenoble: Presses Universitaires

Gay, L.S. and Croft, W.B. (1990) Interpreting nominal compounds for information retrieval. *Information Processing and Management,* **26**,(1), 21-38

Gibb, F. and Smart, G. (1990a) Structured information management: using new techniques for processing text. *Online Review*, **14**,(3), 159-171

Gibb, F. and Smart, G. (1990b) Structured information management processing and retrieval – potential benefits for the offshore industry. In *Proceedings of the Offshore Information Conference* (Edinburgh, 1990) ed. A. Myers, pp. 189-201. Edinburgh: Institute of Offshore Engineering

Gibb, F. and Smart, G. (1990c) Expert systems and information storage and retrieval systems. In *Online Information Retrieval Today and Tomorrow* (Ripon, 1990) eds. C.J. Armstrong and R.J. Hartley, pp. 35-43. Oxford: Learned Information

Gibb, F. and Smart, G. (1990d) Knowledge-based indexing: the view from SIMPR. In *Libraries and Expert Systems*, eds. C. MacDonald and J. Weckert, pp. 38-48. London: Taylor Graham

Gibb, F., Karetnyk, D. and Badenoch, D. (1990e) *ATNs and rule bases for prototype indexing system.* Glasgow: University of Strathclyde. SIMPR-SU-1990-12.2i.

Gibb, F., Karetnyk, D. and Badenoch, D. (1990f) *MIDAS: Ongoing research and development.* Glasgow: University of Strathclyde. SIMPR-SU-1990-12.10i.

Gomez, F. and Segami, C. (1989) The recognition and classification of concepts in understanding scientific texts. *Journal of Experimental and Theoretical Artificial Intelligence*, pp. 51-77

Hahn, U. (1987) Modeling text understanding – the methodological aspects of automatic acquisition of knowledge through text analysis. Presented at *1st International Symposium on Artificial Intelligence and Expert Systems* (Berlin, 1987). University of Passau, MIP - 8709

Hahn, U. (1989) Making understanders out of parsers: semantically driven parsing as a key concept for realistic text understanding applications. *International Journal of intelligent Systems*, **4**,(3), 345-393

Hahn, U. (1990) Topic parsing: accounting for text macro structures in full-text analysis. *Information Processing and Management*, **26**,(1), 135-170

Harman, D. (1987) A failure analysis on the limitations of suffixing in an online environment. In *Proceedings of the Tenth Annual International ACM SIGIR Conference on Research and Development in Information Retrieval* (Cambridge MA, 1987), eds. C.T. Yu and C.J. Van Rijsbergen, pp. 102-108. New York: Association for Computing Machinery

Hein, A.S. (1989) Definite NPs and background knowledge in medical text. *Computers and Artificial Intelligence*, **8**,(6), 547-563

Hendrix, G.G. and Walter, B.A. (1987) The intelligent assistant. *Byte*, **12**,(14), 251-260

Humphrey, S.M. (1987) Illustrated description of an interactive knowledge-based indexing system. In *Proceedings of the Tenth Annual International ACM SIGIR Conference on Research and Development in Information Retreival* (Cambridge MA, 1987), eds. C.T. Yu and C.J. Van Rijsbergen, pp. 73-90. New York: Association for Computing Machinery

Humphrey, S.M. (1989) A knowledge-based expert system for computer-assisted indexing. *IEEE Expert*, **4**,(3), Fall, 25-38

Jacobs, P.S. and Rau, L.F. (1988) Natural language techniques for intelligent information retrieval. In *Proceedings of the Eleventh ACM SIGIR Conference on Research and Development in Information Retrieval* (Grenoble, 1988), ed. Y. Chiaramella, pp. 85-99. Grenoble: Presses Universitaires

Jacobs, P.S. and Zernik, U. (1988) Acquiring lexical knowledge from text: a case study. In *Proceedings of the Seventh National Conference on Artificial Intelligence* (St Paul, Minnesota, 1988). New York: AAAI, 2, 739-744

Karetnyk, D., Karlsson, F. and Smart, G. (1991) Knowledge-based indexing of morphosyntactically analysed language. *Expert Systems for Management*, **4**,(1), 1-30

Karlsson, F. *et al.* (1990). *Natural language processing for information retrieval purposes.* Helsinki: Research Unit for Computational Linguistics, SIMPR-RUCL-1990-13.4e.

Kimoto, H., Nagata, M. and Kawai, A. (1989) Automatic indexing system for Japanese texts. *Review of the Electrical Communication Laboratories*, **37**,(1), 51-56

Krawczak, D., Smith, P.J. and Shute, S.J. (1987) EP-X: a demonstration of semantically-based search of bibliographic databases. In *Proceedings of the Tenth Annual International ACM SIGIR Conference on Research and Development in Information Retrieval* (Cambridge MA, 1987), eds. C.T. Yu and C.J. Van Rijsbergen, pp. 263-271. New York: Association for Computing Machinery

Krovetz, R. and Croft, W.B. (1989) Word sense disambiguation using machine-readable dictionaries. In *Proceedings of the Twelfth Annual International ACM SIGIR Conference on Research and Development in Information Retrieval* (Cambridge MA, 1989) eds. N.J. Belkin and C.J. Van Rijsbergen, pp. 127-136. New York: Association for Computing Machinery

Kuhlen, R. (1983) *Some similarities and differences between intellectual and machine text understanding for the purpose of abstracting.* University of Konstanz, Bericht TOPIC 7/83.

Liddy, E. (1990) Anaphora in natural language processing and information retrieval. *Information Processing and Management,* **26**,(1),

Luhn, H.P. (1957) A statistical approach to mechanized encoding and searching of library information. *IBM Journal of Research and Development*, **1**,(4), 309-317

McKnight, C., Dillon, A. and Richardson, J. (1989) Problems in Hyperland? A human factors perspective. *Hypermedia*, **1**,(2), 167-178

Maller, V.A.J. (1980) Retrieving information. *Datamation*, Sept 1980, **26**,(9), 164-172

Mauldin, M., Carbonell, J. and Thomason, R. (1987) Beyond the keyword barrier: knowledge-based information retrieval. *Information Services and Use*, **7**, 103-117

Metzler, D.P. and Haas, S.W. (1989) The constituent object parser: syntactic structure matching for information retrieval. In *Proceedings of the Twelfth Annual International ACM SIGIR Conference on Research and Development in Information Retrieval* (Cambridge MA, 1989), eds. N.J. Belkin and C.J. Van Rijsbergen, pp. 117-126. New York: Association of Computing Machinery

Metzler, D.P. *et al.* (1990a) Constituent object parsing for information retrieval and similar text processing problems. *Journal of the American Society for Information Science*, **40**,(6), 391-423

Metzler, D.P. *et al.* (1990b) Conjunction, ellipsis, and other discontinuous constituents in the constituent object parser. *Information Processing and Management*, **26**,(1), 53-71

Mikolajuk, Z. and Chafetz, B. (1989) *A domain knowledge-based natural language interface for bibliographic information retrieval.* Presented at ASIS Annual Meeting (San Diego, 1989)

Morris, A. and O'Neill, M. (1990) Library and information science professionals and knowledge engineering. *Expert Systems for Information Management*, **3**,(2), 115-128

Noble, H.M. (1988). *Natural language processing.* Oxford: Blackwell Scientific

Paice, C.D. (1981) The automatic generation of literature abstracts: an approach based on the identification of self-indicating phrases. In *Information Retrieval and Research* ed. R.N. Oddy, pp. 172-191. London: Butterworths

Reimer, U. and Hahn, U. (1988) Text condensation as knowledge-base abstraction. In *Proceedings of the Fourth Conference on Artificial Intelligence Applications* (San Diego, 1988). Washington: IEEE, 338-344

Revie, C. (1990) *SCS: functional specification (document 3).* Glasgow: University of Strathclyde. SIMPR-SU-1990-14.8e.

Revie, C. and Smart, G. (1990) *Classification: theoretical framework (document 1).* Glasgow: University of Strathclyde. SIMPR-SU-1990-14.7e.

Rouault, J. (1985) Linguistic methods in information retrieval systems. In: *Proceedings of Informatics 8 – Advances in Intelligent Retrieval.* (Oxford, 1985). London: Aslib

Ruge, G. and Schwarz, C. (1988) Natural language access to free-text databases. In *Proceedings of the 44th FID Conference and Congress* (Helsinki, 1988), eds. P. Hamalainen, S. Koskiala and A.J. Repo, pp. 164-173. The Hague: FID; Helsinki: Finnish Society for Information Services

Salton, G. (1986) Another look at automatic text-retrieval systems. *Communications of the ACM*, **29**,(7), 648-656

Salton, G. and McGill, M.J. (1983) *Introduction to modern information retrieval.* Tokyo: McGraw-Hill

Salton, G. and Smith, M. (1989) On the application of syntactic methodologies in automatic text analysis. In *Proceedings of the Twelfth Annual International ACM SIGIR Conference on Research and Development in Information Retrieval* (Cambridge MA, 1989), eds. N.J. Belkin and C.J. Van Rijsbergen, pp. 137-150. New York: Association for Computing Machinery

Schwarz, C. (1990) Automatic syntactic analysis of free text. *Journal of the American Society for Information Science* **41**,(6), 408-417

Sievert, M.C. and Andrews, M.J. (1991) Indexing consistency in Information Science Abstracts. *Journal of the American Society for Information Science*, **42**,(1), 1-6

Slator, B.M. (1989) Extracting lexical knowledge from dictionary text. *Knowledge Acquisition*, **1**, 89-112

Slocum, J. (1986) How one might automatically identify and adapt to a sublanguage: an initial exploration. In *Analyzing language in restricted domains: sublanguage description and processing*, eds. R. Grishman and R. Kittredge, Hillsdale: Lawrence Erlbaum Associates

Tong, R.M. *et al.* (1987) Conceptual information retrieval using RUBRIC. In *Proceedings of the Tenth Annual International ACM SIGIR Conference on Research and Development in Information Retrieval* (Cambridge MA, 1987), ed C.T. Yu and C.J. Van Rijsbergen, pp. 247-253. New York: Association for Computing Machinery

Velardi, P. and Pazienza, M.T. (1989) Acquisition of semantic patterns from a natural corpus of texts. In *Computational Intelligence I*, eds. A. Martelli and G. Valle, pp. 151-157. Amsterdam: North Holland

Waltz, D.L. (1987) Applications of the Connection Machine. *Computer*, **20**,(2), Jan, 85-97

Ward, C., Kavanagh, I. and Dunion, J. (1990) *Classification algorithm*. SIMPR-UCD-1991-22.01i.

Winograd, T. (1983) *Language as a cognitive process.* Reading: Addison-Wesley

Zernik, U. (1989) Lexicon acquisition: learning from corpus by capitalizing on lexical categories. In *Proceedings of the Eleventh International Joint Conference on Artificial Intelligence* (Detroit, Michigan, 1989). New York: AAAI, 2, 1556-1562

Zipf, G.K. (1949) *Human behavior and the principle of least effort.* Reading: Addison-Wesley

Chapter 3

Rule-based systems, natural language processing and abstracting

Bill Black

1 Background

This chapter is concerned with the linguistic aspects of the process of accessing sources of information, and with how rule-based techniques can be used to facilitate the process. After a preliminary discussion about the process of storing and searching for information, we first describe how language processing of queries to databases such as OPACs can be implemented within PROLOG's rule-based paradigm, and then discuss the adaptation of these methods to automatic abstracting.

The use of libraries and information centres can be characterized in the following way: the user of the service has an information need, which it is hoped may be met from the contents of the library. The library consists of a collection of books and other documents created by those with information to impart. To help users locate documents which may contain information relevant to their needs, library professionals construct an index to documents based on their contents. Users of the library search through the index, which is organized by key terms or classification codes. Each index card or its equivalent record in a computer-based system contains a brief description of a document identified by the key search. The document descriptions may then be used to filter what seem to the user to be promising sources of information, before source documents are accessed.

In a public or local academic library, relatively little effort goes into describing each individual book, because the books are available on the shelves, and can be browsed through conveniently. However, specialist information centres and computer-based information services leave less to chance in the attempt to make relevant documents available. They do this in two ways: firstly, by describing documents in more detail, and secondly by providing computer-based methods for searching those descriptions. In describing documents in detail, several keywords are assigned to allow alternative entry points to the index, and also, an abstract of the document is provided in the document record, to convey a clear idea of its content and scope.

In providing computer-based searching methods, the most common approach has been to provide a formal query language in which the user can express complex logical search conditions, although more recently, alternative approaches to user–system interaction, such as hypertext, have been developed.

Both document description and query formulation are activities involving intelligence, and particularly language use. Document description, by indexing and abstracting, involves characterizing the topic of the document using linguistic expressions. The indexer or abstractor, in reading the document, applies linguistic as well as 'real-world' knowledge to select the best index terms and to construct the abstract. Similarly, in searching a document database, the user (or library professional intermediary) must characterize the information need in linguistic terms. Where there is only a simple keyword index, as in a public library, then it is necessary to think on the level of keywords – which one or two words can best represent the meaning of the information wanted? In fact it is not so simple: what is needed is not exactly a description of the information sought, but a guess at how an indexer of a relevant work might describe its contents.

2 Systems to help in query formulation

Using a typical computer-based information retrieval system, many more words are used to describe each document in the index, which may, in addition to specifically assigned keywords, also use words from the title or abstract as additional pointers. The fact that many more index entries may easily be made available in a computerized system is at the same time a benefit and a handicap. If keywords are assigned in larger numbers and in a less controlled way, then the number of documents indexed by a particular term will be large, possibly running to hundreds or thousands. It is therefore necessary to ensure that keywords are coordinated in a search, which is likely to specify that two or more keywords must both index a document, for it to be selected. Once we begin to construct searches with conjunctions of terms, we may also be interested in refining searches using other coordinating operators, such as disjunction and negation. The question of constructing appropriately bracketed search expressions then arises. For those untrained in information retrieval or computer database concepts, getting such queries right is difficult, and there is a case for considering whether more natural ways of expressing information need may be possible.

One such natural way might be to let the user describe his information need in free natural language, and use such a statement to begin a dialogue to clarify the need. However, if ultimately index entries are simply keywords, it is difficult to make use of the information about relationships between concepts that may be obtained by analysing free natural language text. For conventional information retrieval systems, there has therefore been little interest in developing natural language interfaces to query facilities.

However, it has long been suggested that future libraries will attempt to go beyond simply storing and indexing documents, but evolve towards fact and knowledge retrieval systems. We may consider a fact retrieval system to be rather like a typical commercial or administrative database, where instead of being encoded in arbitrary natural text, information is structured into records storing descriptions of objects in terms of their attributes. More sophisticated knowledge-processing systems will typically use artificial intelligence knowledge-representation techniques to provide direct access to all kinds of information and pedagogical materials (see for example Norton, 1983), but that is beyond the scope of the present chapter.

A good text on formatted databases is Oxborrow (1986), which uses a library catalogue as the context for many of the illustrative examples. A formatted database stores information about different types of objects or events, each in its own table, but with implicit relationships between them. An example might be the database to support a library issuing system. In such a database, we would need tables about books, storing the class number, author and title of each; a table identifying each borrower and showing the name and address; a table of current loans, identifying each by the pair <borrower, accession number> and showing also the return date. Finally, a reservation table (not shown) could record information about reserved books.

For such formatted databases, the use of natural language queries can be more readily motivated by the difficulty of framing queries involving cross-references between different tables. Figure 3.1 shows an example of a set of tables for an issuing database, and Figure 3.2 is an example of a query in structured query language (SQL) that would find out how many people currently have on a loan a copy of a particular book. Without further argument, we can see that even for simple databases of facts, there is a justification for query facilities that require a little less learning of computer-oriented languages. It, is obviously much better if we can ask such a system: 'How many

BOOK			
isbn	author	date	title
0-8053-0330-8	Allen	1987	Natural Language Processing
0-8623-091-X	Oxborrow	1986	Databases and Database Systems
0-442-31772-7	Black	1986	Intelligent Knowledge-Based Systems

borrower			
borrower_no	name	department	year/status
10123	Green	sociology	3
11223	Browne	physics	pg
10001	Grey	librarianship	staff
12232	Whyte	physics	1

accession	
accession_no	isbn
1A12	0-8053-0330-8
E102	0-8053-0330-8
220A	0-8053-033038
321D	0-86238-091-X
3321	0-442-31772-7

loan		
borrower_no	accession_no	due_date
10001	E102	1-3-90
10001	321D	28-2-90
10123	220A	21-1-90

Figure 3.1 *Example database tables*

copies of Allen's '*Natural Language Processing*' are on loan?' Better still if an interface can answer subsequent questions as in Figure 3.3.

This contrived text helps to illustrate some of the complex issues that need to be addressed in the construction of a natural language interface. In particular, they show that this kind of computer interface is not just a translator which uses a rule-base of English sentence and phrase structure and the corresponding SQL structures, but it is a matter of *pragmatic interpretation* of natural language ut-

```
SELECT COUNT (BORROWER_NO)
FROM LOAN
WHERE EXISTS
    (SELECT LOAN.BORROWER_NO,LOAN.ACCESSION_NO
    FROM LOAN,ACCESSION,BOOK
    WHERE ACCESSION.ACCESSION_NO= LOAN.ACCESSION_NO
    AND
    ACCESSION.ISBN = BOOK.ISBN
    AND
    BOOK.TITLE = 'NATURAL LANGUAGE PROCESSING'
    AND
    BOOK.AUTHOR = 'ALLEN')
```

Figure 3.2 *Database query in a formal query language*

U: How many copies of Allen's 'Natural Language Processing' are on loan?

S: All three.

U: Gazdar and Mellish

S: All four copies of Gazdar and Mellish's 'Natural Language Understanding' are also on loan.

U: When are *they* due back?

S: The seven books are due back at various dates from tomorrow until the 23rd. Unfortunately the two titles have 5 and 7 reservations respectively.
Do you wish to make a reservation?

Figure 3.3 *Example information-seeking dialogue*

terances. Pragmatics refers to the way in which language use and interpretation depends on contextual factors and the general principles of communication. The first system response in the sample dialogue shows a system following Grice's *co-operative principle* (Grice, 1975; Leech, 1983). Grice's principles of communication are specialized into a number of maxims, of which the 'maxim of quantity' guides the communicator to give a useful amount of information in response to a question, irrespective of what is literally asked by the dialogue partner. The user in this case has asked how many are on loan; the system additionally volunteers the information that the number of copies on loan is equal to the total number of copies held.

Of course the mere statement of Grice's principles is not sufficient to get a computer system to behave in this intelligent way. Just to produce the example response shown, it is necessary to reason about the user's goals in asking the question. In the context of a library system, a plausible goal would be to borrow a copy of the book in question. A natural language enquiry system that behaved in this way was GUS (Bobrow, 1986), which could answer enquiries about timetables. GUS would give specific information about the times of departing trains in response to yes/no questions, such as 'Are there any more trains tonight to Newark?', which literally asks for the answer 'yes' or 'no'. The system has to work out what sort of goal the enquirer might have that would presuppose a positive answer to the question.

The techniques underlying such a system involve explicit reasoning about the beliefs of others, and are discussed in Allen (1987), Chapter 15.

: Give me the salary and job title of John Fox
PARSED! (SALARY $35,750 JOB-TITLE systems analyst)

: age and grade
Trying Ellipsis: GIVE ME THE AGE AND GRADE OF JOHN FOX
(AGE 34 GRADE A6)

Figure 3.4 *Sample dialogue with LIFER, showing ellipsis*

The next user utterance, which simply names another pair of authors, can be interpreted in this context as an *elliptical* or abbreviated query about the number of copies of their book out on loan. A well known computer database query system prototype that could do this was LIFER (Hendrix *et al.*, 1978). The LIFER system used a pattern-matching appraoch to compare elliptical fragments with the syntactic or semantic constituents of the previous query, as shown in Figure 3.4. Such pattern matching has to be quite sophisticated, and preferably also supported by pragmatic reasoning about the user's beliefs or goals.

The last user utterance in Figure 3.3 illustrates the problem of *reference*. Pronouns such as 'they' are used for abbreviated reference to objects introduced earlier in the discourse, but in this case as in many others, there is more than one candidate referent for the pronoun. In the context, 'the' could quite likely refer to the Gazdar and Mellish book, mentioned more recently, or to the set of books formed from the two titles referred to within the same focus space. (At any one time only one or a small number of objects or actions is in focus in a dialogue, and therefore available for abbreviated reference via pronouns). As before, the system generates a response motivated by cooperative principles and reasoning about what purposes the answer to the user's question could serve, and this necessarily involves resolving the reference of all referring expressions, including pronouns.

The foregoing discussion set out to establish some of the knowledge-based processing which must be done in addition to grammatical analysis. However, this does not mean that we can build intelligent dialogue systems without grammatical analysis. In fact, we can regard natural language understanding as subjecting utterances to a series of levels of analysis, as indicated in Figure 3.5. Morphology refers to the structure of words – both the way prefixes and suffixes can systematically alter words, and the way in which words are inflected for agreement. A morphological analysis of a word such as 'liking', for example, would separate it into a stem 'like' and a morpheme 'ing'. Note that morphological analysis deals with rules

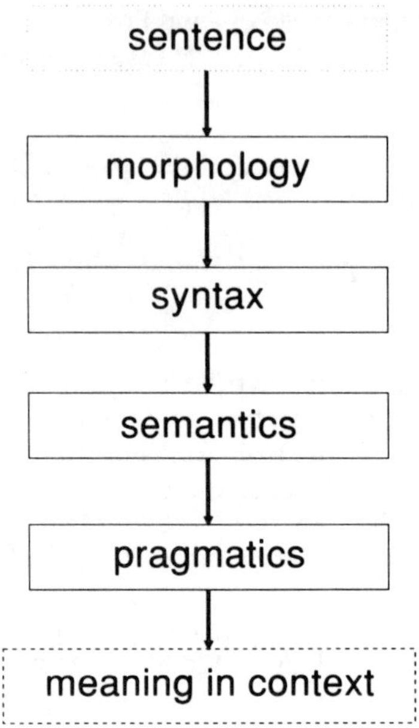

Figure 3.5 *Levels of linguistic analysis*

such as those which change the root (in this case by dropping the 'e') when particular suffixes are added. In a dictionary, for example, it suffices to give the infinitive form of a verb (the one that is preceded by 'to'), relying on the user's knowledge that the other forms e.g. *likes, liked, liking* are predictable. In a morphological analyser, the standard endings are identified, then rules for identifying the roots are applied. Exceptions (e.g. *choose: chose, chosen*) must be identified before applying the standard endings and rules.

In English, noun and verb morphology does not exhibit the same variety as the declensions and conjugations of many other languages, such as Latin, French and German, not to mention Finnish. However, many words in our vocabulary are derived from other words by the addition of prefixes and suffixes. For example, the ending *-ly* usually indicates an adverb derived from an adjective, and the ending *-tion* is usually a noun derived from a verb. In many applications of natural language processing in information management, it is quite useful, because we are dealing with unrestricted texts, to be able to guess the likely usage of a word that is not in the dictionary of the system. This can often be done quite effectively using a mixture of clues from the context and the 'derivational morphology' of the word.

Syntax is the level of analysis which deals with the structure of sentences. We may observe that sentences appear to have a hierarchical structure, and can be decomposed at the first level into two major parts, often known as the subject and the predicate. A simple sentence 'John slept' has 'John' as the subject and 'slept' as the predicate. We can replace either of these constituents of the sentence with many alternatives, and still get a structure that is grammatical (although we do not regard any of the alternatives as equivalent in meaning). For example, in place of 'John', we could have 'The boy', 'The old man', 'The older of the two African elephants' – any of these substitutions still makes a grammatical sentence. We can do the same for the predicate: an infinite range of alternative predicates can be substituted for 'slept', giving grammatical sentences. We can therefore write a rule that says a sentence consists of one item we shall call a noun_phrase followed by another that we shall call a 'verb_phrase':

sentence →noun_phrase verb_phrase

Of course, we have not yet said what either of these subphrases is, so we must rectify this deficiency with additional rules which show how phrases are ultimately realized by words of the language. Such a set of rules is a *grammar* for a language. Figure 3.6 is an illustration of such a grammar. These rules always have a standard form, where a left-hand side and a right-hand side are separated by an arrow. The left-hand side is always the name of a grammatical category, such as *sentence, noun group* or *adjective.* The right-hand side is either such a symbol or it is a *terminal.* A terminal is one of the actual strings of characters used in the language – a literal word. In the examples below, these have been distinguished by enclosure in quotation

noun_phrase	→ pronoun
noun_phrase	→ determiner noun_group
noun_group	→ adjective noun_group
noun_group	→ noun
verb_phrase	→ intransitive_verb
pronoun	→ 'he'
determiner	→ 'the'
adjective	→ 'old'
noun	→ 'sheep'
intransitive verb	→ 'slept'

Figure 3.6 *A simple phrase structure grammar*

marks. There is a whole mathematical discipline of formal language theory which studies the way in which different restrictions on grammar rules (for example whether the left-hand side may have more than one symbol, or whether the right-hand side of each rule must always start with a terminal) may delimit interesting formal classes of language, and what precisely are the restrictions on possible human languages. Interesting as these matters are, we will not dwell on them here but stick to rules of the structure indicated above, with one non-terminal symbol on the left-hand side of each rule.

Let us compare this kind of rule with the rules in an expert system, as described in Chapter 1. These rules are just like expert system production rules, in that each associates a number of conditions with conclusions about some abstract concept or object. The linguist's concepts *sentence*, *noun* etc. are abstract concepts in just the same way that a disease is an abstract concept in the domain of a medical rule-base, for instance. When we analyse a sentence, we can say that our goal is to establish the presence of a sentence in the data, in just the same way that we might have a goal to prove that a set of patient data justifies the conclusion that a patient has appendicitis. The sentence goal is provable whenever we find the constituent phrases of a sentence in the linguistic data (i.e. the string of words). A minor difference is that in an expert system, we may ask the user about the basic factual data; in analysing a sentence, we have the data already available as a list of words.

We can say for example that the noun_phrase rule satisfied there is either a pronoun or a determiner and a noun group. One difference between the rules in a grammar and those in an arbitrary knowledge base is that there is a strict ordering of the conditions in a grammar, whereas there is not in a knowledge base. For example in a noun phrase, the determiner *precedes* the noun_group (we cannot say *dog the*). By contrast, the conditions in an expert system rule form a simple logical conjunction where there is no constraint on the order in which conjoined conditions may be satisfied.

Let us continue with the parallel between an expert system rule base and a grammar. In applying the rule base against a set of data, an expert system's inference engine uses a general computational mechanism, such as forward chaining or backward chaining. Equally, a sentence analyser, or parser, tries the syntax rules in a systematic way to check if a string of words is a sentence in the language. It may therefore come as no surprise to observe that parsing of sentences can be approached in the same basic way as inference in an expert system. That is, it can be either hypothesis-driven or data-driven. We can start by posing the question 'is there a sentence here?', which leads in turn to the subsidiary questions 'is there a noun_phrase?' and then 'is there a verb_phrase?', which lead eventually to questions that can be answered directly about the presence of words in the input string. Alternatively, we can start by asking 'what types of phrase can start with the word 'the'?'. Conventionally, we refer to top-down parsing and bottom-up parsing instead of backward and forward chaining, respectively, but the concepts correspond.

Just as a simple expert-system shell can be built in PROLOG using the inherent theorem-proving mechanism of the language, so we can use PROLOG's theorem prover directly for sentence analysis. If we start with a simplified set of noun_phrase rules, we can translate them directly into PROLOG with a few very minor changes of notation. We will give an example, including two clauses for terminals*, and then explain the notation below:

```
noun_phrase(S, Rest) :- determiner(S,S1), noun(S1,Rest)
determiner([the| Rest],Rest).
noun([dog | Rest],Rest).
```

You will notice that each of the non-terminals in the first rule is written as a structured PROLOG term with two variable arguments. To see the purpose of these arguments, we again consider the similarities and differences between grammar rules and those in an expert system rule base. The terminals in a grammar correspond to the factual conditions in an experts system. In a rule-based expert system, these basic facts can either be obtained from a database or by asking the user. In a grammar, each time we consider a terminal on the right-hand side of a rule, we are looking to the next symbol in the string of words for analysis (and if the rule matches successfully, we must be able to pass on the remainder of the string to the next rule). Rather than store this information in the PROLOG database, or ask the user what is the next word, we pass strings of words from one rule to another as 'difference lists'. Each time we match a word with a terminal on the right of a rule, we remove that word from the string that is passed on to successive rules.

In the PROLOG clause for 'the', it can be seen that the second argument is the same list of words which followed 'the' in the first argument. When one of these clauses is called as a PROLOG goal, the first argument represents the input data, and the second is the out-

---

* recall that in a grammar, *terminal* symbols are those which are not capable of further analysis, i.e. words and not phrases.

```
| ?- trace.

yes

| ?- noun_phrase([the,dog],R).
(1)  1 Call: noun_phrase([the,dog],_5) ?
(2)  2 Call: determiner([the,dog],_65637) ?
(2)  2 Exit: determiner([the,dog],[dog])
(3)  2 Call: noun([dog],_5) ?
(3)  2 Exit: noun([dog],[ ])
(1)  1 Exit: noun_phrase([the,dog],[ ])
R    = [ ]

yes
```

Figure 3.7 *Trace of the DCG parsing a NP*

put. Thus, the clause for 'the' expects to get a list starting with the atom *the*, and if that is so, it leaves the tail of the list as its output*. It is only the clauses like this in a grammar which actually consume symbols from the input.

In the noun_phrase rule, the existence of a determiner was the first condition and that of a noun the second and last. Notice that the input to the determiner goal was the same PROLOG variable as that for the noun phrase. Also note that the output of the determiner goal becomes the input of the noun goal, and that the output of the noun goal is identical to that of the noun phrase as a whole. In each goal, the first argument corresponds to the string to be analysed, and the second to the string that is left after the goal has been proved. So if we present the noun_phrase rule above with the input string [the,dog,barks], we would expect after analysis that the second argument would be instantiated to [barks]. Similarly, if the input string is the list [the,dog], the remainder in the second argument would be [] or the empty list. This is precisely what happens in the trace in Figure 3.7 where PROLOG has been called to see if the string 'the dog' constitutes a noun phrase according to these rules: the top level rule was called with the whole string as its first argument in line 1 of the

---

* If you are not familiar with the symbol | in PROLOG list pattern matching, and you feel you need to understand this point in detail, you will need to study the list processing chapter of a PROLOG textbook.

trace, and the second argument was an uninstantiated variable, R. (This variable could have been instantiated to the empty list, [], if we were concerned that the *whole* string should be a noun phrase, in which case PROLOG would have answered 'yes' without showing the variable binding R = []).

In translating a grammar rule into PROLOG, the general pattern is exactly the same as in our noun_phrase rule. The right-hand side of a non-terminal rule always has a difference list in each of its subclauses. If you follow the arguments of the noun_phrase example rule, you can see that we have a noun_phrase from the whole string to the string containing Rest if there is a determiner spanning from the start to a point S1, and a noun spanning from S1 to Rest. This pattern is quite general: if we have *n* conditions on the right-hand side of a grammar rule, then the difference lists are chained through *n*-1 intermediate variables. For example:

```
1hs(S,E) :- rhs1(S,S1),rhs2(S1,S2),rhs3(S2,S3),rhs4(S3,E).
```

Because it is quite a mechanical procedure to translate from a standard grammar rule notation into standard PROLOG, we can let the computer do it. PROLOG has a special grammar rule notation that hides the details of difference lists from the grammar rule writer. Non-terminal rules do not have any arguments for difference lists at all, and rules introducing terminal symbols have the next word from the input stream enclosed in a pair of brackets. So, instead of

```
noun_phrase(S,Rest) :– determiner(S,S1), noun(S1,Rest).
```

we write

```
noun_phrase → determiner, noun.
```

and instead of

```
determiner([the|Rest],Rest).
```

we write

```
determiner → [the].
```

As the trace above showed, our example grammar only allows one noun phrase to be recognized – 'the dog'). This can easily be rectified by adding more rules such as

```
determiner → [a].
noun → [man].
noun → [ball].
```

etc.

The rules we have illustrated so far only allow us to take a yes/no decision about whether a phrase is a noun_phrase. Using an expert system, we might be quite pleased with a yes/no answer to a question such as 'Is there a massive petroleum deposit in my back garden', but it is difficult to imagine a practical use for a sentence analyser which goes through a text and says 'yes, this is a sentence' and nothing more. We are more likely to want to find out about the structure of the sentence, or more likely still, to want to translate it into an explicit representation of its meaning, say in a logical notation or a query language like SQL.

If we want to build up a structural analysis of a sentence, we can do this in a definite clause grammar by exploiting PROLOG's versatile pattern matching to progressively instantiate a complex pattern which represents the structure.

The kind of structure we might want to capture could be the tree structure used by grammarians to show the composition of a sentence (although we can use essentially the same principles to translate directly to predicate logic for example. In this structure, terminal symbols appear at the leaves of the tree, and non-terminals at the root of the tree and its subtrees. The tree shows which rules in the grammar were used in the analysis computed by the parser. Now, with modern bit-mapped graphics, we can draw this sort of graph on a computer screen or a printer, but for each hardware environment the programming involved is different and inconvenient. Standard software such as PROLOG is happier with a textual form of output which can be made up entirely using the printable characters. Fortunately, there is a formally equivalent notation that we can use – that of labelled bracketing. The diagram in Figure 3.8 can be rendered by the following string without loss of information:

```
np(det(the),n(dog))
```

We can build such an analysis using PROLOG structures with variable component parts, and making these structures an additional parameter in each clause. The left-hand side shows the label it assigns to the root of the local tree, and denotes each branch with a

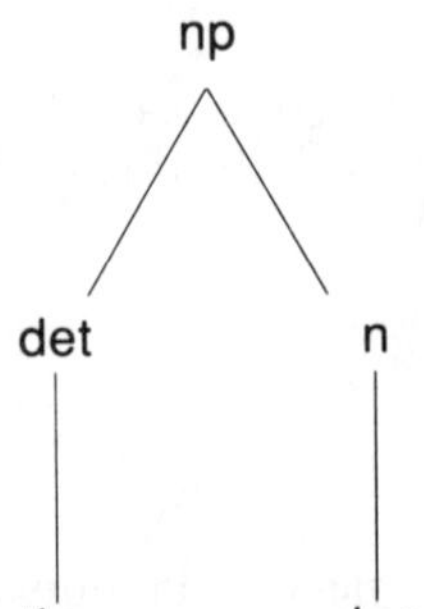

Figure 3.8 *Simple syntax tree*

variable. The right-hand side associates each branch variable with a rule which will establish the structural description for the corresponding branch of the tree. For example, the sentence rule in the grammar below labels the whole structure 's' and assigns an internal structure of two branches, NP and VP. The structure of the NP is to be obtained by whichever NP rule matches the input string, and that of the VP from a rule with left-hand-side verb_phrase.

```
sentence(s(NP,VP)) → noun_phrase(NP), verb_phrase(VP).
noun_phrase(np(D,N)) → determiner(D), noun(N).
noun_phrase(np(P)) → propern(P).
determiner(det(the)) → [the].
noun(n(dog)) → [dog] .
propern(pro(fido)) → [fido].
```

When we now ask PROLOG if 'the dog barks' is a sentence, we get more information in response:

```
?– sentence(S,[the,dog,barks],_).
S = s(np(det(the),n(dog)),vp(iv(barks)))
```

This structure corresponds directly to a conventional syntactic parse tree, with each functor being the label on the root of a subtree. The sentence 'fido barks' would have received the analysis

```
S = s(np(pro(fido)),vp(iv(barks))).
```

In general, as PROLOG parses sentences top-down, the structural analyses are built up 'outside in' with the label or functor established when the rule is called, and the detailed internal structure only established when terminals have been matched.

A final convenience for the grammar writer is the ability to remove some redundancy in the grammar. In particular a lot of typing can be saved if we can reduce the terminal rules to simple clauses, supported by a single rule for each class of word or part of speech. Take an example such as:

```
propern(pro(fido)) → [fido].
```

where you may have noticed that the same information 'fido' appears on both sides, suggesting there might be some redundant information. In a typical system, we would expect to have many times more terminals or lexical entries than there would be different grammar rules. It would be much better if we could write these facts down as simple PROLOG facts, such as *is_pro(fido)*.

In fact we can do this, because the grammar writer is allowed to call any PROLOG goal in place of a grammar rule on the right-hand side of a grammar rule, by enclosing the goal in a pair of braces {}. Such goals are not translated by the addition of the difference list arguments when the program is read in by the PROLOG interpreter and its grammar rule preprocessor.

If we use one general rule per word class as follows:

```
pronoun(pro(W)) → [W], {is-pro(W)}.
```

we can now write any number of simple PROLOG clauses to list the members of this class of words, for example:

```
is_pro(fido).
is_pro(john).
is_pro(london).
```

Another useful feature of definite clause grammars (DCGs) that constituents in rules can be annotated with *features* to encode constraints on grammaticality (such as number agreement in English) or record information that might be relevant to meaning (such as tense). Figure 3.9 is an example of a DCG which uses features both to enforce number agreement and to store information about tense. Most implementations of PROLOG include grammar rule notation as an extension to the language. In case they do not, a PROLOG program to preprocess a file of grammar rules so that they are stored in memory as standard PROLOG clauses is listed in Pereira and Shieber (1987: Appendix A3), Gazdar and Mellish (1989: Chapter 4) and Clocksin and Mellish (1981: Chapter 9). These texts are also recommended for a detailed appreciation of the use of the DCG notation for constructing grammars and parsers.

```
sentence(s(Tns,NP,VP))                   → noun_phrase(Num,NP),
                                           verb_phrase(Num,Tns,VP).
noun_phrase(Num,np(DET,N))               → det(DET),
                                           common_noun(Num,N).
noun_phrase(sing,np(N))                  → proper_noun(N).
verb_phrase(Num,Tns,vp((V,Tns),NP))      → verb(Num,Tns,V),
                                           noun_phrase(N2,NP).

/* lexical rules and clauses for verbs */

verb(plur,pres,v(W))                     → [W], {is-verb(W)}.
verb(sing,pres,v(W))                     → [W], {pl(W,W1), is_verb(W1)}.
verb(Num,past,v(W))                      → [W1], {past(W,WI), is_verb(W)}.
pl(kicks,kick).
is_verb(kick).
past(kick,kicked).
```

Figure 3.9 *Sample DCG grammar with lexical rules*

In the context of a system for interpreting natural language enquiries to a database, it will be necessary to provide a reasonably comprehensive grammar and dictionary. The dictionary will include an element of general vocabulary, and also a specialist vocabulary of terms relevant to the particular information domain. The grammar will have to have additional sentence formation rules, in particular those for questions, and it should record in the parse structure whether a sentence is a question or a declarative sentence, by means of features.

In order to process the query, the parse needs to be translated into an expression in the database query language. This language will typically be a language close to predicate logic. One way to do the translation would be to write rules to translate from a parse tree into the query language. However this is not necessary, as the facility in the DCG PROLOG notation we used to build the parse tree is quite general enough to build other structures too. Clocksin and Mellish (1981: Chapter 9) show how to do a direct translation to predicate logic as an alternative to building up a syntactic parse tree. Gazdar and Mellish (1989: Chapter 8) show additionally how a translation to a database query language can be accomplished, and how the query language can in turn be evaluated over a database also written in PROLOG. This approach to semantics is termed *compositional semantics*, based as it is on the building of the sentence semantics from the semantics of constituent words and phrases in direct correspondence to the rules of syntactic composition An example of a database query system in the literature, based on this approach is Warren and Pereira (1982).

However, as we have seen in the earlier discussion, the literal meaning of an utterance is not a sufficient analysis, and pragmatic factors need to be taken into account.

3 Text processing and abstracting

We now turn to the application of rule-based natural language processing techniques to the problem of analysing texts – the other half of the problem of matching information sources to information needs. Just as conversations are structured according to principles of pragmatics, on top of the levels of syntax and semantics, so texts are organized according to a set of textual and rhetorical principles.

3.1 Text structure and discourse

When two or three sentences are written together, not every permutation of them forms a coherent discourse. Consider the following example:

1 Pronouns are anaphoras.

2 Pronouns can be used in place of proper nouns.

3 Anaphoras are abbreviated referring expressions.

This sequence of sentences is less acceptable than would be the sequence 1,3,2. This can be explained by reference to such concepts as the focus and theme of the sentences. The theme may either remain the same in two successive sentences or it may progress to a new topic which has been introduced in the preceding sentence. In sentence 1, 'pronouns' is the *theme* of the sentence, and 'anaphoras' is a *potential focus.* The next sentence is allowed to use either the theme or the potential focus as its theme, so that either sentence 2 or 3 is an acceptable next sentence. However, sentence 3 is not a good successor to 2, because its theme was neither the theme nor the potential focus of its immediate predecessor.

3.2 Rhetoric

A further structuring principle is that the sentences of a text are related by rhetorical principles. Rhetoric was one of the ancient Greeks' disciplines for the study of language and its use, and was complementary to the study of logic and of grammar. Today, we tend to use the term pejoratively for artful tricks of persuasion, but the essential meaning of rhetoric is the study of the use of language for purposes such as explanation and argumentation. There are particular rhetorical relationships between sentences which can be used as part of a strategy for developing an explanation or an argument. For example, in the three-sentence text above, we can see the whole text as an attempt to explain the concept of an anaphora. A typical explanation links a class of objects to other objects (in sentence 1, 'pronouns', because the writer can reasonably assume 'pronoun' to be a more familiar concept). So a schema for an explanation of a new concept might include identification of its class membership, followed by an attribute description, and examples of the new concept. Such an approach to rhetorical structures in text is used in research into the generation of coherent natural language text (McKeown, 1985). Other rhetorical structures include those that are used in constructing an argument to convince the hearer/reader of some conclusion. Clearly, both identification and argumentation are rhetorical structures we would expect to find in scientific literature.

3.3 Text grammar

Texts also have structure at the highest level. Van Dijk (1980) has referred to this level as macrostructure. It is often proposed that a typical scientific paper has the schematic structure: problem statement; methods adopted; findings; conclusions; normally in that order. Certainly, this is the case for many papers in experimental sciences such as biology and psychology, but it does not encompass all that can be published in other disciplines such as computer science.

Janos (1979) attempted to relate the notion of macrostructure to the principles of thematic progression discussed earlier. He used the term 'theme' as we have done above to refer to the topic the sentence is about, and the term 'rheme' to refer to the predication about the theme. He noted that in sentence grammar, a variety of syntactic devices, e.g. cleft sentences 'it is ... that ...'), can be used to signal explicitly marked rheme instead of relying on the default principle of end-focus (that the item at the end of a sentence is the focus of the next sentence). He then sought to generalize this notion to the level of the text, where he posited the existence of an *extended theme* and an *extended rheme*. In a scientific paper, he suggests that extended themes might be exemplified by characterizing the broad background of the work and characterizing the author's approach to it; extended rhemes would be the formulation of a hypothesis; description of method; experimental results; formulation of conclusions. As with sentence-level themes and rhemes, the theme(s) link the text to already known information, and the rheme(s) provide additional information. What Janos also noted was that the extended themes and rhemes, forming as they do major partitions of a long text, are often explicitly bounded by what he termed *metatext*.

3.4 The indicator phrase method of abstracting

Paice (1981) has taken up this notion of the importance of metatext in signalling thematic boundaries, calling such explicit signals of purpose and content *indicator phrases*. Indicator phrases are structures such as 'the results of this study imply that ...' which indicate that the remainder of the sentence will state something of importance within the context of a scientific paper. The sentence which best indicates (according to a scoring scheme) the topic and results reported in the paper is the starting point for the composition of a readable abstract. It is then consolidated by selecting sequences of adjacent sentences from the document. To render the abstract readable, it is necessary to ensure that the selected sentences contain no referring expressions (pronouns, descriptive noun phrases, etc.) which refer back to things not mentioned within the abstract. Such referring expressions are called *anaphoras*. Clearly, the text of the abstract will be incoherent if there are anaphoras which refer to some object mentioned in a sentence that has not been selected for inclusion. This in turn requires an ability to recognize those uses of potential anaphoras that are actually functioning as anaphoras. For example, 'it' is not anaphoric in the constructions 'it follows that...' or 'it is easy to...'.

```
indicator(Ntotal)    →    [the],
                          emphasis(N), indic1(N1), emphasis2(N2),
                          ([of,this]; [of,the]; [in,this]),
                          indic2(N3),indic3(N4),
                          ([that],{N5 = 1};
                          {true, N5 = 0}),
                          {Ntotal is N + N1+ N2 + N3 + N4 + N5}.
indic1(N)            →    skip(3,Ind), {ind1(Ind)},!,{N is 3}.}
```

Figure 3.10 *Sample rules for identifying indicator phrases*

3.4.1 IMPLEMENTING THE INDICATOR PHRASE METHOD

Implementing the indicator phrase method for resolving anaphoras breaks into two stages: first, extracting content-indicative sentences by pattern matching for indicator phrases, and second, checking for unresolved anaphoras. This program was developed to identify sentences which contained an indicator phrase. Although Paice and Husk (1987) developed a special rule formalism for writing indicator phrase rules, Johnson (1988) found it possible to encode the relevant information in DCG rules. In using the DCG notation for indicator phrase recognition, there is no need to build a parse of the whole sentence. The more limited goal is to recognize an occurrence of the indicator phrase and to compute a score based on its constituents. In doing so, a 'grammar' for indicator phrases was written which differs in several ways from the standard grammar for recognizing general sentence structures.

Firstly, this grammar could use terminal symbols that were directly motivated by the concepts of indicator phrase patterns, and not the names of conventional syntactic phrase types (e.g. noun, verb, etc.). Secondly, some of the rules permit following words to be skipped up to some set limit. Thirdly, the rules use the facility of arbitrary PROLOG computations enclosed in braces to directly implement the scoring attached to particular rules. Embedding arbitrary PROLOG goals allows the calculation of an overall weighting for the sentence, based on the weightings of the different indicator and emphasis words. For example, a sentence beginning 'The results of this study into automatic indexing confirms that...' matches the rules in Figure 3.10.

The rule *indic1* allows up to three words to be skipped, and expects the next word to be an indicator of category *ind1*. This in turn is satisfied by any of a set of PROLOG unit clauses, such as *ind1(results)*. Several synonyms are also treated as equivalent to 'results'. A weighting of 3 is carried forward through the variable *N* to be added to weights associated with other parts of the indicator rule. The rules for *indic2* and *indic3* similarly allow intervening words to be skipped. In the example sentence, *indic3* matches 'confirms' after skipping 'into automatic indexing'. The application of the rule proceeds in this manner until a final weighting of *Ntotal* can be calculated for the sentence as a whole. The scoring allows the sentence which has the 'best' indicator phrase to be selected as the basis for the abstract. Prior sentences are then selected while the current sentence contains anaphoric pronouns, or until the beginning of the paragraph is reached.

Alternative approaches could be envisaged which recognized special metatext patterns for each distinct component of the text (the method, conclusions, etc.), and thereby sought to apply the notion of a text grammar (as discussed above) of scientific papers. However, such a notion would presuppose that scientific texts have a standard text structure, and that all subdivisions of the text are metatextually indicated. The advantage of Paice's technique is that being based on domain-independent metatextual features, it requires only a modest rule base, and no adaptation for a particular knowledge domain. This is of course also a disadvantage, because the technique relies on the author using such metatextual clues, and allows no alternative approach to sentence selection which might be able to exploit domain knowledge. We will return to this theme later, after examining the way in which DCG rules also play a part in determining whether referring expressions are functioning anaphoras.

Paice (Paice and Husk, 1987; Paice, 1988) has recently developed computer-based implementations for some of the rules required to recognize functioning anaphoric occurrences of 'it' in texts. The problem with expressions such as the pronoun 'it' is that they do not always function as anaphoras. For example the 'it' in 'it is raining' or 'it is easy to...' are not functioning anaphoras. Paice and Husk's rules were formulated so that they could distinguish between those occurrences of 'it' that were not anaphoric; anaphoric with an antecedent in the same sentence; anaphoric with an antecedent in the preceding sentence.

Paice's rules for anaphora detection were tested against a large corpus of texts and those for 'it' found to be about 95% accurate in identifying those that function as an anaphora. Liddy *et al.* (1987) formulated the following rules for 'that': THAT

- is non-anaphoric after a cognitive or emotive verb such as know, think, believe, feel, where it introduces an embedded sentence
- after the nominalization of a cognitive or emotive verb, e.g. assumption, suggestion, hypothesis , etc. when it introduces an embedded sentence

- when it is part of a subordinating conjunction in the constructions but that, in that, such that, etc.
- as a relative pronoun, after a noun phrase
- as the determiner in a noun phrase

THAT is anaphoric when it serves none of the above functions.

4 Future developments

Paice's computer-based system (Paice and Husk 1987) was able to deal with anaphora recognition rules for 'it' and some other pronouns, and also some simple cases of noun phrases starting with 'the'. Like the rules for selecting indicator phrases, these were written in the special notation they devised. Paice and this author are now embarked on further research to improve the ability to identify referring uses of noun phrases.

Definite noun phrases, such as 'the experiment' occur frequently in scientific papers (this one caused trouble in one of Johnson's trials, where her program proposed an abstract made up of three successive sentences with occurrences of this phrase, but where it turned out that three different experiments were being referred to). When a noun phrase is marked as definite by the use of 'the', it is likely to be referring to some entity or concept introduced earlier. Some early natural language processing programs took the simplifying assumption that a noun phrase introduced by 'a' always introduces a new individual into the discourse, and a noun phrase with 'the' is always referring back to an already introduced individual. Things are by no means so straightforward. One exception to this rule is the definite description 'The present prime minister of Canada' or the so-called homophor (such as 'the weather'), neither of which need have been previously introduced in the text – it is simply that the writer assumes the reader to know how to identify the referent. Another complexity is that an indefinite (or definite) phrase may not be talking about an individual but a class of objects (for example 'a submarine is a naval vessel', 'the submarine is a type of naval vessel', but *cf* 'a submarine was entering the harbour').

The ultimate goal of our work on abstracting is to produce good quality abstracts from unseen texts, whose vocabulary and range of expression are beyond the scope of a predefined dictionary and grammar. However, to identify occurrences of noun phrases and then classify their referring function, we face a much harder task than identifying pronouns and their usages. The pronoun is a single word, but the noun phrase, although its start may be easy to identify, can be of almost arbitrary length, and may comprise many different structures of pre- and post-modification.

The method we are adopting is first to use morphological clues and a dictionary of function words (e.g. articles, conjunctions, prepositions, verbal auxiliaries) to identify the part of speech of most words, and to try to determine the others from constraints derived from grammar rules. The phrases so identified are then analysed by reference to a new set of anaphora detection rules for noun phrases. The rule base is not yet developed, but it is expected that the premises of the rules will be based mostly on syntactic clues, for example the use of the copula verb 'is', tense, and presence of prepositional phrases. The aim in the short term is to see to what extent we can build a system for this task which does not need the vast background knowledge that would be needed by a genuine 'artificial intelligence' approach. This new development is being implemented in PROLOG for the rule-based part, and C for efficient text segmentation and morphological analysis. If these methods for identifying referring and co-referring expressions turn out to be successful, we will then be able to look towards uncovering chains of reference and other aspects of textual structure. This in turn may lead to the possibility of evolving our abstracting methods towards those simulating some kind of 'understanding' of the text rather than mere skimming. Other goals for the future will include knowledge acquisition from textual sources (a more substantial goal than abstracting).

References

Allen, J. (1987) *Natural language understanding.* Menlo Park: Benjamin Cummings.

Black, W.J. and Johnson, F.C. (1988) A practical evaluation of two knowledge-based automatic abstracting techniques. *Expert Systems for Information Management*, **1**,(3), pp 159-177.

Bobrow, D. (1986) GUS, a frame-driven dialogue system. In *Readings in natural language processing*, eds. Grosz, B.J., Sparck-Jones K. and Webber, B.L., pp. 595-604. Los Altos, Morgan Kaufmann.

Clocksin, W.F. and Mellish, C.S. (1981) *Programming in PROLOG.* New York: Springer-Verlag.

Gazdar, G.G. and Mellish C.S. (1989) *Natural language processing in PROLOG.* London: Addison-Wesley.

Grice, H.P. (1975) Logic and conversation. In *Syntax and Semantics, Vol. 3: Speech Acts*, eds. Cole P. and Morgan, J.L. Academic Press, New York.

Hendrix, G.G., Sacerdoti, E.D., Sagalowicz, D. and Slocum, J. (1978) Developing a natural language interface to complex data. *ACM Transactions on Database Systems*, **1**, (2), pp 105-147.

Janos, J. (1979) Theory of functional sentence perspective and its application for the purposes of automatic extracting. *Information Processing and Management*, **30**, (1), 19-25.

Johnson, F.C. (1988) A practical evaluation of two automatic abstracting methods. MSc Dissertation, UMIST, Manchester, 1988, *see also* Black and Johnson (1988).

Leech, G.N. (1983) *The principles of pragmatics*, London: Longman

Liddy, E., Bonzi, S., Katzer, J. and Oddy, E. (1987) A study of discourse anaphora in scientific abstracts. *Journal of American Society for Information Science*, **38**, (4), 255-261

McKeown, K. (1985) Discourse strategies for generating natural language text. *Artificial Intelligence*, **27**, 1-41

Norton, L.M. (1983) Automated analysis of instructional text. *Artificial Intelligence*, **20**, 307-344

Oxborrow, E. (1986) *Databases and database systems*. Bromley: Chartwell-Bratt

Paice, C.D. (1981) The automatic generation of literature abstracts: an approach based on the identification of self-indicating phrases, In *Information retrieval research*, Oddy, R.N. *et al*, eds. pp. 172-191, London: Butterworths

Paice, C.D. (1988) *The automatic generation of abstracts of technical papers*. Dept. of Computing, University of Lancaster, Final Report to British Library Research and Development Division.

Paice, C.D. and Husk, G.D. (1987) Towards the automatic recognition of anaphoric features in English text: the impersonal pronoun 'it'. *Computer Speech and Language*, **2**, 109-132

Pereira, F.C.N. and Shieber, S.M. (1987) *PROLOG and natural language analysis*, CSLI Lecture Notes No. 10, University of Chicago Press

Van Dijk, T.A. (1980) *Macrostructures*. Hillsdale, N.J.: Lawrence Erlbaum.

Warren, D.H.D. and Periera, F.C.N. (1982) An efficient easily adaptable system for interpreting natural language queries. *American Journal of Computational Linguistics*, **8**(3-4), 110-122

Chapter 4

Expert systems in reference work

Roy Davies, Alastair G. Smith and Anne Morris

1 Introduction

1.1 Definition and purpose of reference work

Before considering the application of expert systems to reference work, it would be useful to consider the definition of the concept of 'reference' in the library/information context. Rothstein (1953) traced the development of reference work, or reference service as he called it. In the earlier part of the 19th century the emphasis in libraries was on collections, and it was almost an after thought that librarians would have some knowledge of the information resources of their libraries and a responsibility to facilitate their use by clients. Until the 1890s the implication of the name 'Reference Department' in a library meant that the books therein were for reference only, and it was not until 1893 that the term 'reference' acquired its present meaning of providing an information service using that reference collection, or, indeed, any of the library's resources that may be used in answering enquiries.

Why is a reference service necessary? For very small collections it might not be, but such collections would not satisfy a wide range of needs. All other things being equal, the larger the collection the more likely it is that it will contain what any particular enquirer needs, but the larger the collection gets the more difficult the task of finding the right material becomes. Catalogues have severe limitations as guides to stock; some material such as periodical articles and many government publications are not usually catalogued, and even for material that is, subject access is vitiated by the low number of subject headings or class numbers assigned to each item and often, particularly in the case of class numbers, by their lack of specificity. Bibliographies and abstracts journals, in printed form, CD-ROM or online, are useful for subject access to many forms of literature, but online searching is usually too complicated or, when connect-time charges are involved, too costly for inexperienced end-users, while in the case of printed or CD-ROM versions the reader still has the task of selecting the appropriate tool and then of using it properly, which may be difficult where complex tools such as *Chemical Abstracts* are involved.

In any case, enquirers often want information rather than documents and the use of subject bibliographies may not be the best way of finding it. 'Save the time of the reader' is one of Ranganathan's 'laws' of library science (Ranganathan, 1963). In organizations served by special libraries it is not cost-effective for highly paid staff to spend long periods searching the literature when the task can be delegated to information scientists. In academic institutions students need to be shown or taught effective means of finding information, and in libraries of any kind it is a waste of resources to build up collections which are not properly exploited. Reference librarians exist to ensure that enquirers' needs are satisfied using library resources, and their efforts are beginning to be augmented by the use of expert systems.

Generally, in considering the application of expert systems to reference work, writers are considering the provision of reference services based on printed materials. For instance Richardson (1990) considered the effect of CD-ROM and online: he wondered if the effort of creating a model of knowledge relating to the reference question domain is wasted, if the paper-based sources that he covered in his model have been replaced by their CD-ROM and online versions. But are online and paper-based reference that far apart? Essentially they contain the same information, and the mechanisms for choosing between them will be based on similar assumptions. Granted, access points will be different, and this will have to be included in the knowledge base, but none the less an expert system for chemistry reference will need knowledge about *Chemical Abstracts*, and whether this is of its online, CD-ROM or paper versions will not be fundamentally different.

While later on in this chapter implementations of expert systems for selecting online databases will be treated separately from implementations for general reference work, there is still significant common ground. The potential difference lies in the interaction of the expert system with sources. With online and CD-ROM sources, there is the potential for direct interface between the system and the source.

1.2 Motivation for expert systems in reference work

1.2.1 BETTER UNDERSTANDING OF THE REFERENCE PROCESS

One reason for investigating the application of expert systems to reference work is that the analysis of the process in order to encapsulate it in an expert system may lead to a greater understanding of reference work. That this is happening is shown for example in publications by Parrot (1989b) and Richardson (1989; 1990) that will be referred to later.

1.2.2 BETTER USE OF REFERENCE LIBRARIAN'S TIME/STAFF RESOURCES – THE 'CRISIS IN REFERENCE SERVICE'

There is some dissatisfaction with reference services expressed in the literature. Miller (1984) discussed a 'darker side of reference life' where overwork and burnout prevents reference librarians from giving their clients the service that they deserve. Miller mentioned the advantages of automating the duller clerical tasks involved in reference work, allowing reference staff to concentrate on more interesting professional tasks and the development of new programs. Herñon and McClure, (1987) raised questions, based on unobtrusive testing of reference services, about the effectiveness of reference librarians. Too often they are unfamiliar with the range of reference sources available to them, conduct superficial reference interviews and provide 'half-right' answers to test questions.

Crews (1988) surveyed more than 30 reference accuracy studies and identified a wide range of variables (collection size, budgetary restraints) that may affect performance. He concluded *inter alia* that 'understanding the details that bear on reference, services is increasingly important as libraries grow in complexity'. This raises the possibility that, as in other disciplines, routine enquiries and tasks can be dealt with by an expert system, or a paraprofessional aided by an expert system, freeing the human reference expert for more challenging and demanding tasks.

Some studies indicate that typical ready reference enquiries may be dealing with a relatively limited knowledge base of reference works. For example a Maryland survey of public library reference services (Gers and Seward, 1985) quoted in Richardson (1989) indicated that seven reference works were used to answer 87.5% of a sample set of questions asked. This indicates that an expert system that can encapsulate the knowledge about a relatively small number of reference sources should be able to answer a high proportion of ready reference questions.

Richardson (1989) has considered systematically the pros and cons of reference expert systems for different groups involved in reference service. These include:

- end users
- reference librarians
- reference department paraprofessionals

- reference department heads
- library directors
- library school faculty
- library school students
- reference book authors and publishers

In general terms, the potential advantages of the application of expert systems to reference work (as adapted from Richardson) are:

- an after-hours service could be provided, when only paraprofessional staff may be available
- an independent option could be offered to users who may be inhibited from approaching a human reference librarian for assistance
- staff could be freed from repetitive, boring queries, thus reducing risk of burnout
- they could have a role in teaching students and paraprofessionals
- the reference service could be made more consistent, preserving the 'corporate memory' through changes of reference staff
- they could help to identify new reference tools that are required

Disadvantages include:

- the absence of human contact
- the need for an adequate supply of machines
- the potential threat to job security
- the possibility of staff losing familiarity with basic reference work
- the large amount of investment required in staff time to set up and maintain the expert system(s)

1.2.3 MANAGEMENT INFORMATION

Collecting reference statistics in a real library environment is notoriously difficult. Busy staff do not tend to record accurately the numbers of queries dealt with, let alone other characteristics. Smith and Hutton (1984) described the use of an after-hours reference advisory system at Purdue University to collect statistics on the nature of the queries it was used for. They suggest that this gives management an insight into the information needs of users who for various reasons do not approach reference staff.

2 The reference process

The classic model of knowledge engineering for the development of an expert system begins with a thorough understanding of the skills and knowledge possessed by the human expert. Therefore an investigation of the applications of expert systems to reference work must draw on studies of the reference process.

Frequently the reference librarian will be unable to give an immediate answer to the enquirer's question as it is initially stated. A clarifying dialogue or reference interview is often necessary when any of the following conditions listed by Jahoda (1976) apply:

- the real query may not be asked
- the librarian is unfamiliar with the subject of the query
- the query statement is ambiguous or incomplete
- the amount of information needed is not specified
- the level of the answer is not specified
- the query takes more time than the librarian can spend on it
- the answer to the query is not recorded in the literature
- the language, time period or constraints regarding geographical area or type of publication need to be added to the query statement

The task of determining whether or not the real query has been asked can be difficult. Subjecting all enquirers to interrogation would waste time and would also irritate some readers, and therefore the reference librarian must rely on clues to tell whether or not an interview is necessary. Jahoda and Braunagel (1980) have described various clues in enquiry statements (e.g. requests for a particular reference tool or for a particular type of publication) that might indicate that the subject of the real query has not been stated.

2.1 Models of the reference process

2.1.1 TAYLOR (1968)

How can the reference librarian ascertain the enquirer's real need? One of the earliest and most influential models of the reference process is that proposed by Taylor, who looked at the negotiation process that takes place as a seeker for information works through a librarian intermediary. Taylor's work was based on a series of relatively unstructured interviews with reference librarians, which closely parallel the pattern of a knowledge-acquisition interview for an expert system development project.

Clients must develop their queries from a visceral need, through the conscious and formalized query stages to a 'compromised' need or query which matches the resources of the information system. In order to help the client arrive at the compromised need, the librarian must apply a number of filters, to determine the client's:

- subject of interest
- motivation
- personal characteristics
- the relationship of the expressed query to the information system's file organzation
- anticipated or acceptable answers to the query

These filters are not necessarily applied in a linear, sequential fashion. Data for several may be embedded in a single statement by the enquirer. It may be necessary to repeat certain steps if the results of the search are not satisfactory – a point also discussed by Shera (1964), whose account of the reference process emphasized its cyclical nature and the importance of evaluation in determining its course.

Interestingly, Taylor also considered the potential for using computers in the reference process. He looked at how a natural language processing program of the ELIZA (Weizenbaum, 1966) type could be used for eliciting additional concepts, phrases and search terms from an enquirer. He concluded that the systems available at the time were 'not sophisticated enough to do much with the information in response to such questions'. He also described early automated bibliographic instruction systems using computer and microfilm technology, and mentioned early artificial intelligence work 'on the augmentation of human intellect by computers' which 'may generate interesting systems in the future, but appears to have little pertinence at this time to the problems under consideration here'.

Minor modifications to Taylor's model, emphasizing the distinction between those stages in the reference process that involve the enquirer alone and those involving both the enquirer and the librarian, were proposed by Markey (1981), who also discussed the possibility of testing her modified model. Actual tests of a model have been conducted by Jahoda (1977), but in general, the subject of testing has not attracted much attention, possibly because it might be difficult to make falsifiable predictions that would enable the validity of one model as opposed to another to be clearly demonstrated.

2.1.2 LYNCH (1978)

Lynch (1978), motivated to some extent by 'discontent' with the work of Taylor and that of Penland (Penland, 1970), who advocated the use of counselling techniques used in other disciplines, carried out content analysis of tape recordings of reference interviews and allocated them to four classifications:

1. Directional transactions – relating to locations, policies and services of the library. Taylor did not consider these to be true reference questions.
2. Holdings transactions – to locate the whereabouts of a known item.
3. Substantiative transactions – for factual information, subject searches, bibliographic verification etc.
4. Moving transactions – for transactions which are altered in the course of the reference process to another class of transaction.

Lynch developed two clarification procedures, or models, for the reference interview. These are the holdings model (for the location of a discrete bibliographic item) and the substantiative model (for a subject query).

In a holdings model, a librarian would ask for the following kinds of information:

- bibliographic description – facts about the document, spelling, the citation or source of information
- function – for what purpose the enquirer requires the item, for instance in order to determine whether another item will be useful instead
- action taken – to determine whether the enquirer had already searched the catalogue or the shelves for the item
- location requirement – relating to the status of the material, for instance whether a reference or a loan copy is required
- other – relevant experience of the enquirer, or other information

In a substantiative model, these kinds of information would be requested:

- subject definition – narrowing down the query to a more specific one
- fact gathering – what the enquirer already knows about the subject, what source(s) of information the enquirer has already used, what the purpose of the enquiry is
- answer specification – the amount of information needed, any deadline, acceptable sources, the possible loan status of sources, the time period required, how information is to be

presented, the level of difficulty, whether a particular answer has satisfied the question

- action taken – what sources the enquirer has used and how they were used, what sources they have experience with, kinds of material found
- other – any other relevant information

It is worth noting that Lynch's study challenged some of the assumptions of reference work, for instance by finding a lower rate of actual reference interviews than had been assumed, that open and non-directive questions were asked infrequently, and that clients asked more precise questions than expected.

2.1.3 KATZ (1982)

In his seminal textbook on reference work, Katz (1982) introduced three important search procedures which depend on the reference librarian's own knowledge:

- automatic retrieval (case 1) where the librarian already knows the answer (for example to a directional query); in general this will apply to Lynch's directional queries
- automatic retrieval (case 2) where the librarian has a simple procedure for answering the query (for instance consulting a particular reference tool); this will be true of many ready reference questions
- translation devices, which link a query, after clarification in the reference interview, with aspects of the information system, for instance:
    - types of information sources
    - subject field
    - time period
    - language

2.1.4 INGWERSEN

In Denmark, Ingwersen (1982, 1984, 1986) has investigated the links between user needs, negotiations and search procedures with the aim of improving our understanding of the complete process, so that students of librarianship and inexperienced or less-skilled staff can be taught the approaches that skilled reference librarians adopt intuitively, and also because such an analysis is necessary to identify the features that would, ideally, be required in reference expert systems. Whereas Lynch noted without criticism that open questions were not used as frequently as might be expected, Ingwersen concluded that insufficient use was made of them in elucidating the real need when, as is often the case, the enquirer's statement consists largely of a few out-of-context terms which may be more generic than the true need. Ingwersen (1982, 1986) argued that closed or leading questions are generally used at too early a stage, whereas their use should be restricted to delimiting and confirming the reference librarian's picture of the enquirer's need. The actual need may fall into one of three categories:

1. Verificative or locational information problems. The enquirer wants to verify bibliographic references or find the location of specific items.

2. Conscious substantiative information problems. The enquirer wants to clarify, review or pursue specific topics.

3. Muddled substantiative information problems. The enquirer is looking for new ideas but has difficulty in explaining the problem, e.g. a scientist might want to trace analogous theories or solutions to analogous problems in other disciplines, but has no idea what these might be.

Ingwersen (1986) has outlined the different types of knowledge which a reference librarian or an expert system should employ in each of the above cases.

2.1.5 DERVIN

Dervin, writing from the standpoint of an expert in the study of communication, has criticized the way in which librarians and information scientists tend to regard individual users as conforming to stereotypes of certain groups who ask certain types of questions: the uniqueness of each person is disregarded (Dervin, 1989, Dervin and Dewdney, 1986, Dervin and Nilan, 1986). She and her associates argued that most questions people ask in troublesome situations had some relation to themselves or others, rather than being questions that could be answered satisfactorily with facts from reference tools, and she developed a 'situations–gaps–uses' model of how information needs should be met. Dervin's work is obviously relevant to the tasks of citizens' advice bureaux and to librarians concerned with the provision of community information. However, she has claimed that it is relevant to reference interviews in general, and a number of librarians in the United States and Canada have been trained in the use of this approach, so that they would ask enquirers about their life situations and what brought them to the system or enquiry desk, rather than pose the traditional questions that attempt to specify what portion of the system's resources are relevant to the user's needs (Dervin and Dewdney 1986).

It should be noted, however, that questions about the reasons why particular information is wanted may be regarded as intrusive by the enquirer (Jahoda and Braunagel, 1980). Wilson (1986) suggests that there is a lot to be said for taking non-bibliographic requests (i.e. those for information on specific subjects) at face value and only asking probing questions in connection with bibliographic requests (i.e. those for specific publications or types of publication).

Nevertheless, if Dervin's criticisms of the way in which librarians traditionally operate are valid, they will also apply to expert systems designed to emulate that way of working, and they also have implications for the issue of whether user models should be based on stereotypes or on the characteristics of the individual person (Rich, 1983).

2.1.6 BELKIN

Belkin and his colleagues have also undertaken investigations in which enquirers were encouraged to describe their problems rather than being asked a series of closed or leading questions (Belkin, Oddy and Brooks, 1982a, 1982b). Their work is based on the belief that the underlying motivation for queries is usually the recognition of some inadequacy or anomaly in the enquirer's knowledge. Whereas the conventional approach to information retrieval is to try to get the enquirer to describe as accurately as possible what it is that he or she does not know, and then draw up search statements consisting of Boolean combinations of terms which are then matched with document descriptions consisting of similar combinations of terms, the approach advocated by Belkin and his collaborators is to identify the category to which the enquirer's anomalous state of knowledge (ASK) belongs and then choose a search strategy appropriate to that type of ASK. The classification of ASKs used in their initial work was descriptive in nature, not theoretically based, and some of Belkin's subsequent work has concentrated more on analysing reference negotiations in great detail, with the aim of specifying the functions to be performed by the various components of an expert system for information retrieval (Belkin and Windel, 1984).

2.1.7 FRANTS AND BRUSH (1988)

Whereas Belkin and his associates advocated the creation of a detailed taxonomy of user needs, Frants and Brush suggested that a very meaningful distinction may be drawn between concrete information needs (CINs) and problem-oriented needs (POINs). A CIN, e.g. a query such as 'what is the melting point of lead under standard conditions?' has a clearly defined boundary, whereas a POIN does not. A typical example of the latter would be a request for information on 'the application of statistical methods in interpreting experimental results'. Frants and Brush claimed that because the thematical boundaries of a POIN cannot be precisely defined, individuals requesting information on what seems to be exactly the same topic may not be satisfied by the same documents. Like Dervin's views, this could be used as another argument in favour of the creation of individual user models for use in expert reference systems. The differences between CINs and POINs are summarized below:

CIN	POIN
1. The thematic boundaries are clearly defined.	1. The thematic boundaries are not clearly defined.
2. The request can be put into exact words so that it corresponds to the thematic limits.	2. As a rule the request does not conform exactly to the POIN.
3. To satisfy a CIN only one pertinent document is needed.	3. As a rule the POIN cannot be completely satisfied even with every pertinent document existing in the system.
4. Judgement of relevance is objective.	4. Judgement of relevance is subjective.
5. As soon as the pertinent document is found the CIN disappears.	5. As soon as pertinent documents are read the thematical limits of the POIN may be changed and the POIN may remain for a long time.
6. Can be satisfied by handbooks, tables, dictionaries, encyclopaedias etc.	6. Can be satisfied (partially) by primary literature.

2.1.8 WHITE (1983)

White developed a model of the reference interview that is based on the schema ideas proposed by Minsky and other theorists in cognitive processing and artificial intelligence. Minsky stated that a frame could be regarded as 'a collection of questions to be asked about a hypothetical situation' (Minksy, 1975 p.246), a description which clearly suggests its relevance to the reference process. Assuming that schema ideas are valid in this context, the librarian's master interview frame probably contains slots for goals, role relationships, participants, the kind of information needed to achieve goals, operational procedures, and perhaps common problem areas. White pointed out that Taylor's filters are likely slots. An experienced searcher might have differentiated master interview frames with subframes for specific types of reference interviews, e.g. developing an SDI profile or planning a retrospective search. In contrast, an inexperienced user approaching the interview with the librarian might use an inappropriate frame, based predominantly on encounters with library personnel at the circulation desk, and therefore the librarian would probably have to spend more time probing the user's needs and explaining what could be done to satisfy them than would be the case with a more experienced user.

During the negotiation process various slots in both the librarian's and the user's frames are filled by the transfer of information or, more simply, by default. When a sufficient number of slots has been filled the actual search begins. Whereas some writers have cautioned against excessive reliance on transcripts of negotiations for studying the reference process since non-verbal communication is ignored, White drew attention to a second reason: because of the importance of default assumptions the transcripts will give an incomplete account of what really happened.

Some of the more complex reference expert systems, e.g. PLEXUS and REFSIM, do use frames to formulate search statements in a manner similar to librarians (White, 1983).

2.2 Bates' idea/search tactics

The reference negotiation process frequently continues during the search, but whether it does or not, changes in the direction of the search are very common. Bates (1979a) identified 29 tactics used to guide a search strategy in information searching. These were divided into:

1. Monitoring tactics to guide the progress of a search, such as PATTERN, to be aware of and assess a common search pattern.

2. File structure tactics to utilize features of the sources and files being used: an example is SCAFFOLD. To combine several sources to find an answer; for instance to find a person's phone number by looking them up in a source that lists the organization they belong to, then looking up a directory that lists the organization's phone number.

3. Search formulation tactics to aid the development and modification of search strategy. An example is REDUCE, to limit the number of query elements included in the search formulation in order to increase recall.

4. Term tactics, which aid the selection and modification of search terms. Examples are SUPER, SUB and RELATE, that use broader, more specific or related terms in the file vocabulary.

Bates saw these tactics firstly as practical tools for use in everyday searching, and secondly as a teaching model. The utility of the tactics is emphasized by the use of capitalized verbs, denoting actions to be taken in the course of a search. In general the tactics are usable both in print and online sources. However, many of them, particularly the search formulation and term tactics, depend on access to the internal structure of the source, and thus are less appropriate for use by an expert system that does not have direct access to electronic versions of the sources.

2.3 Parrott's paradigm of reference knowledge

Parrott (1989b) reviewed much of the existing body of knowledge relating to the reference process and attempted to identify the knowledge and skill associated with it. The structure of reference knowledge, particularly that derived from Taylor, Lynch and Bates, has been embodied in his REFSIM system (Parrott 1989a).

He identified seven types of knowledge used in reference work:

1. Typical information for question type – the knowledge of what kind of information is associated with, and is necessary to answer, a particular type of question. For instance a company information query may have associated with it information about the country the company operates in, its products, whether it is listed on the stock exchange, etc.
2. Librarian's model of client – the knowledge about the client, his/her skills and attitudes.
3. Action specification – knowledge about actions that may form a search strategy.
4. Scope of sources – knowledge about the scope of information contained in a source. Parrott in fact makes a distinction between the knowledge of information types in sources, and the scope of knowledge in those sources. However the information types contained in a source could be regarded as part of its scope.
5. Index types in sources – knowledge about index structure and points of access.
6. Strengths of coverage of sources – knowledge about the comprehensiveness of a source.
7. Conceptual links – knowledge of the semantic links of the sort contained in a thesaurus.

Parrott then matched these types of knowledge against Taylor's filters,

Lynch's categories, Katz's search procedures and Bates' search tactics. From this he synthesized what he called a 'paradigm of reference knowledge' (see Figure 4.1).

2.4 Tasks for expert systems for reference work

Work on models of the reference process from Taylor onwards demonstrates what a complex activity it is. It would appear to be impracticable, at least in the short term, to produce an expert system capable of dealing with as wide a range of queries as a good reference librarian, and consequently, if automation is to be useful it will be necessary to identify some reasonably limited tasks which could be tackled successfully before setting more ambitious goals. Unfortunately, although libraries often keep statistics of the number of queries answered, they rarely record the topics in any detail and there is a paucity of published information on this subject (Richardson, 1989). In setting goals it is necessary to distinguish various categories such as:

- queries that take up the most time
- queries that are irksome and irritating
- queries that are repetitive
- queries that reference librarians enjoy dealing with

To elucidate the knowledge required for answering the most time-consuming queries would be difficult, as they would probably require considerable expertise and therefore it would be natural to concentrate first on frequently asked, and irritating, questions. Relieving librarians of these would improve their job satisfaction, but if the intention is to improve services when the appropriate individuals are not available, it will eventually be necessary to tackle the other categories too.

Conventional computing techniques would be adequate for answering locational queries (graphics would be particularly useful for these) concerning the bookstock or facilities such as photocopiers, toilets etc., and for routine enquiries, about library services and policies, e.g. ones about opening hours and loan periods, as well as some of the simpler subject enquiries, whereas for those of any real difficulty it is likely that AI techniques would be required. The answers to queries concerning locations, policies and services would vary from one library to another, but systems for answering substantiative queries might be useful in many different libraries if they were based on the most important and commonly available sources of information in each subject. The creation of such systems requires a thorough analysis of the knowledge used for answering enquiries.

Knowledge type involved	Taylor's filters	Lynch's holdings categories	Lynch's substantive categories	Katz's reference search procedures	Bates' tactics
TYPICAL INFORMATION TYPES FOR QUESTION TYPE	Subject; Motivation/ objective; Acceptable answers	Bibliographic description; Function; prior action taken; Location requirement; other (Client's expertise with item)	Subject definition; Fact gathering; Answer specification; Action taken		
LIBRARIAN'S MODEL OF CLIENT	Client characteristics	prior action taken; other (client's expertise with item)	Answer specification (level of difficulty); Action taken		
ACTION SPECIFICATION	modify question (to fit inquiry to file organisation)			Automatic retrieval 1 (from librarian's memory); Automatic retrieval 2 (librarian has simple procedure); Translation devices	PATTERN; STRETCH; SCAFFOLD; SUPER; WEIGH
ACTION SPECIFICATION — confidence factor for success of					PATTERN; STRETCH; SCAFFOLD; SUPER; WEIGH
FACTUAL INFORMATION				Automatic retrieval 1 (from librarian's memory)	
SOURCES — scope of information types in				Automatic retrieval 2 (librarian has simple procedure)	STRETCH; SCAFFOLD; SUPER; WIEGH
SOURCES — index types for					SCAFFOLD
SOURCES — degree of coverage for					WEIGH
CONCEPTUAL LINKS				Translation devices (to subject terms of information system)	SUPER

Figure 4.1 *Paradigm of reference knowledge*

2.5 Levels of knowledge

The knowledge associated with a task can be regarded as being of three types (Richardson, 1990, Parrott, 1989b):

1. Surface (or heuristic or subordinate) knowledge, which consists of the rules-of-thumb or short cuts and specific strategies learnt through experience in a task. This would include the knowledge that a specific source will answer a particular class of query.
2. Intermediate (or basic) knowledge, which consists of general strategies, for instance that a particular type of question is best answered by encylopaedias.
3. Deep knowledge, which involves first principles, axioms and laws. Generally this will be learned from books or in education. Surface knowledge can be regarded as compiled deep knowledge.

It is likely that surface knowledge will be first applied to a task since this type of knowledge is likely to yield quick results if successful, and then if this fails, intermediate and finally deep knowledge will be applied.

Richardson (1990) applied the distinctions between intermediate level knowledge and surface knowledge to the knowledge required for ready reference work. He excluded deep knowledge because its practical relevance in this field is still uncertain. Without the foundation of deep knowledge, much of it tacitly acquired, it would probably be difficult if not impossible to acquire skills in reference work, since it would be hard to appreciate the purpose of it all. However, even when acquiring those skills the deep knowledge remains very much in the background. The novice librarian is unlikely to make conscious use of it and the experienced one is even less likely to. Once the skills have been acquired, surface knowledge seems to be adequate. (Nevertheless, according to Parrott, codification of deep knowledge could have important benefits, as explained later in this section).

Richardson's objective was to identify:

- the surface-level rules for selecting specific print sources for answering ready reference, fact-based queries (he concentrates particularly on dictionaries)
- the intermediate-level rules and general strategies for particular classes or formats of information

He identified two stages of a ready reference enquiry:

1. Using intermediate level knowledge of the kind:

IF query relates to basic information about words
THEN use a dictionary

to establish the general class(es) of reference source appropriate to the query.

2. Using surface knowledge of the type:

IF query relates to information for a young person
THEN use World Book Encyclopedia to identify a specific source.

As part of a Council on Library Resources funded study, Richardson has been systematically identifying surface knowledge of this latter type, and expressing it in IF ... THEN rules. He has suggested that the intermediate rule base of procedural knowledge used in the first stage appears to be largely private, embodied in the personal knowledge and experience of reference librarians. In this it contrasts with the public fact base used in the second stage, which is declarative knowledge of the kind embodied in Sheehy's *Guide to reference books.* The intermediate-level rules or knowledge he generalized as 'Richardson's Principle', that 'All reference questions can be categorized by type of source (i.e. format, class of reference tools, or literature)' and consequently he propounded the 'General Reference Rule' which states: 'Classify the reference question by type of source and then by specific source'.

The topic of deep knowledge for reference work has been investigated by Parrott, according to whom it involves:

- categories of questions
- rules describing motivations of the creators, editors, finders and users of information
- factual information
- conceptual links for subject terms, geographical terms etc.

To show how deep knowledge and surface knowledge are related, Parrott gave the following example of a surface rule and the corresponding deep rules:

Surface Rule: IF the type of ready-reference question is biography, the person is dead, and the occupation was academic, THEN consult indexes of academic journals for obituaries.

This rule can be derived from about 20 deep rules as shown in Figure 4.2.

Deep knowledge is far more complex and takes longer to use. Why then bother to articulate it? Parrott gave three reasons. By using deep knowledge it is possible for:

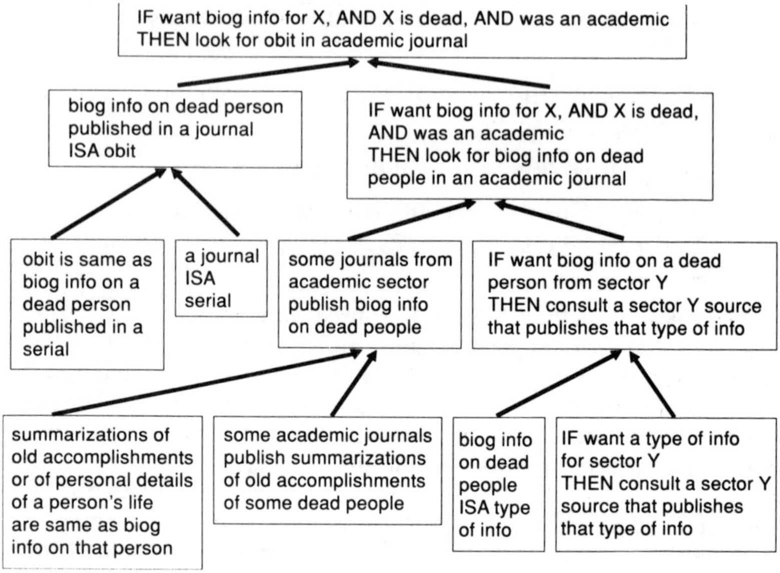

Figure 4.2 *Deep structure of a rule*

- a system to give explanations of explanations (i.e. to explain the relevant surface rules instead of simply displaying them)
- an intelligent computer-assisted instruction (ICAI) system to identify subtle errors (called deep cognitive errors) made by a student using the system
- a system to generate additional surface knowledge for prescribing strategy when the surface knowledge is exhausted. This is done by searching for consequences of the deep knowledge that have not yet been compiled into surface knowledge

2.6 Knowledge acquisition of the reference process

How can the knowledge of expert reference librarians be codified in rules? Richardson (1989) considered some possible methods:

- textbooks in reference work – these offer relatively little guidance
- record an interview between a novice and an expert reference librarian about a reference question scenario
- interviews with practitioners – how are they to be selected? Does a researcher ask what a librarian would do, or determine what is actually done?

Some developers of expert systems for reference are systematically acquiring knowledge from experts. Newham, in developing an expert system for online business database selection (Morris, Tseng and Newham, 1988), carried out knowledge-acquisition interviews with expert searchers. Kelly's personal construct theory (Kelly, 1955) and inductive learning methods could possibly be used to elicit the relevant knowledge and express it as rules (Richardson, 1989). In fact, personal construct theory has been used in comparing and contrasting different books, but they were not reference works (Keen and Bell, 1980).

An interesting approach to knowledge acquisition is taken by McDonald (1990) in his DISTREF system, which he is developing for advising distance education students on sources related to their coursework. DISTREF allows a user to browse a 'discipline map' which shows relationships between topics in a course. The discipline map has been created from 'item maps' derived from contents pages and indexes of textbooks which have been edited by a subject specialist, normally the lecturer in the course. The process of creating and editing the discipline map is controlled by a number of expert-system modules such as the 'knowledge integrator' and the 'knowledge editor' which question the subject specialist about relationships when these are not clear from the relationships expressed in the textbooks.

There is a tendency for reference librarians developing their own systems to prefer to organize and analyse their own knowledge. This approach is advocated by Ardis (1990) and by Hanfman, (1989). However, experts tend to perceive a task as proceeding in the way that they would like it to, rather than in the way that it actually does. This means that, to quote Alberico and Micco (1990): 'Serving as one's own knowledge engineer is analogous in many ways to acting as one's own lawyer, and probably about as advisable'. Nevertheless, if there really is a shortage of knowledge engineers it is likely that many librarians who wish to get involved in this field will have to ignore that warning.

3 Design issues

3.1 Limiting the domain

It is generally acknowledged that an expert system should be limited to a specific area of knowledge, or domain. How have implemented systems limited the domain? This has been done:

1. By subject. The PLEXUS system (Vickery *et al.*, 1987) limits its knowledge base to a set of reference works about

gardening. Materials Librarian (Carande, 1989) is focused on the topic of materials engineering.

2. By type of material. The POINTER system (Smith, 1989) restricts its advice to locating material in US Government Publications, and Ardis's 'Patent Information Assistant' (Ardis, 1990) is concerned with patent information.

3. By client group. DISTREF, a system under development by McDonald (1990), is concerned with the information needs of distance education students using the Charles Sturt University library. PLEXUS is also limited by client group, in that it is oriented to public library clients.

3.2 Shells vs languages

A number of authors describing implementations debate the pros and cons of shells vs languages. Carande (1989) pointed out that there is a compromise of the versatility of a language such as LISP or PROLOG versus the ease of creation using an expert system shell.

Implementors of reference expert systems have taken both approaches. PLEXUS (Vickery *et al.*, 1987) has been written in PASCAL, POINTER (Smith, 1989) was originally written in LISP but subsequently rewritten in BASIC, the 'Patent Information Assistant' (Ardis, 1990) was written in C, PASCAL and BASIC, and REFSIM (Parrott, 1989a) was written in Arity PROLOG.

As shells have increased greatly in availability (particularly for microcomputers) and ease of use, more recent implementations have tended to use them. A large number of systems has been implemented using shells, for instance Answerman (Waters, 1986) and Aqaref (Hanfman, 1989) using 1st Class, and INDEXES (Carande, 1988) using EXSYS. Vedder *et al.*, (1989) described a comparison of creating expert systems for business reference using EXSYS, 1st CLASS, GURU, PC Easy and PC Plus. Sarangapani (1990) described ChemRef, a reference expert system using VP-Expert. Trautman and von Flittner (1989) used GURU for their online database selection system.

Alberico (1988b) compared the advantages and disadvantages of the shell-versus-language approaches by comparing the VP-Expert shell with the PROLOG language. In another article (1988a) he pointed out that very cheap shareware shells are available.

In using shells or languages, an interface to a database management system is often necessary because it is more efficient to hold information about, for instance, a range of sources, in a database management system than in an expert system. For instance, the PLEXUS system (Vickery *et al.*, 1987) uses the MIRABILIS database package to store references to sources.

3.3 User interfaces

Richardson (1989) observed that most systems have used the 'Socratic mode' of either yes/no (binary) interfaces or menus. He listed the advantages of menus as:

- typing is not required
- spelling is not critical
- interfacing with other programs is straightforward, presumably because input has been standardized

The Socratic mode is limited to closed questions; the information about the query that can be obtained from the user by this approach will always be limited. It should be remembered, however, that more options can be presented in a single menu than would be given normally in any single question by a librarian during a reference interview. Open-ended questions, with the results subjected to some form of natural language processing, is more attractive as this style of questioning is favoured by many of the writers on the reference process whose views were discussed earlier, (e.g. Ingwersen, Dervin and Belkin) but good natural language interfaces are much more difficult to create.

Whatever form of interface is chosen, it is important that the system is easy to use. Many people are unwilling to expend much effort on finding information; they will simply do without it if using the information system takes much trouble – an observation known as 'Mooers' law' (Mooers, 1960). Cooper, (1978) with his 'Why bother?' theory made much the same point. This consideration is probably valid for expert systems as well as manual and conventional computerized ones.

3.4 Access to external databases

The logical extension of advising on search strategy is for the expert system to have access to an external database, for instance on CD-ROM, or on a database vendor such as DIALOG. This can be achieved in a relatively primitive fashion by allowing a user to enter a search string, which is then uploaded via a communications program to a database host. This approach was taken by Ardis (1990) in her 'Patent Information Assistant' which uploads, for instance, a patent number or an inventor's name to one of the patent databases on DIALOG. Aquaref (Hanfman, 1989) allows access to databases on CD-ROM and to DIALOG. However these implementations do not appear to involve any expert system processing of the input provided by the user.

Ideally the expert system would carry out some processing on the request offered by the user. This would greatly increase the scope of knowledge about search strategy that can be bought to bear, but also increases the complexity. For instance, some form of natural language handling will be necessary to transfer, and perhaps process, search terms from the user to the external database. Once the expert reference system becomes a front end to an external database, it could be argued that the logical next step is that the database is organized as a knowledge base, of which the knowledge about search strategy is just a part, and the distinction between database and front end will disappear.

PLEXUS has been used as the basis for the commercially sold system TOME Searcher (Vickery, 1988) which assists the searching of online databases in specific subject areas (for instance electronics) where the appropriate vocabulary has been programmed into the system (Vickery, 1988).

External databases of course include Online Public Access Catalogues (OPACs). Ercegovac (1989) examined how the concepts of information search tactics and idea tactics, as developed by Bates (1979a, 1979b) could be (and have been) incorporated into an OPAC user interface.

Chisman and Treat (1984) describe an implementation of a Dataphase OPAC that provides hierarchical menu access to subject groupings of reference books. Micco and Smith, (1989) proposed a system in which a workstation would give access to both an OPAC and a CD-ROM jukebox holding both full-text reference works and controlled vocabularies. These systems are described more fully in Section 4.

3.5 Use of reference expert systems for bibliographic instruction

A number of systems have as part of their goal the education of users in library systems. For instance Ardis. (1990) used her 'Patent Information Assistant' to provide information about the patent system to users unfamiliar with it.

REFSEARCH (Meredith, 1971) was the first attempt to use a 'knowledge base' about reference sources to train reference librarians.

ORA (Parrott, 1988), was a reference expert system primarily designed for bibliographic instruction. A later system, REFSIM, (Parrott 1989a,b) was considered by its developer to be an example of intelligent computer-assisted instruction (ICAI).

REFSIM, which is discussed in more detail in Section 4.3, works in both a consultation mode which assists in answering reference queries, and three ICAI modes:

- a presentation-oriented tutor
- a Socratic tutor

- a simulation-based coach which emulates the behaviour of either librarians or library users

Parott pointed out that a potential problem is that existing expert systems may function fairly well by using fairly superficial knowledge, rather than the deep knowledge which an ICAI should be concerned with. Therefore REFSIM includes metarules which enable the ICAI mode to present overall strategy as well as specific tactics.

3.6 Use of models of the reference process

To what extent is the identified knowledge about the reference process embodied in implementations? Relatively few implementations of reference expert systems are based on an understanding of the reference process. Parrott, in his REFSIM system, has drawn heavily on the work of Taylor and Lynch. A number of others have concentrated on the structure of the knowledge in the domain: PLEXUS with its embodied thesaurus relationships, and the various systems which embody a classification of reference works to organize the knowledge base.

3.7 System validation

Sarangapani (1990) carried out a literature review on the evaluation of expert systems and found that they were informal, subjective and testimonial. Butkovich *et al.*, (1989) conducted a basic performance evaluation of their 'Technical Writing Assistant'. While this showed a high degree of user satisfaction, one third of the students could not find what they were looking for, primarily, it seems, because of shortcomings in the database. Some systems make provision for feedback from users, e.g. Aquaref (Hanfman, 1989) allows users to store evaluations on the hard disk. In perhaps the most thorough attempt to date to evaluate a reference expert system, Sarangapani, (1990) used both formative and summative evaluation on the ChemRef reference advisory system. In the formative evaluation, domain experts evaluated the system according to the criteria of:

- soundness – were the conclusions correct?
- completeness – had all truths been derived?
- precision – was an appropriate level of precision expressed?
- usability – how good was the user interface?

They also made comments on ways to improve the design. A cycle of formative evaluations and modifications was carried out until the system met expectation, and then a summative evaluation was completed.

For the summative evaluation, the recommendations made by

ChemRef for a set of sample questions were compared to those of experienced reference librarians. This showed that the system recommended more sources than the experts (this may or may not be an indicator of high quality advice) and showed a high correlation with those sources that the experts agreed on.

Wade *et al.* (1988) carried out a comparison of the semantically based retrieval of the PLEXUS system with the statistically based information retrieval system INSTRUCT. They found that the best results were obtained by using the terms suggested by PLEXUS for an INSTRUCT search.

It is difficult to compare isolated, non-standardized user evaluations of differing systems in a range of environments, and obviously there is some need for a consensus on what a reference expert system is trying to achieve, and how this can be evaluated.

4 Systems implemented or under development

The first experiments in the automated provision of reference services began in the 1960s. A method of characterizing biographical reference books for the purpose of retrieving those most likely to answer particular biographical queries was developed at the University of Chicago (Weil, 1968) while at Berkeley REFSEARCH was based on a careful analysis of the characteristics of reference questions, such as how topics are qualified, and the functions of the works used to answer them, e.g. the topics may be defined, identified, discussed, chronicled, quantified etc. (Meredith, 1971). Consequently it could be claimed that REFSEARCH embodied a more realistic model of the reference process, albeit one that has received little attention in the literature, than some of the simple shell-based systems that were produced later. It is interesting to note that moves have been made recently to revive the REFSEARCH project. White and Woodward (1990) proposed to build a new version using Insight 2+ software on a microcomputer which would include ranking of sources and modelling of the question negotiation.

A variety of systems for answering reference enquiries have been developed. Most of these vary considerably in their functions and complexity. This section will briefly consider systems which provide routine information about library policies and services and those which enhance the catalogue's usefulness as a reference tool, before going on to discuss those which seek to make available expertise in particular subject areas or in answering reference queries in general.

4.1 Answering routine enquiries

One of the earliest systems of this type was REFLES1 (Reference Librarian Enhancement System) developed at the University of California, Los Angeles (UCLA) in the late 1970s (Bivins and Palmer, 1980). It was a microcomputer-based system for in-house data files of information about library facilities, services and operations, and also gave details of specific types of library materials along with some 'how to use' comments on the catalogue, abstracting services etc. An enhanced version of REFLES1, called REFLINK, was subsequently produced at Linköping University in Sweden (Bivins and Eriksson, 1982).

In 1983 Purdue University Undergraduate Library in Indiana, USA, introduced its Reference and Information Station for public use (Smith, 1989). An analysis of questions received at the reference desk showed that the most frequently requested could be grouped into nine categories, with another nine subcategories, and these were used in the design of a menu-based system which runs on both Apple and IBM microcomputers. Most of the menu choices provide general information about library facilities, but those in the Reference and Index categories do give details of publications that might assist readers with work in particular subject areas. Statistics on the menu paths chosen are kept automatically, and the system also has a 'suggestion box' feature so that users can provide feedback to library staff.

Another microcomputer-based, menu-driven ready reference system known as the Information Machine was produced at the University of Houston Library (Fadell and Myers, 1989). Graphics are used to illustrate floor layouts to help with directional enquiries. A lot of thought was put into the design of the menus, as it was intended that the user should be able to tell whether the information being sought was actually in the presentation by at least the second screen. Like Purdue's system, the Information Machine keeps statistics on the number of enquiries on different topics but it also asks the user to answer 'yes', 'no' or 'partly' to a question about whether or not he/she found the information that was wanted. Evaluation of the statistics and feedback has shown that the least successful module is the one on finding articles on a topic. It would have been possible to provide more detailed guidance but the designers did not think that the Information Machine was a good vehicle for that purpose, since many combinations of indexes would have to be catered for by the menus and several screens would have to be changed every time an index was added, deleted or physically moved to another location. Therefore an expert system for selecting reference works is being developed and it will be linked to the Information Machine. Other expert systems for recommending reference works also provide information about library facilities and services, e.g. ORA and REF-SIM, and these will be considered later.

4.2 Catalogue-linked systems

One of the problems encountered with the Information Machine at Houston was that some users mistook it for the online catalogue, despite a disclaimer on the first screen. Therefore there would be advantages for libraries in using their OPACS as a medium for providing assistance in answering common queries. In general, catalogues are rather unsatisfactory reference tools because they simply identify books (by author, title, subject etc.) without distinguishing between them according to their usefulness for different purposes. The first generation of automated library housekeeping systems did not include OPACS; catalogues continued to be produced on cards or microfiche, but online access to bibliographic files was required for circulation control. At Bowling Green State University in North Carolina in the early 1980s it was realized that the library's DataPhase (ALIS II) circulation system could be used to improve the quality of the reference service if catalogue records were enhanced to explain the reference uses of particular items (Chisman and Treat, 1984). Therefore descriptions of about 1000 reference works in the science library were included in the notes fields of the MARC records, and the Online Reference System (ORS) was designed to provide menu access to these records by subject (using broad categories based on the Library of Congress Classification), type of material, or course name and number. This latter facility is particularly useful in the case of class assignments, which are a major source of repetitive enquiries.

Records retrieved by the ORS are presented to the user in the same order that reference librarians often use in recommending material to enquirers: first, basic non-technical works covering the whole of a subject, then more technical material on that subject and finally works covering specialized areas of the subject. This order is probably more suitable for students than researchers, but ORS, like most other reference systems, does not employ user models for adapting the presentation to the individual.

Chisman and Treat regarded the circulation-based ORS as a model for the OPACS and integrated library systems which were then still a novel feature of the library scene, but this use has been slow to develop, as research on OPACS has tended to concentrate on improving subject access and user-friendliness. However, the LS/2000 integrated library system at Carnegie–Mellon University was enhanced to include an Information Function, which provides access via menus not only to details of library services and policies but also the text of in-house guides to the literature on different subjects (Diskin and Michalak, 1985).

While developments such as ORS and the Information Function represent important enhancements of the online catalogue that are achievable using conventional programming rather than AI techniques, they can only perform a very limited part of the librarian's role. Ercegovac has proposed using Bates' 'idea tactics' and 'information search tactics' to improve subject access and suggested that research is needed to determine which tasks could be most usefully mediated by the computer, and which might be left to the user acting with the assistance of displays of options and suggestive prompts from the machine (Ercegovac, 1989).

One way to provide assistance in the choice of search terms is to use 'discipline maps' as does DISTREF, a prototype reference system for students taking courses by distance learning offered by Charles Sturt University in Australia (McDonald, 1990). DISTREF is not an enhancement of an online catalogue as such, but expert system which it is intended to link to a union catalogue on CD-ROM of the holdings of a wide range of libraries in New South Wales. The discipline maps show the relationships between specific topics and serve to stimulate concept formation, so that students accessing DISTREF using PCs with modems are enabled to express their search requirements accurately. From the maps displayed the enquirer selects terms for use in searching the union catalogue. The amount of detail shown in the maps is determined by a user model based on the courses being taken and other details from the student's enrolment record.

The Workstation for Information Seekers planned by Micco and Smith is intended to provide access to thesauri and, like DISTREF, to maps of terms. The system would be used for searching reference works which would be stored, along with the thesauri and catalogues of various collections, on a CD-ROM jukebox. Tables of contents would be used as the sources of terms for enhancing MARC records and for creating the maps which would be implemented using hypertext. Search strategies employing expert systems techniques, including user modelling, would be used to narrow the search space (Micco and Smith, 1989). Preliminary experiments were conducted by Micco and Smith at Chatham College in Pittsburgh, USA, and a more detailed feasibility study was undertaken by Micco during a period spent working at the Australian Defence Force Academy in Canberra.

4.3 Standalone expert systems

Most of the expert systems for reference work developed so far have been microcomputer-based ones which are not integrated with the main computer systems of any library, though some do have links to CD-ROM or online databases. Where development has been undertaken as an educational exercise, shells have commonly been used, e.g. Richardson's dictionary guide, that was briefly described in the section on surface knowledge, used ESIE (Richardson, 1989). Five different shells were used by teams of MBA or PhD students to construct systems for answering business enquiries at the University of North Texas Libraries, as an exercise in evaluating such software tools. It was concluded that only two of the shells tested, PC Plus and GURU, would probably have proved suitable for a worthwhile business adviser (Vedder *et al.*, 1989).

One of the first systems to be used routinely was POINTER, which was developed at the State University of New York at Buffalo for providing assistance in finding US government publications where regular library staff members were not available (Smith, 1986, 1989). POINTER was initially written in LISP, then rewritten in BASIC. In planning the system, a list of questions asked during the previous 18 months was used by the designers. Two types of searches are catered for by POINTER: enquirers wanting specific documents are given their SuDoc numbers; subject searching is also possible but the designers had difficulty in devising a suitable conceptual framework for the organization of the menus.

In scientfic domains it is probably easier to produce a conceptual framework that makes sense to the user, but even then problems arise. The Materials Librarian at San Diego State University is a guide to reference tools in materials science, and is written in PROLOG (Carande, 1989). The main menu is a mixed list of types of literature, such as journal articles, conference proceedings etc., and types of organization on which information might be desired, e.g. manufacturers and research centres. In the second menu, various types of material are listed, e.g. plastics, ceramics, metals etc. If the enquirer was interested in metals, a third menu would list the various kinds included. Carande suggested that systems such as this could be linked to cover a much wider area, but he did point out that it would then be better if the subject menus preceded the ones for the type of information, since many subjects have their own unique types of information, e.g. star charts in astronomy. Even so, the enquirer would still be required to know what kind of literature would be useful and some sort of guidance might prove necessary if users with widely varying levels of knowledge were to be catered for. However, the Materials Librarian was designed for a quite homogenous group of users – working materials engineers – and furthermore, Carande argued that for certain types of enquiry, e.g. requests for physical data, user models are not necessary.

Patents are a domain where there is not the complication of a variety of different forms of literature, as in materials science, and literature searching conforms to certain standard approaches, giving the field a clear conceptual framework in contrast to the situation regarding government publications. The 'Patent Information Assistant' was developed at the University of Texas at Austin because of the time-consuming and repetitive nature of patent enquiries (Ardis, 1990). It is menu-driven and allows searches by patent number, inventor's name, assignee name, class/subclass, and keyword. Access is provided to external databases chosen according to the type of search. An interesting feature of the Patent Information Assistant is its trouble-shooting facility. If a search is unsuccessful the enquirer is offered a menu of choices describing the situation, and these lead to advice as to the appropriate course of action.

Expert advisory systems with links to external databases have also been produced by the National Agricultural Library in the US. The first of these, Answerman, was created for demonstration purposes in 1986 using the shell 1st-class (Waters, 1986). Its domain is ready reference enquiries in agriculture which it answers by giving details of relevant books, sometimes including specific page numbers, or by allowing the user to search a database such as Agricola. The user indicates the subject of the enquiry first by making choices from a hierarchical series of menus, and then indicates the type of information required (e.g. statistics, legal documents etc.) in a similar way. As a result of experiences with Answerman the staff of the National Library of Agriculture decided to create a new system, AquaRef, with a similar design but covering a narrower domain, namely aquaculture, as a pilot project to determine the usefulness of expert advisory systems in more specialized areas (Hanfman, 1989). One of the limitations of 1st-class is that the maximum capacity of a single file is 31 different results, but separate programs can be linked together automatically by a process called 'chaining' which makes it possible to connect thousands of knowledge bases into a complex whole. The chaining facility also permits cooperative updating and independent development of knowledge bases to occur. A specialized knowledge base on crawfish produced by staff of Louisiana State University has already been chained to the corresponding module in AquaRef. Various specialized Information Centres at the National Library of Agriculture are planning systems based on the AquaRef prototype, covering fields such as food and nutrition, herbs, and critical agricultural materials, and it is possible that these could all be integrated to form a full-scale agricultural expert system.

As discussed in the section on evaluation, most of the systems described so far have been evaluated either informally or by carrying out satisfaction surveys among users, but a more systematic assessment has been attempted in a few cases, most notably ChemRef, a guide to reference sources in chemistry that was developed at Nova University in Florida (Sarangapani, 1990). Comparisons with the performance of experienced reference librarians showed, so it was claimed, that ChemRef is capable of operating at a level comparable to or better than library staff. However, the tendency of the system to recommend a much greater number of titles than librarians would for the same enquiries might exacerbate the problem of information overload. Improvements planned to ChemRef include the addition of hypertext and a program to access CD-ROM databases. As the shell used – VP-Expert – can support up to 100 files, much larger systems should be feasible.

ChemRef uses windows for a clear presentation of its recommendations. Most of the expert systems for reference developed so far use very simple menu selection interfaces, and only a few use natural language instead as the principal method of interaction. Among the exceptions are the Technical Writing Assistant, the business reference system designed by Krulee and Vrenios, PLEXUS and REFSIM. Any system for assisting technical writers would ideally have to cover a wide range of disciplines; the prototype produced at Texas A&M University for the use of students in technical writing classes has a domain which includes reference sources in business, science and engineering (Butkovich *et al.*, 1989). Maintaining menus in a broad domain can be difficult, as was pointed out by the designers of the Information Machine, and natural language understanding is a possible alternative. The Q&A shell was selected for the development tool for the Technical Writing Assistant because it was inexpensive and was thought to have a good capability for natural language. A typed request such as 'I need indexes on electronics' results in a Boolean search for records containing the terms 'indexes' and 'electronics'. It should be pointed out, though, that Q&A's natural language facilities are not on a par with the more sophisticated abilities of PLEXUS, which is discussed later. However, the response by users of the system was very favourable and consequently it was decided to enlarge the domain. Nevertheless, one problem with vocabulary was encountered in the original version: the Technical Writing Assistant can question users about words it does not recognize and allow them to teach these to the system. However, it was found that users might not understand the proper way of doing this, and that could cause problems for subsequent users whose enquiries included words that the system had been mistaught.

In order to cope with phrases and non-grammatical sentences, natural language interfaces used for reference purposes have been based on semantics, not syntax, and therefore the quality of performance is almost totally dependent on the extent and appropriateness of the vocabulary chosen by the system designers. What criteria can be used for deciding which terms to include? A simple solution was adopted by Krulee and Vrenios for the small system, written in LISP, that they created covering 36 reference works on business. They took their vocabulary from the relevant parts of the Dewey Classification and its Relative Index (Krulee and Vrenios, 1989). The schedules with their tree structure constitute a list of broader, narrower and related terms, while the index provides many additional terms. Such a solution might be reasonably satisfactory in a system with a small database of records in a limited domain, but problems with ambiguous terms could be expected in more ambitious systems and in such cases words would have to be categorized in some way and a method of assigning words to their correct categories would have to be devised.

Taking gardening as an example, the word 'blossom' could mean either the process 'to blossom' or 'a blossom' i.e. part of a plant. Consequently the designers of PLEXUS, a microcomputer-based expert system written in PASCAL for answering the kind of queries on gardening that a public library might receive, devised rules for determining the meanings of ambiguous terms (Vickery, Brooks and Vickery, 1986). In the case of 'blossom' the rule is:

IF there is another process present

THEN assume blossom is a part

ELSE if there is an operation concept present

THEN assume blossom is a part

ELSE if there is an object7 or object1 present
[i.e. a general term like plant or tree or a specific plant name]

THEN assume blossom is a process

ELSE assume blossom is a part.

Why go to all this trouble? The reason is that instead of simply searching for the keywords found in the enquirer's initial statement, PLEXUS attempts to ascertain the user's problem and, if necessary, asks questions to obtain further details just as a librarian does in the reference interview (Vickery *et al.*, 1987). Queries about the best time to plant a type of seed and diseases of plants might both contain the word 'plant' or 'plants', but the supplementary questions that a librarian (or an expert giving advice on gardening) would ask would be quite different in the two cases. So that queries can be correctly interpreted, PLEXUS uses a dictionary of gardening terms with their semantic categories (which are subdivided) and frames showing which categories are likely to be found together in properly formulated queries, e.g. in an enquiry about an operation such as pruning, the object of the operation such as 'roses' would normally be stated, and if it was omitted from the initial statement the system would query the user about it.

In order to cater for singular and plural forms of nouns, different conjugations of verbs etc., the dictionary entries are based on word stems. Hierarchical relationships between terms are represented by a classification based on the FID/UNESCO Broad System of Ordering (BSO) and synonyms are linked using semantic nets, each of which is identified by a number. To each subcategory of term there is a corresponding type of frame, with slots for the term, its class number and, if it has synonyms, semantic net number as well as slots for the other categories of terms likely to be found with it in a properly formulated query. A separate frame is created for each term in the query statement that PLEXUS recognizes, and the system tries to fill some of the empty slots before querying the user by copying terms from one type of frame to another in accordance with certain rules, e.g. an empty object slot in an operation frame might be filled by copying the term name from an object frame if one has been created.

Of course not all enquiries are equally complex, and therefore it is not necessary to fill every slot in every frame but, depending on the type of frame, a certain number has to be filled before the enquiry is considered to be properly formulated. PLEXUS only asks the user for information to fill empty slots if they are essential. When all the frames are sufficiently complete, PLEXUS creates a search statement by connecting all the terms from the various frames with Boolean 'AND' operators and eliminating any duplicate terms. If any of the terms has synonyms in the semantic nets, these are incorporated in the search statement using 'OR' operators. A database of books and other sources of information on gardening is then searched, and if too many or too few references are retrieved the search strategy is modified automatically. For instance, if it is necessary to broaden the search this can be done by replacing 'AND' by 'OR' in cases where it links two terms in the same category, by dropping ANDed terms in accordance with certain rules (e.g. locations and attributes that would be unlikely to be used as index terms would be dropped first) or by finding broader terms in the classification and linking them to the original terms using 'OR'.

PLEXUS is an experimental system that has demonstrated the usefulness of AI techniques in formulating and revising search strategies. It also served as a prototype for the development of a commercial product – Tome Searcher – which is an intelligent interface for online searching of databases on remote hosts, the initial version covering the domains of electrical/electronic engineering, computer science and information technology (Vickery, 1988). No prior referral system employed such a range of knowledge representation techniques – semantic nets, frames and rules – and PLEXUS was also distinctive in its use of a user model to control the explanations given by the system, and to order the output of references so that those in the most accessible libraries or other centres were given first. Later systems employing user models include DISTREF (McDonald, 1990), described in the section on catalogue-linked systems, and REFSIM (Parrott, 1988, 1989a).

REFSIM was designed by Parrott to simulate both the librarian and the enquirer, so that it can be used not only for answering queries but also as a tutorial system for instructing users, including novice librarians. Reference librarians, particularly in academic libraries, spend a lot of time explaining how to use particular bibliographic tools for finding information, and this task could be performed, at least to some extent, by computer-assisted instruction (CAI), which could also be used for in-service training of library staff just as it has been used in teaching students in library schools (Starks, Horn and Slavens, 1972). As the use of expert systems is also motivated by the desire to alleviate the burden on reference librarians or to provide cover when they are not present, Parrott suggested that it would be logical to combine both the consultation and the educational functions in the same system. The knowledge base of the expert system could also serve in an intelligent computer-aided instruction (ICAI) system that would be more responsive to user needs than one using traditional CAI techniques. The inclusion of metarules, or rules of strategy, or fairly general tactics based on intermediate or deep level knowledge, would improve the intelligibility of the explanations given by the system in both the consultation and the tutoring modes, and in conjunction with a user model would also facilitate the detection of deep cognitive errors.

The prototype version of REFSIM was developed by Parrott at the University of Waterloo, Ontario, Canada, and is written in Arity PROLOG and runs on an IBM PC-XT. REFSIM is the successor to the Online Reference Assistance system (ORA) (Binkley and Parrott, 1987) which was a menu-driven system but of a more complex nature than most referral systems of that kind, e.g. in enquiries about the library's holdings ORA would use an expert system for interpreting citations in cases where the enquirer could not distinguish properly between the different fields in the bibliographic reference (Parrott, 1986). In both holdings transactions and complex substantive ones, the menu sequences were modelled on the reference interview. In the case of the latter type the client would first choose the subject and then ORA would ask about the purpose of the request, and would check whether or not the material desired was of a brief or introductory nature, in which case references to dictionaries, handbooks or encyclopaedias would be given.

REFSIM differs from ORA in that it uses natural language, it has a user-modelling facility, and it has three ICAI modes. As stated in Section 3.5 these are:

1. A presentation-oriented tutor which presents the knowl-

edge and tests the individual student's comprehension of it.

2. A Socratic tutor which reveals and resolves paradoxes in a student's understanding of a topic.

3. A simulation-based coach that plays the role of a client during interaction with a novice librarian and the system, and then evaluates the recommendations made by that librarian.

In the ICAI modes there are several user models. One tailors the interface to the user, as does the one employed in the consultation mode. In the simulation mode, a user model allows a novice librarian to choose the characteristics of the client being played by the system. There is also a student model which tracks the progress of the person being instructed and determines which material or questions to present.

When used in consultation mode, REFSIM, like PLEXUS, uses a parser to scan the client's question for words indicative of the question type, e.g. 'patent', 'address' etc. Then a frame corresponding to the question type is invoked and the system asks the client questions to determine the value of each empty slot in the frame. Next, rules representing knowledge about the appropriate classes of reference books to consult are activated, and relevant titles are retrieved from a database.

The metarules used by REFSIM in dealing with ready-reference transactions are based mainly on Bates' tactics, especially the PATTERN tactic which prescribes categories of tools to be used for particular question types. However, if there is no suitable PATTERN tactic, REFSIM uses the STRETCH tactic of employing a tool, which could contain the information, for a purpose for which it was not intended. The SCAFFOLD tactic – of consulting tools which will not give the answer but will give additional information that can be taken to other tools that will give the answer – is implemented as a single rule, and because of the complexity of this tactic Parrott expects that REFSIM will handle it more effectively than human intermediaries do. Finally, REFSIM also uses the WEIGH and SORT tactics to assess the probable effectiveness of the other tactics and determine the order in which they are recommended to the user.

5 Future directions

To date, a significant number of small-scale expert reference systems have been created. Although most of these are rather primitive, they serve to highlight the potential of such systems in aiding interested users and paraprofessional staff in answering queries when time or workload make professional reference librarians unavailable. The expert reference systems of today, therefore, show much promise for the future. Ideally one can look forward to much larger, better interfaced, more user-friendly systems that contain significant deeper levels of reference knowledge and the ability to interface with electronic information sources.

Most of today's systems are too narrow to offer an effective reference service; much larger systems are needed if this approach is to become viable. In some cases, where shells have been used, it would be possible to add similar modules and link them together to create systems covering broader domains. Such systems might reduce the 'brittleness' in current expert systems which suffer sudden and drastic deterioration in performance, rather than graceful degradation when the boundaries of their knowledge bases are reached (Walters and Nielsen, 1988). When this occurred the enquirer would simply switch to another module. However, this raises the question of how the universe of knowledge should be divided up into modules and, as librarians know only too well, no classification is likely to meet the needs of all enquirers.

Another difficulty that could be encountered in a large reference expert system might be the problem of navigation. The user might get lost in a forest of menus. Natural language interfaces would be better in such circumstances, but the broader the knowledge base the greater the problem of terms which have different meanings in different disciplines, and consequently the more difficult it would be to design a satisfactory interface. Further work needs to be undertaken into the processing of natural language queries from users, as pioneered by the development teams of PLEXUS and Tome Searcher. The use of hypertext could also be explored. Possibly hypertext technology together with expert system technology could be used to link reference sources into a 'Database of Everything', in which the distinction between individual sources would appear seamless to the user (Bevilacqua, 1989).

Many other systems could also be improved by links to online catalogues, for dealing with enquiries concerning holdings and for ensuring wider dissemination of information about library policies and services. Interfaces to external databases would also be a worthwhile enhancement to systems in which they are currently lacking. A local catalogue, external databases and an expert system for referral could all perform useful functions when used separately, but enquirers would find it rather tedious to make notes and switch from one to the other, particularly if it meant using different terminals or workstations. Integration would enhance all three functions. Moves in this direction will become increasingly important as the normal format for reference sources becomes electronic (online and CD-ROM) rather than paper.

By the standards of the various models of the reference process that have been proposed, most of the reference expert systems developed so far are deficient in that insufficient provision is made for ensuring that the enquiry is properly formulated, the search strategies adopted tend to be simple and inflexible, and variations in the characteristics of users are not taken into account. Of the current systems PLEXUS probably best exemplifies the approach needed for ensuring that enquiries are correctly formulated, while REFSIM shows that it is possible to implement a variety of search tactics. Possibly the most critical feature lacking in the majority of systems is user modelling, and this is therefore a promising area for research.

It is one thing to identify differences in the needs of various types of user and another thing to devise ways of ensuring that those needs are met, just as it is one thing to retrieve information relevant to a problem and another to know how to use it to solve that problem. Therefore Harmon's (1987) suggestions for identifying heuristics used by elite researchers and using them in systems for answering enquiries are worth pursuing, as is the work by Swanson (1986, 1989, 1990) on how hypotheses leading to original discoveries can be inferred by means of information retrieval. (This latter topic has been reviewed by Davies (1989).)

The task of developing systems exhibiting a high level of expertise in reference work is one which will necessitate a deeper understanding of such expertise. Because so much of the procedural knowledge involved consists of private and poorly understood heuristics, expertise has to be acquired through experience rather than study, making its acquisition a slow process. Furthermore, knowledge that is private is not cumulative but dies with the individual. Research on reference expert systems should help to make knowledge in this domain cumulative, thereby enabling librarians and information scientists to do more to assist the growth and dissemination of knowledge in all domains.

The indications are, therefore, that it will be a long time before the richness of experience and skills that human reference librarians bring to reference services can be completely incorporated in knowledge bases. In fact, studies of the application of artificial intelligence to reference work may further knowledge of human reference skills as much as they extend the boundaries of artificial intelligence. This may prove to be a development in the exploration of reference and information work as important as the development of the concept of 'reference services' with which we started this chapter.

References

Alberico R. (1988a) User-supported artificial intelligence. *Small Computers in Libraries*, **8**,(2), 4-9

Alberico, R. (1988b) Software for expert systems – languages versus shells. *Small Computers in Libraries*, **8**(7), 4-12.

Alberico, R. and Micco, M. (1990) *Expert systems for reference and information retrieval.* Westport, CT: Meckler

Ardis, S.B. (1990) Online patent searching: guided by an expert system. *Online* **14**(2) 56-62

Bates M.J. (1979a) Information search tactics. *Journal of the American Society for Information Science*, **30**, 205-214

Bates, M.J. (1979b) Idea tactics. *Journal of the American Society for Information Science*, **30**, 280-289.

Belkin, N.J., Oddy, R.N. and Brooks, H.M. (1982a) ASK for information retrieval: part 1, background and theory. *Journal of Documentation*, **38**, 61-71

Belkin, N.J., Oddy, R.N. and Brookes, H.M. (1982b) ASK for information retrieval: part 2, results of a design study. *Journal of Documentation*, **38**, 145-164

Belkin, N.J. and Windel, G. (1984) Using MONSTRAT for the analysis of information interaction. In *Representation and exchange of knowledge as a basis of information processes: Proceedings of the Fifth International Research Forum on Information Science, 1983, Heidelberg, Germany* ed. H.J. Dietschmann, pp. 359-382. Amsterdam: North Holland

Bevilacqua, A.F. (1989) Hypertext: behind the hype. *American Libraries* **20**(2), 158-162

Binkley, R.D. and Parrott, J.R. (1987) A reference-librarian model for computer-aided library instruction. *Information Services & Use*, **7**, 31-38.

Bivins, K.T. and Palmer, R.C. (1980) REFLES: an individual microcomputer system for fact retrieval. *Online Review*, **4**, 357-365

Bivins, K.T. and Ericksson, L. (1982) REFLINK: a microcomputer information retrieval and evaluation system. *Information Processing and Management*, **18**, 111-116

Butkovich, N.J., Taylor, K.L., Dent, S.H. and Moore, A.S. (1989) An expert system at the reference desk: impressions from users. *Reference Librarian*, **23**, 61-74

Carande, R. (1988) INDEXES: a micro-based expert system. *Small Computers in Libraries*, **8** (December), 26-27

Carande, R. (1989) Reference Advisory Systems (RAS): some practical issues. *Reference Services Review*, **17**, 87-90

Chisman, J. and Treat, W. (1984) An online reference system. *Reference Quarterly*, **23**, 438-445

Cooper, W.S. (1978) The 'Why bother?' theory of information science. *Journal of Informatics*, **2**, 2-5

Crews, K.D. (1988) The accuracy of reference service: variables for research and implementation. *Library and Information Science Research*, **10**, 331-355

Davies, R. (1989) The creation of new knowledge by information retrieval and classification. *Journal of Documentation*, **45**, 273-301

Dervin, B. (1989) Users as research inventions: how research categories perpetuate inequities. *Journal of Communication*, **39**, 216-232

Dervin, B. and Dewdney, P. (1986) Neutral questioning: a new approach to the reference interview. *Reference Quarterly*, **25**, 506-513

Dervin, B. and Nilan, M. (1986) Information needs and uses. In *Annual review of information science and technology*, ed. M.E. Williams, pp. 3-33. New York: Knowledge Industry Publications

Diskin, G.M. and Michalak, T.J. (1985) Beyond the online catalog: utilizing the OPAC for library information. *Library Hi-Tech*, **3**, 7-13

Ercegovac, Z. (1989) Augmented assistance in online catalog subject searching. *Reference Librarian*, **23**, 21-40

Fadell, J. and Myers J.E. (1989) The Information Machine: a microcomputer-based reference service. *Reference Librarian*, **23**, 75-112.

Frants, V.I. and Brush, C.B. (1988) The need for information and some aspects of information retrieval systems construction. *Journal of the American Society for Information Science*, **39**, 86-91.

Gers, R. and Seward, L.J. (1985) Improving reference performance: results of a statewide survey. *Library Journal*, **110**, 32-35.

Hanfman, D. (1989) AquaRef: an expert advisory system for reference support. *Reference Librarian*, **23**, 113-133

Harmon, G. (1987) Toward expert inquiry systems. In *Current trends in Information*, ed. B. Katz and R. Kinder, pp. 95-106. London: Haworth

Hernon, P. and McClure, C.R. (1987) Library reference service: an unrecognised crisis – a symposium. *Journal of Academic Librarianship*, **13**, 69-80

Ingwersen, P. (1982) Search procedures in the library analysed from the cognitive point of view. *Journal of Documentation*, **38**, 165-191

Ingwersen, P. (1984) A cognitive view of three selected online search facilities. *Online Review*, **8**, 465-492

Ingwersen, P. (1986) Cognitive analysis and the role of the intermediary in information retrieval. In *Intelligent information systems: progress and prospects*, ed. R. Davies, pp. 206-237. Chichester: Ellis Horwood

Jahoda, G. (1976) *The reference process: modules for instruction.* Talahassee: Florida State University

Jahoda, G. (1977) *The process of answering reference questions: a test of a descriptive model.* Washington DC: US Dept. of Health, Education and Welfare

Jahoda, G. and Braunagel, J.S. (1980) *The librarian and reference queries: a systematic approach*. New York: Academic Press

Katz, W. (1982) *Introduction to reference work. 4th ed. Vol. 2: Reference services and reference processes.* New York: McGraw-Hill

Keen, T.R. and Bell, R.C. (1980) One thing leads to another: a new approach to elicitation in the repertory grid technique. *International Journal of Man–Machine Studies*, **13**, 25-38

Kelly, G.A. (1955) *The psychology of personal constructs.* New York: Norton

Krulee, G.K. and Vrenios, A. (1989) An expert system model of a reference librarian. *Library Software Review*, **8**(1), 13-15

Lynch, M.J. (1978) Reference interviews in public libraries. *Library Quarterly*, **48**, 119-142

McDonald, C. (1990) *DISTREF: a prototype distance referral system.* Libraries and Expert Systems: proceedings of a conference and workshop held at Charles Sturt University, Riverina, Wagga Wagga, Australia, July 1990 ed. C. McDonald and J. Wechert, pp. 28-37. London: Taylor Graham

Markey, K. (1981) Levels of question formulation in negotiation of information need during the online presearch interview: a proposed model. *Information Processing & Management*, **17**, 215-225

Meredith, J.C. (1971) Machine-assisted approach to general reference materials. *Journal of the American Society for Information Science*, **22**, 176-186

Micco, M. and Smith, I. (1989) Designing a workstation for information seekers. *Reference Librarian*, **23**, 135-152

Miller, W. (1984) What's wrong with reference: coping with success and failure at the reference desk. *American Libraries*, **15**, (May), 303-322

Minsky, M. (1975) A framework for representing knowledge. In *Psychology of computer vision*, ed P.H. Winston, p.211-277. New York: McGraw-Hill

Mooers, C.N. (1960) Mooers' law, or why some retrieval systems are used and others are not. *American Documentation*, **11**,ii

Morris, A., Tseng, G.M. and Newham, G. (1988) *The selection of online databases and hosts – an expert systems approach.* Online Information 88: Proceedings of the 12th International Online Information Meeting. London, 1988, pp. 139-148

Parrott, J.R. (1986) Expert systems for reference work. *Microcomputers for Information Management*, **3**, 155-171

Parrott, J.R. (1988) Simulation of the reference process. *Reference Librarian*, **21**, 189-207

Parrott, J.R. (1989a) Simulation of the reference process, part 2: REFSIM, an implementation with expert system and ICAI modes. *Reference Librarian*, **23**, 153-176

Parrott, J.R. (1989b) *Using expert systems in reference services: course notes.* Waterloo, Ontario: University of Waterloo

Parrott, J.R. (1990) Implementation of reference models in expert systems. In *Expert systems in libraries*, ed R. Aluri and D. Riggs, pp. 64-75. Norwood, NJ: Ablex

Penland, P. (1970) *Interviewing for counselor and reference librarians.* Pittsburgh: University of Pittsburgh

Ranganathan, S.R. (1963) *The five laws of library science.* London: Asia Publishing House

Rich, E. (1983) Users are individuals: individualizing user models. *International Journal of Man–Machine Studies*, **18**, 199-214

Richardson, J. (1989) Toward an expert system for reference service: a research agenda for the 1990s. *College and Research Libraries*, **50**(2), 231-248.

Richardson, J. (1990) *The logic of ready reference work: basic and subordinate level knowledge.* Libraries and Expert Systems: proceedings of a conference and workshop held at Charles Sturt University, Riverina, Wagga Wagga, Australia, July 1990 ed. C. McDonald and J. Wechert, pp. 7-16. London: Taylor Graham

Rothstein, S. (1953) The development of the concept of reference service in American libraries, 1850–1900. *Library Quarterly*, **23**, (1), 1-15

Sarangapani, C. (1990) Development and evaluation of a reference expert system in chemistry. In *Proceedings of the 11th National Online Meeting*, New York. May 1-3 1990 ed. M.E. Williams, pp. 355-362. Oxford: Learned Information

Shera, J. (1964) Automation and the reference librarian. *Reference Quarterly*, **3**, 3-7

Smith, D.E. (1989) Reference expert systems: humanizing depersonalized service. *Reference Librarian*, **23**, 177-190

Smith, D.E. and Hutton, S.M. (1984) Back at 8.00 a.m.: microcomputer library reference support programs. *Collegiate Microcomputer*, **2**, 289-294

Smith, K.F. (1986) Robot at the reference desk? *College and Research Libraries*, **47**, 486-490

Smith, K.F. (1989) POINTER vs Using Government Publications: where's the advantage? *Reference Librarian*, **23**, 191-205

Starks, D.D., Horn, B.J. and Slavens, T.P. (1972) Two modes of computer-assisted instruction in a library reference course. *Journal of the American Society for Information Science*, **23**(4), 271-277

Swanson, D.R. (1986) Undiscovered public knowledge. *Library Quarterly*, **56**, 103-118

Swanson, D.R. (1989) Online search for logically-related non-interactive medical literatures: a systematic trial-and-error strategy. *Journal of the American Society for Informnation Science*, **40**, 356-358

Swanson, D.R. (1990) Medical literature as a potential source of new knowledge. *Bulletin of the American Library Association*, **78**, 29-37

Taylor, R.S. (1968) Question negotiation and information seeking in libraries. *College and Research Libraries*, **29**, 178-194

Trautman, R. and von Flittner, S. (1989) An expert system for microcomputers to aid selection of online databases. *Reference Librarian*, **23**, 207-238.

Vedder, R.G., Fortin, M.G., Lemmermann, S.A. and Johnson, R.N. (1989) Five PC-based expert systems for business reference: an evaluation. *Information Technology and Libraries*, **8**,(1), 42-54

Vickery, A. (1988) The experience of building expert search systems. in *Online Information 88: Proceedings of the 12th International Online Meeting*, London, 1988. pp. 301-313.

Vickery, A. and Brooks, H.M. (1987) PLEXUS – the expert system for referral. *Information Processing and Management*, **23**, 99-117

Vickery, A., Brooks, H.M. and Vickery, B.C. (1986) An expert system for referral: the PLEXUS project. In *Intelligent information systems: progress and prospects*, ed R. Davies, pp. 154-183. Chichester: Ellis Horwood

Vickery, A. *et al.* (1987) A reference and referral system using expert system techniques. *Journal of Documentation*, **43**, 1-23

Wade, S. *et al.* (1988) A comparison of knowledge-based and statistically based techniques for reference retrieval. *Online Review*, **12**, 91-108

Waters, J. and Nielsen, N.R. (1988) *Crafting knowledge-based systems*, pp. 297-299. New York: Wiley

Waters, S.T. (1986) Answerman, the expert information specialist: an expert system for retrieval of information from library reference books. *Information Technology and Libraries*, **5**, 204-212

Weil, C.B. (1968) Automatic retrieval of biographical reference books. *Journal of Library Automation*, **1**, 239-249

Weizenbaum, J. (1966) ELIZA, a computer program for the study of natural language communication. *ACM Communications*, **9**, 36-45

White, H.D. and Woodward, D. (1990) A model of reference librarians' expertise: reviving Refsearch on a microcomputer. In *Expert systems in libraries* ed. R. Aluri and D. Riggs, pp. 51-63. Norwood, NJ: Ablex

White, M.D. (1983) The reference encounter model. *Drexel Library Quarterly*, **19**, 38-55

Wilson, P. (1986) The face value rule in reference work. *Reference Quarterly*, **25**, 468-475

Chapter 5

Expert systems and cataloguing

Roy Davies

1 Introduction

The catalogue is a medium by which the librarian communicates to the reader information concerning the library's holdings. This information is intended to answer questions about the existence in stock of specific works, such as a book by a particular author, or groups of related works, e.g. all the books by that author (Verona, 1971). (The catalogue is also used to find works on particular subjects, but classification and subject indexing are major topics in their own right and will not be considered in this chapter). Despite the apparent simplicity of these questions, the process of creating and maintaining the catalogue is surprisingly complex, and has evolved gradually since the practice first received serious scrutiny in the middle of the 19th century. As befits a task whose performance requires a significant amount of specialized knowledge, cataloguing has attracted attention as a possible area of application for expert systems. Cataloguing has been described as a pseudo-formalized task (Ercegovac, 1986). It is regulated by a large body of rules which might give the impression that it is an orderly, almost mechanical process, but in reality it is a rather more subtle activity. Existing codes say nothing about the order of application of the rules, and although algorithms for that purpose have been designed they do not describe the way in which cataloguers actually work. Rules by themselves are not enough. Many rules involve decisions which require the possession of, or access to, diverse types of knowledge. The cataloguer also relies on examples and analogies with previous decisions and therefore, according to Ercegovac (1986), cataloguing is a non-deterministic activity in which complementarity of rule-based and case-based reasoning prevails. Consequently, because of the intrinsic difficulties of the domain, and also the greater financial importance of non-library areas for the application of AI techniques, most of the work done on expert systems for cataloguing so far has been of an exploratory nature.

Computers have been used for many years now for sharing, copying, manipulating and providing access to catalogue records but, important as their impact has been, they merely implement the decisions of the cataloguer. Making records available through bibliographic networks such as OCLC has greatly reduced wasteful duplication of effort by cataloguers in different libraries – amending records for local use takes much less time than the creation of the records in the first place – but a considerable amount of original cataloguing still takes place. Even in the very early days of library automation the reduction of the intellectual and not just the clerical work required in cataloguing was regarded as a possible goal. In a discussion during a conference held at the Library of Congress in 1965, Pauline Atherton suggested that cataloguing rules should be systematized in such a way that title page data could be dealt with by following an algorithm like those used in programmed instruction (Atherton, 1965). Four years later Fred Kilgour (1969), the founder of OCLC, proposed extracting information from title pages automatically, to make the process faster, and shortly afterwards the Library of Congress also considered that possibility (Avram, 1972), but the simpler task of converting data from old card catalogues into machine-readable form proved very difficult with the optical character recognition (OCR) technology of that period. Even if successful, capturing data directly from title pages would not make cataloguing an automatic process unless a computer could be programmed to interpret the information and apply rules just as the cataloguer does. This was also envisaged at an early stage, long before the terms 'expert systems' and 'knowledge-based systems' became common.

In the late 1960s, Sandberg-Fox (1972) began an investigation, for which she was awarded a doctorate, comparing the ease of simulating the process of making decisions concerning the main entry or access point using the then new *Anglo-American Cataloguing Rules (1967)* (AACR1) and the older *American Library Association (ALA) Code* (Beetle, 1949). Her work did not attract the attention it deserved until the mid 1980s. However, the issue of automatic cataloguing was briefly considered in a paper given by Wellisch (1980) at a conference in the late 1970s, in which he suggested that it was not then feasible for three reasons. Firstly, existing cataloguing rules were not designed for machines and are often ambiguous or illogical; secondly, the irregular layout of title pages would make identification of the relevant information difficult; and thirdly, the data on the title page would have to be printed in a type font capable of being read by an OCR device.

Nevertheless, in the early 1980s people's notions of what was feasible to automate were broadened considerably as a result of the publicity surrounding expert systems. Most of these were developed, not with the aim of taking over the human role, but of simplifying it. Typical medical consultation systems such as MYCIN still required medical personnel to identify symptoms and answer questions about the results of tests before the machine made the diagnosis. The proven technical feasibility of this approach indicated that a similar one might work in cataloguing. Although the process would not be fully automatic, it would have the advantage of completely circumventing the second and third problems identified by Wellisch. Title page interpretation would remain a human task but the choice of rules to execute would be made by the computer.

This was the approach that was taken by Brian James (James, 1983; Davies and James, 1984) in a project for an MPhil degree at the University of Exeter, to investigate the feasibility of automating part 2 of the *Anglo-American Cataloguing Rules*, 2nd edition (AACR2) (Gorman and Winkler, 1978), which consists of instructions concerning the choice and form of headings or access points. While the work in Exeter was in progress, a project was started at Linköping University in Sweden, which resulted in the creation of two expert systems using shells, but the researchers were not aiming to produce systems for practical use. Instead they were more interested in studying the cataloguing code by discovering what was entailed in creating a knowledge base, and they found that the process of using AACR2 for that purpose was far from simple (Hjerppe and Olander, 1985, 1989). Their work demonstrated the importance of the first problem identified by Wellisch (1980) – ambiguous or illogical rules – and indicated the desirability of designing any successor to AACR2 as a knowledge base if full advantage of computer technology was to be taken. The first of the Swedish systems, based on EMYCIN, produced actual bibliographic records, whereas the second, based on Expert-Trees, informed the user of the conclusions drawn from the relevant rules. Other experimental advisory systems were developed at the Polytechnic of North London (Eyre, 1986) and Teesside Polytechnic (Black, Hargreaves and Mayes, 1985). Later on, an expert system with extensive explanation facilities, as would be desirable in teaching students to catalogue, was produced at Strathclyde using the shell ESP/Advisor (Gibb and Sharif, 1988) which had also been used at Teesside, and in the late 1980s two innovative systems both using Apple's Hypercard environment were developed at the University of California, Los Angeles. One, MacCat, is intended for establishing headings, together with their MARC field codes, in accordance with AACR2 while the other, MAPPER, is of a more specialized nature and gives advice concerning cartographic publications (Ercegovac, 1990a).

In addition to these experiments, some work of a purely theoretical nature was published during the early to mid-1980s. Burger (1984) compared the reasoning process used in authority control (checking the forms of names or other access points) with some commonly used in artificial intelligence, while de Jager (1985) discussed the types of knowledge required in constructing and using existing and possible future forms of catalogue. The possibility of complete automation was considered again, this time by Yaghmai and Maxine (1984) who pointed out that the advent of electronic publishing had brought the prospect closer by eliminating the problem of data capture, and the subject of interpreting title pages, which had been rather neglected in the years following Sandberg-Fox's (1972) thesis, received fresh attention. Hjerppe and Olander (1985) had noted various irregularities that might cause difficulties for any automatic system, but possible heuristics for recognizing various bibliographic features were proposed by Schwarz (1986) and by Davies (1987) while Jeng (1986,1987) gathered statistical data on title pages and Svenonius, Baughman and Molto (1986) investigated the problems posed by names. These theoretical studies were followed in the mid to late 1980s by the first experiments in fully automatic cataloguing. In the United States OCLC carried out trials using data of a kind that could be acquired by optical scanning, assuming that OCR technology had reached a sufficiently advanced stage (Weibel, Oskins and Vizine-Goetz, 1987,1989) while in Darmstadt in Germany a system known as AUTOCAT was developed for the purpose of cataloguing articles in journals on nuclear physics (Rauth and Schnellbach, 1987).

Thus during the 1980s three quite different approaches to automating the intellectual processes involved in cataloguing were introduced. The simplest is to give advice on the application of the rules, as was tried with one of the Swedish systems and also those produced at the Polytechnic of North London, Teesside Polytechnic, the University of Strathclyde and the University of California, Los Angeles. A somewhat more ambitious approach would be to have the computer not only select the rules to apply, but also to execute them and create the necessary records, as was intended in Exeter and achieved by one of the systems developed in Linköping. Most ambitious of all would be a fully automatic process as envisaged by the researchers at OCLC and in Darmstadt. This would entail the automatic acquisition and interpretation of data, as well as selection and execution of the rules. Each of these three approaches will now be discussed in more depth.

2 Advisory systems

Of the early advisory systems, Eyre's at the Polytechnic of North London was unusual in not being based on a shell. It was written in PROLOG and was developed as an exercise in learning about that language rather than as a serious attempt to design a useful system (Eyre, 1986). Eyre found that PROLOG handled the task well, and it proved easy to make amendments to the program, as might be expected of a language which in comparison with more conventional ones allows the programmer to concentrate more on what is to be done and less on the precise means by which the objectives are to be achieved. The knowledge base was derived from Chapter 22 of AACR2 concerning the forms of names of persons. By selecting options from a series of menus, the user indicates the conditions that apply in the case of the item being catalogued and the system then gives instructions about the forms of names to be used as headings.

Despite the fact that the program worked satisfactorily, Eyre was not convinced that an advisory system of this type would be worthwhile: negotiating a long chain of menus might prove much slower than the direct access offered by the published hardcopy. Nevertheless he did point out that one of the curious features of PROLOG is that any clause having a prefix can be accessed directly, so it would be possible to allow experienced users to by/pass irrelevant menus, e.g. if 'conference' were used as a prefix, then by typing that word the user could jump directly to the part of the program dealing with the names of conferences. However, Eyre did not explore the possible uses of this facility to any significant extent and therefore was not certain how helpful it would be in a complex system.

At Teesside Polytechnic, the library was originally interested mainly in the possibility of providing advice to users of the online catalogue and other information services. In order to test the feasibility of using expert systems for this purpose, it was decided to conduct preliminary experiments in a field that did not involve library users but was similar to the intended domain, namely cataloguing (Black, Hargreaves and Mayes, 1985). An attempt to develop from scratch a shell suitable for the various related domains of interest to the polytechnic library proved too time-consuming, and consequently a switch was made to commercially available shells. In contrast to Eyre, Black and his colleagues claimed that an advisory system would have two advantages over the printed version of the cataloguing code. Firstly, assuming that the knowledge base could be searched by the user, the appropriate rule could be retrieved more easily, just as online databases make information easier to find than do the printed abstracting publications upon which they are based. Secondly, the text can be 'animated' so that instead of simply presenting the rules for inspection, they are applied to give the user an answer to a specific problem.

Using the shells ESP/Advisor and SAGE, two versions of an expert system (called HEADS) were created which allowed the user to browse through the text of the code or to obtain advice regarding a particular field in a record, or to work through the complete cataloguing procedure. Neither shell was ideal, as they both had poor string-handling facilities and therefore conditions involving strings, e.g. in rules concerning hyphenated surnames, could not be recognized by the system, which instead had to question the user about the presence of those conditions. (It would have been possible to write string-handling subroutines in some language and interface them with the shell, but the only external procedures used were some, written in PROLOG, for operations involving numeric fields such as the ISBN and accession number). The developers of HEADS concluded that an advisory system would be far more useful if it was integrated with software for the production of catalogue records rather than being a standalone application. This could be accomplished in four different ways:

1. A new program is written to combine the functions of both data entry and of advice on rules.
2. The advisory facilities are invoked as one or more subroutines of the data capture program.
3. The data capture program is implemented as a subroutine of the advisory program.
4. There are two autonomous programs, preferably in an environment using windows so that the user can move back and forth between them at will.

For educational purposes, integration with other software would be less important. At Strathclyde University a system known as CATALYST was produced as a prototype of a possible expert system, for use both in operational environments and for teaching students of cataloguing (Gibb and Sharif, 1988). CATALYST was developed during research into the suitability of various shells for bibliographic classification, and although none of those examined proved very satisfactory it was realized that for one of them cataloguing would be a far more suitable domain. This was ESP/Advisor, which had also been used at Teesside in the development of one version of HEADS. With this shell, a system was produced using menus based on one of the algorithms of Shaw *et al.* (1980). One of the strengths of CATALYST is its explanation facilities, which are clearly vital in an educational role. Information interpreting the menu choices and explaining the meaning or scope of the terms used, as in Figure 5.1, can be dis-

```
THE ESP ADVISOR .  Vers 2.02    Copyright © 1984   Expert  Systems  International
Goal:  spec category              SECTION: part 37
----------------------------------------------------------------------------------

Which of the following options applies?  The work is:-

 (1) - of a legal nature
 (2) - of a religious nature
 (3) - a related work
 (4)  - none of the above

----------------------------------------------------------------------------------
Enter the number of the relevant entry  :  EXPLAIN
----------------------------------------------------------------------------------
```

```
THE ESP ADVISOR .  Vers 2.02    Copyright © 1984   Expert  Systems  International
Goal:  spec category              SECTION: part 37
----------------------------------------------------------------------------------
Further information
-----------------------

Legal works INCLUDE:
 - laws
 - treaties
 - court rules etc.
But NOT
 - legal textbooks
 - commentaries etc.

----------------------------------------------------------------------------------

----------------------------------------------------------------------------------
                          PRESS ANY KEY TO CONTINUE
```

Figure 5.1 *Example of the explanation facilities in CATALYST*

played on request. This was felt to be far more valuable to novices than the justification facilities, which often amount to no more than a trace of executed rules, commonly provided by expert systems.

In the design of the help system for MacCat at the University of California, Los Angeles, Maccaferi also placed considerable emphasis on explaining concepts. In addition to the scope notes in the help screens, definitions from a glossary may be displayed. However, the most significant advance over earlier systems is probably the interface. MacCat is implemented on the Apple Macintosh and therefore full advantage is taken of the mouse and icons for entering commands. Furthermore, as it makes use of Hypercard, Apple's hypertext software, MacCat is far more flexible than earlier expert cataloguing systems, many of which forced the user to work through chains of menus one step at a time. In contrast, if the user of MacCat knew that a heading for a pope was required, then instead of going right through the complete cataloguing procedure, a few clicks of a button on the Macintosh's mouse to display MacCat's table of contents and select 'popes', would take the user straight to the first page of the decision sequence for establishing the heading for a pope. MacCat not only creates headings but also assigns the correct MARC field and subfield codes to them. The initial version was limited to dealing with certain types of corporate headings (for cataloguing purposes, names of religious officials acting in their official capacity are treated as subheadings of the names of the appropriate religious bodies), but it is intended to expand its capabilities to cope with other types of headings.

Another system which makes extensive use of windows has been designed by Piotr Murasik, of Gdansk University in Poland. The first prototype of this system called APEX (Access Point EXpert), which is written in PROLOG, was completed early in 1991. APEX asks a series of questions, one at a time, but like MacCat it does allow short cuts: users can select a mode of interaction that allows them to volunteer information. To use this information effectively it might be necessary for the system to make certain assumptions, e.g. if it is told that three or fewer authors are involved, APEX will assume that it is dealing with a case of shared authorship (as opposed to mixed authorship, where the individuals concerned make contributions of a different nature, e.g. a writer and an illustrator) and this assumption will be displayed. This reduces the chances of mistakes occurring when short cuts are taken, since the cataloguer should notice if the information volunteered is not interpreted in the manner he intended.

All the advisory systems discussed so far have knowledge bases which are of a fairly general nature, in that they deal with the choice or form of access points to documents rather than the problems posed by specific types of material. They are also somewhat superficial in that the knowledge is derived exclusively or predominantly from the rules in the relevant parts of AACR2, even though, as Ercegovac (1986) pointed out, real expertise in cataloguing cannot be founded solely on the basis of a knowledge of the formal rules. In her work for her doctoral thesis in Los Angeles, Ercegovac (1990a) has designed and implemented a more specialized system, termed MAPPER, which gives advice on the descriptive cataloguing of certain classes of cartographic publications. Instead of simply studying the relevant rules in AACR2, she also made a detailed study of the ways in which expert map cataloguers make their decisions (Ercegovac, 1990b). Records for nearly 500 maps that had been catalogued by the Library of Congress were identified using the OCLC union catalogue. From this sample, the records of 128 maps held in the Map Library plus a further 50 in the Library of Congress were selected and carefully analysed, with particular attention paid to inconsistencies, and the inclusion of cataloguing decisions that could not be explained by conventional bibliographic practices and formal cataloguing procedures. Expert map cataloguers at the Library of Congress were then interviewed about these inconsistencies, and the unpublished knowledge elicited from them was expressed in rules which were used, along with the formal rules of AACR2, in a knowledge base. Next, a survey was made of students of librarianship who had just completed a course on the cataloguing of books, in order to learn more about the kind of assistance they would need in cataloguing maps, and on the basis of that survey and the existing literature on human information processing, MAPPER's interface, like MacCat's, was designed and implemented in the Hypercard environment. During their studies, few library school graduates acquire the knowledge to become proficient map cataloguers and therefore they may need a long apprenticeship with an experienced map cataloguer. MAPPER could save some of the time that experts would otherwise have to spend helping novices, or could serve as a substitute in libraries where there were no experienced map cataloguers. Similar systems would be desirable for other materials requiring cataloguing expertise that was in relatively short supply, e.g. computer files, archives and some audiovisual materials.

A very different advisory system, ESSCAPE/Expert-Trees, had been produced a few years earlier at Linköping University in Sweden (Hjerppe and Olander, 1989). This was one of two systems developed as tools for studying the rules and processes of cataloguing, but it will be considered along with the other one, which produced actual records, in the next section.

3 Record creation systems

The developers of HEADS at Teesside Polytechnic concluded that the benefits gained from an advisory system would be much greater if it were fully integrated with a system for the production of catalogue records (Black, Hargreaves and Mayes, 1985). This approach had, in fact, already been tried at Exeter University (Davies and James, 1984) and although that aim was not achieved, owing to problems with the software used, the case for doing more than providing advice remains strong. An advisory system would be used only when the cataloguer was aware of a problem to which he was uncertain of the solution, but such an awareness would be dependent to a certain extent on a knowledge of the cataloguing code. No matter how good the advisory system, incorrect records would still be produced if it was only consulted when deemed necessary by the cataloguer. Why, for instance, should a novice suspect that the names of television stations might require different treatment (in accordance with rule 24.11) from those of other corporate bodies? Furthermore, an advisory system would not expedite record production in the straightforward cases which account for a large proportion of the workload in most libraries, and would therefore have only a limited effect on the economics of the process. In contrast, a system for creating catalogue records would ensure greater consistency (although it would not altogether prevent users from responding inconsistently to the prompts) and might speed up the cataloguing process, not only by reaching decisions more quickly in difficult cases, but also by eliminating the entry of redundant data, e.g. names belonging to the statement of responsibility area would not need to be input again in the added entry fields of the MARC record. However, in simple cases the time taken by the computer to gather from the user the information determining which rules apply might partially negate, or even totally offset, these gains and therefore the quality of the interface would be a major factor in determining the economics of an expert record creation system (Davies, 1986a).

In the attempt at the University of Exeter to create a prototype of such a system, James developed a menu interface so that interaction would not be slowed down by the need to answer 'no' to irrelevant questions: instead the user would simply indicate the condition that applied, the choices in each menu being mutually exclusive. (Even so this would be quite inflexible compared to the Hypercard-based interfaces adopted later for MacCat and MAPPER). The process of menu selection would continue until the system had acquired enough information to determine precisely the type(s) of access points required, and then the bibliographic record would be created. For the purpose of deciding what should be included in the menus and how the different menus should be linked, the flowcharts produced by Shaw *et al.* (1980) were consulted. It was envisaged that at the data entry stage the user would be guided by a screen form though a series of prompts which would probably be just as useful. Figures 5.2, 5.3 and 5.4 show the cataloguing process for a book purportedly dictated by a spirit to a medium. Initially the ISBN would have been input so that the system could check that the book was not already listed in the catalogue, and the default values of the place of publication and the publisher's name would be inferred from the ISBN prefix.

Whatever its precise form, the content of the screen display for

1 = Unknown, uncertain, or unstated authorship
2 = Erroneous or fictitious authorship
3 = Work is a collection
4 = Mixed authorship
5 = Shared authorship
6 = Authorship attributed to a single personal author/corporate body
7 = Why?

Figure 5.2 *Menu for types of authorship (reprinted with permission from Information Processing and Management,* **23***, (2), Roy Davies, Outlines of the emerging paradigm in cataloguing, copyright (1987), Pergamon Press PLC)*

data entry would depend on the choices made during the menu selection process. Therefore, if it had been ascertained that the work was a monograph by four or more authors and the principal one was not indicated, the system would prompt the user to enter the surname and forenames or initials of the first-named only, whereas in the case of the proceedings of a conference the name, number (if any), place and date of the conference would be requested. This detailed guidance could be provided by using frames to represent the structures of the various possible types of record. Some of these frames could be of a very specific nature, e.g. there could be a general one for government publications, then more specialized ones for different countries and, if necessary, for the publications of individual ministries and agencies of the governments of those countries. In addition to indicating to the user what type of information was required, frames could, in the absence of evidence to the contrary, supply some simple bibliographic data by default, e.g. in a British

Main Entry Distinction - Mixed Authorship

1 = Collaboration between an artist and an author
2 = Report of an interview
3 = Spirit communication
4 = Academic disputation
5 = Other
6 = Why?

Figure 5.3 *Menu for mixed authorship (reprinted with permission from Information Processing and Management,* **23***, (2), Roy Davies, Outlines of the emerging paradigm in cataloguing, copyright (1987), Pergamon Press PLC)*

Enter title	
Subtitle	
Edition (if not the 1st)	
Enter Name of Spirit	
Name of Medium	
Enter Place	(filled by default)
Publisher	(filled by default)
Date	
Enter No. of Pages	
Enter Series Title	
Enter Circulation System No.	
Enter Class No.	
Press C/R to skip inapplicable fields	

Figure 5.4 *Screen form for data entry (reprinted with permission from Information Processing and Management,* ***23****, (2), Roy Davies, Outlines of the emerging paradigm in cataloguing, copyright (1987), Pergamon Press PLC)*

library it might be assumed that a government publication was probably also British.

PROLOG was the language chosen for the rule-based operations of the Exeter system (though input/output was handled using PASCAL, which was also the language in which the PROLOG interpreter was written) but the interpreter of the particular version of PROLOG used had very poor garbage collection facilities, so that areas of working memory that were no longer being used were not automatically reclaimed and reallocated while the programs were running. This problem of insufficient memory could have been overcome by making extensive modifications to the interpreter, or by making a fresh start using different software (and perhaps hardware too), but as neither of these courses could be pursued in the time available for a Master's degree project, the planned system was never actually implemented. Nevertheless, the project helped to awaken interest in the potential of expert systems for cataloguing and some worthwhile lessons about the domain were also learned, as is often the case when familiar problems are looked at from a fresh angle.

No code is self-sufficient. Difficulties of interpretation do arise and consequently some libraries use local codes of practice to ensure that different cataloguers make consistent decisions. For instance, at Exeter local guidelines are followed for the publications that accompany Open University courses, and while advising James on cataloguing it was realized that these instructions could be replaced by a pair of decision tables embodying seven rules for choosing between different model entries. Therefore it would be quite feasible to codify local practices as rules which could be added to the knowledge base of an expert system (Davies and James, 1984). Nevertheless there is a limit to how much could be achieved in this way. Wittgenstein (1958) showed that there is a philosophical problem concerning the application of rules in any field: namely the fact that although there may be rules guiding the application of other rules, this process does not terminate in rules which unequivocally determine their own applications. Rules, Wittgenstein concluded, are just signposts and a signpost is in order if, under normal circumstances, it fulfils its purpose. However, even if the idea of a completely self-explanatory body of rules is chimerical, it would be foolish to assume that the balance between clarity and complexity in AACR2 is optional.

Another point that emerged is so obvious that it is normally taken for granted, and that is the great variations in the types of knowledge required for understanding different rules. Some require little more than an ability to count names (e.g. 21.6C1), others require a knowledge of what particular names represent, e.g. a fictitious character (21.4C1), a disembodied spirit (21.26), a radio station (24.11) or a ship (24.5C4), and could possibly be executed automatically given access to large authority files; still others require the exercise of human judgement, e.g. the provision in rule 21.30K1 that an added entry should be made under the name of the translator if the main entry heading might be difficult for catalogue users to find. However, the rules of cataloguing are not laws of nature and may be changed. Therefore, before a cost-effective expert system could be devised, the cataloguing process and the nature of the rules themselves would have to be considered carefully. By coincidence, an investigation of the suitability of AACR2 as a knowledge base had begun in Sweden while the project at Exeter was still in progress.

This work by Hjerppe and Olander (1985, 1989) at Linköping University had various aims, the most general being to become thoroughly acquainted with expert systems and create prototypes in order to assess their relevance to libraries. In the domain chosen – cataloguing – it was hoped that expert systems would prove useful tools for studying the tasks involved and that a simplified, reduced set of rules yielding records compatible with those based on the complete code would be produced. This last objective was not achieved, but when the time eventually comes for planning a successor to AACR2, Hjerppe and Olander's work will repay careful study because of their use of knowledge engineering in an attempt to answer the questions 'how does one start analysing a set of prescriptive rules?' and 'what would characterize a "bad" versus a "good" set of rules?' Two very different shells, EMYCIN and ExpertTrees, were used in a project known as ESSCAPE (Expert Systems for Simple Choice of Access Points for Entries) and the systems produced were denoted by appending the name of the shell to the project name, e.g. ESSCAPE/ExpertTrees. EMYCIN is the shell derived from MYCIN, probably the most influential of all the early expert systems, and is used for tasks involving a similar sort of reasoning process. Identifying a disease is a classificatory task, and identifying the type of bibliographic record required for a document can be regarded in the same light. Expert-Trees is very similar to PAL and the shell Expert-Ease, which is well known for its use in machine learning for deriving rules from examples.

Knowledge in systems based on EMYCIN is expressed in the form of production rules having premises consisting of a fact, or two or more facts combined in a Boolean expression. Each fact is represented by three associated features: an object, an attribute of that object, and the value of the attribute. The objects are the physical or conceptual entities of the domain, e.g. in medicine these might include patients, organisms, cultures etc., while one attribute of the object 'patient' would be sex and its value 'male' or 'female. Objects are also known as contexts, because the relationships between them define the conceptual structure of the knowledge base and determine the flow of action. This conceptual structure is a hierarchy, e.g. organisms are found in cultures belonging to patients. In ESSCAPE/EMYCIN three contexts are used: the highest or most general is known as CATALOGUING as that is what the system is for, while the middle and bottom contexts, DESCRIPTION and HEADING, also have names indicative of the goals of the rules associated with them.

In a session using ESSCAPE/EMYCIN the user is prompted to enter a brief bibliographic description of the item to be catalogued, starting with the title. The system then asks how many authors there are, as this information tells it how many names to prompt for and will also be needed in deciding on access points. When the bibliographic description is complete the system asks questions to establish the type of authorship, and on the basis of the number and type of authors selects the appropriate headings and generates the record. As it stands, ESSCAPE/EMYCIN does not attempt to establish the correct forms of the headings, nor can it cope with works of mixed responsibility where different persons or bodies make intellectual or artistic contributions by performing different types of activity, e.g. writing, adapting, translating, illustrating etc.

Although the rules of part 2 of AACR2 are all to do with conditional courses of action, it was not possible to transfer these instructions directly into production rules; to preserve the meaning of the rules it was necessary to rewrite them to include explicitly bibliographic conditions that would normally be implicitly assumed by cataloguers. For instance, compare the part concerning main entry in rule 21.5A with its ESSCAPE/EMYCIN equivalent:

Rule 21.5A. If a work is of unknown or uncertain personal authorship, or if it emanates from a body that lacks a name, enter it under title.

In ESSCAPE/EMYCIN this becomes:

If:
1. the item is not a work of personal authorship
2. the item is not a work emanating from a corporate body
3. the item is not a work or collection of works produced under editorial direction
4. the item is a work of unknown or uncertain authorship according to the statement of responsibility

Then: It is definite (1.0) [where this figure is a certainty factor] that the title proper is the main heading under which the item is entered in the catalogue.

Hjerppe and Olander did not discuss the differences in much detail, but clauses 3 and 4 of the ESSCAPE/EMYCIN version are needed to exclude cases covered by other rules. The original AACR2 form of the rule does not cover the case of an edited version of a work by authors whose identity is unknown or uncertain. Clause 4 is presumably necessary because a different rule (21.4C1) applies in cases where the statement of responsibility is erroneous or fictitious, irrespective of whether or not the true identity of the author is known.

In contrast there was no need for this sort of analysis when Expert-Trees was used as a shell, since it is designed to discover rules for itself. Rule induction from examples is particularly useful in domains where experts have difficulty in stating correct rules but can identify the facts upon which the rules would be based. They do not even have to know for certain which facts are relevant and which are not, since as long as none of the relevant ones is overlooked the program will, given enough examples, discover which facts are pertinent. In using Expert-Trees to create a cataloguing system, a spreadsheet-like matrix was set up in which the rows represented examples of individual documents and the columns, except for the last, represented the bibliographic attributes displayed by those documents, e.g. type of work, type of authorship etc. The last column represented the actual outcome, i.e. the decision concerning access points according to Chapter 21 of AACR2. When the number of examples was considered satisfactory, a decision tree was generated and then menus based on the tree were set up so that it could be used as an expert system, although lacking explanation facilities.

In any expert cataloguing system intended for practical use, speed would be of major significance as there would be no economic advantage in using it unless productivity was increased (or the task deskilled), and therefore the order in which the rules are considered is of major significance. The fewer irrelevant ones involved the better. When Expert-Trees generates a decision tree it arranges the branching points in the sequence that leads most quickly to the results. Furthermore, since as Ercegovac (1986) observed, case-based reasoning is important in cataloguing, it might be advantageous to have a systematic method of studying examples, particularly in situations where AACR2 does not provide sufficient guidance for different cataloguers to produce consistent entries.

As a result of their experiments, Hjerppe and Olander (1989) concluded that the development of an expert system with comprehensive coverage of the cataloguing rules would be technically feasible but not cost-effective, as the computer resources required would stretch far beyond the means of libraries in the 1980s. Technological progress might change the situation, but in the meantime more modest systems covering routine cases could free cataloguers to deal with the more difficult items, or alternatively systems for particular types of material based on subsets of AACR2 could be developed. (One such system, MAPPER, for cataloguing maps, is currently under investigation at the University of California, Los Angeles (Ercegovac, 1990a).) However, to equal the performance of a human cataloguer, access to an authority file and/or catalogue would be required, with all the ensuing problems of retrieval. Even a system like ESSCAPE/EMYCIN which did not deal with the forms of access points could be cumbersome to use in a real-life setting, because of problems with contradictions and lack of clarity in AACR2.

The ESSCAPE project showed that the cataloguing rules should be rationalized if full advantage is to be taken of computer technology. However, existing codes have their roots in the era of the card catalogue and were designed with linear files in mind, not the convoluted interlinking paths of hypertext, and therefore Hjerppe (1986) decided that it would be better to reassess the form and function of the catalogue before doing any more work on devising a code more suitable for use as a knowledge base.

4 Fully automatic systems

The suitability of different cataloguing codes (in this case AACR1 and ALA) for automatic application had been a theme of Sandberg-Fox's work in the late 1960s and early 1970s, and she was the first to tackle the major obstacle to the development of fully automatic systems: the problems of title-page interpretation. Her doctoral dissertation was on the simulation of the intellectual process of identifying the main entry heading and did not address the question of added entries (Sandberg-Fox, 1972). Since the main entry headings are either names (of persons or bodies) or titles, she attempted to categorize the different ways in which titles and statements of responsibility may be represented on title pages. Next, on the basis of format and syntax, rules were developed for recognizing all the names occurring in statements of responsibility, or in the title when that served to indicate responsibility, as is often the case with autobiographies, diaries, correspondence etc. Recognizing names is not enough. It is also necessary to decide whether the main entry should be under the title or a name, and in the latter case which name if there is more than one. This too was accomplished using rules based on format and layout.

Decision trees for both the recognition and selection tasks were created and were tested by using them in cataloguing. Although the trees were not intended as a model of the cognitive processes that actually take place, it is not unreasonable to regard title-page interpretation as being equivalent to answering a series of questions of the form 'is an author's name given?', 'if there is more than one author, is one name emphasized by typography or layout?' etc.. Sandberg-Fox used the decision trees to simulate the application of subsets of rules from both the old *American Library Association Code* (ALA) and the first edition of the *Anglo-American Cataloguing Rules* (AACR1) to test the hypothesis that it would be easier to simulate decisions based on the new code. In fact, the directed tree graphs or decision trees for both codes proved to be highly, and almost equally, accurate. The last finding was somewhat surprising, as the Anglo-American rules are based on a set of principles, in contrast to the older code which was based on an enumeration of specific problems. Recently Sandberg-Fox (1990) has applied the same techniques to a subset of the second edition of the Anglo-American Rules (AACR2), with similar results.

Over a decade was to pass before the automatic interpretation of title pages was to become a topic for research again. Hjerppe and Olander (1985) briefly noted some of the difficulties that would have to be overcome, and other writers discussed possible solutions. In Germany, Schwarz (1986) argued that a large memory and the ability to recognize patterns are the aspects of intelligent behaviour most relevant to the cataloguing problem. With the exception of the article by Burger (1984) on authority control, memory has been relatively neglected by workers in this field, but it can greatly simplify the task of recognizing some bibliographic features. People can usually recognize names for what they are simply by comparison with similar names in their memory, e.g. even if you have never heard of anybody called 'Philip Shaw' you would know that it is a personal name as the two words are a common Christian name and surname, respectively. An automatic system would be even better than people at making such inferences if it had access to a large authority file of names from many different countries and linguistic groups. If names of corporate bodies were identified as such, or were stored in a separate file, they too might be recognized in a similar manner. Even titles might be detected by comparison with words found in the title fields of records in an online catalogue: words like 'handbook', 'introduction' and 'textbook' would be obvious clues. It might prove necessary to determine the language of the book, but that could be inferred from the presence of certain characteristic words, e.g. 'the' in English, or the place of publication, though that would be less reliable. Given a system designed for parallel processing, Schwarz suggested that it would be feasible to carry out simultaneous searches of files of personal names, corporate names, titles, publisher's names etc., to ascertain the nature of any character string.

However, the nature of a character string does not uniquely determine its function. A personal name may belong to an author, an editor, translator etc., or, as in some of the examples considered by Sandberg-Fox, it may be part of the title. Similarly, a sequence of words that is indicative of a title might occur in the title proper, subtitle, parallel title or series title. Consequently, after identifying the general nature of a character string its exact function must be determined, and this could be done taking into account the clues offered by title page layout and syntax. Unlike Sandberg-Fox, who, in order to make the simulation task more tractable, studied only those cases where the statement of responsibility followed the title, Schwarz chose examples of a variety of formats in order to analyse some of the different problems that can arise, and to discover clues that might be useful in recognizing the functions of different character strings. She suggested that many more clues could be enumerated, perhaps about 100 altogether, and statistics on their applicability could be gathered. Then, possibly using machine-learning techniques to discover patterns in the data, rules could be formulated and an expert system created which would be capable of scanning a title page, preparing a record and, if necessary, prompting the human operator to supply any missing data.

While Schwarz's investigations were in progress, a similar study was under way in Exeter in an attempt to find a way past the limitations of systems such as the one James had worked on there, which would depend totally on the cataloguer for interpreting data. Sets of rules for data interpretation were drawn up but they were of a very tentative nature and were not tested, as the intention was merely to show that possible clues for recognizing every bibliographic field represented on title pages could be enumerated (Davies, 1987). These clues were based on layout, typography, syntax and semantics. Some features would be fairly easy to recognize: the date of publication would be a four-digit Arabic number, probably beginning 19-, in relatively small print near the foot of the title page. Titles would obviously be far more variable, but are usually either the most prominent or second most prominent feature in terms of position and typography, and can often be distinguished from other prominent features such as authors' names by the use of grammatical clues, e.g. the presence of a definite or indefinite article, conjunction or preposition or the suffix 'ing', which in English is indicative of the present participle of verbs.

The problems of recognizing significant features received much more detailed attention from Jeng (1987) in her doctoral thesis at the University of Texas at Austin. She studied a sample of 203 books to gather data on both the grammatical and the visual characteristics of different bibliographic elements. (The visual features included position, relative typesize, typefont, darkness, case, punctuation, spacing etc..) Her two initial hypotheses, that the words and phrases found on title pages have specific linguistic properties and that these differ from one bibliographic element to the next, were both confirmed by the results (Jeng, 1988) and she also concluded that frames of different levels of abstraction would be suitable for representing the visual properties of title pages (Jeng, 1991a). Statistical data such as those Jeng gathered would, she pointed out, be of value not only in formulating rules for the knowledge base of an expert system, but also in revising AACR2 so that the code's instructions concerning the use of title pages would be based on detailed factual knowledge of their properties. Since completing her thesis Jeng has begun another empirical investigation – this time of AACR2. In a pilot study covering the provisions governing titles and statements of responsibility, data on the applicability or frequency of use of different rules were collected, and from the results she concluded that the smallest units in any knowledge base for cataloguing should be condition/action pairs, rather than the individual AACR2 rules (Jeng, 1991b).

Jeng (1986) had previously considered the question of how information about title pages could be processed, and as lists can be linked to form data structures of great complexity she advocated their use. Three different types of list were suggested: one to represent distinguishable units of the title page, another to represent the physical characteristics of these units, and a third to represent words. Any title page consists of a number of blocks of patterns separated by spaces or lines. One block might be the title and subtitle, another would be the publisher's name and the place and date of publication. For each block a record, acting as a node in a list, would be created consisting of the number of words in the block, a pointer to the memory address of the first node in the corresponding word list, a pointer to the first record in a list of physical attributes of that block, an 'interpretation value' assigned by the system and used in deciding what type of bibliographic feature the block represents, and finally a pointer to the next block. Each node in the word list would contain the following information: the position of the word within the block, its content, i.e. the characters making up the word, the part of speech (noun, verb etc.), the interpretation value, and a pointer to the next word node. The distinctive contents of the attribute node would be physical characteristics, such as typeface and dimension, and their values in the case of the block to which the node related e.g. italic for typeface. Sometimes two different sizes of typeface may be used in the title, so that the most important word or phrase can be emphasized. In that case a second attribute node would be linked to the first by a pointer. These lists could be expanded indefinitely, and therefore the data structure proposed by Jeng, illustrated by Figure 5.5, has the flexibility needed for coping with the great variations shown in title page displays.

Whereas the early part of Jeng's work concentrated on titles, a study undertaken at the University of California, Los Angeles, by Svenonius, Baughman and Molto (1986) gathered information about the occurrence of names in title pages and other significant places (i.e. covers, preliminary pages, versos of title pages, contents lists

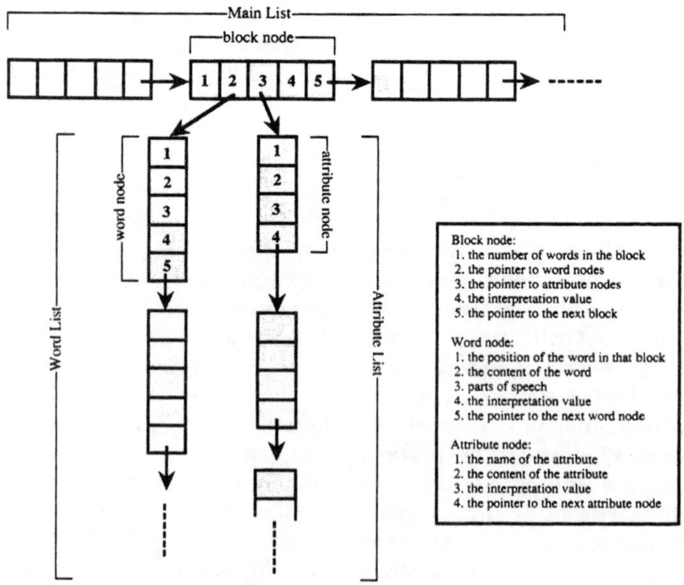

Figure 5.5 *Data structure for title page information (reprinted with permission from Cataloguing Classification Quarterly, Vol.* **7** *(2), The Haworth Press Inc., 10 Alice Street, Birmingham, NY 13904)*

and colophons) in order to ascertain the possibility of simplifying the rules concerning the selection of names as access points. Could the Gordian knot of AACR2's complex prescriptions be severed at a stroke by making every name an access point? This was regarded as unacceptable, since it is necessary to distinguish between books by a person and those about that person, and because by including many more names the amount of work involved in checking authority files would be greatly increased. Consequently it was decided that only the names classifiable as belonging to an author, editor, illustrator, emanator or publisher should be included. The study confirmed the pre-eminence of the title page as the most useful source of access points. Contents lists would provide more names but would probably treble the size of the catalogue, while enhancing access to only a relatively small proportion of publications, e.g. conference proceedings. The other sources considered were not very productive. Of the names which according to AACR2 should be used as access points, only a small proportion would be missed by adopting the simple rule of including all those occurring in particular locations and identifiable as belonging to certain specified categories, e.g. author, editor, illustrator etc. If that were not the case, then research into fully automatic as opposed to machine-aided cataloguing would be a waste of time, but as their findings suggest that the goal is not infeasible in principle, Svenonius and Molto (1990) have followed up their original study by investigating rules for recognizing names and treating them in accordance with the provisions of AACR2. The issue of feasibility has also received attention from OCLC (Weibel, Oskins and Vizine-Goetz, 1987, 1989; Vizine-Goetz, Weibel and Oskins, 1990), the organization which in the 1970s and 1980s probably did more than any other in the world to transform the practice of cataloguing.

The motivation of the OCLC research was the long-term prospect that automatic cataloguing would reduce backlogs, expedite recataloguing of older material for which machine-readable records are not available, and make it economical to catalogue material such as internal technical reports, correspondence etc., on which the expenditure of human time and effort is not justified (Weibel, Oskins and Vizine-Goetz, 1989). Preliminary experiments with commercially available OCR devices were unsatisfactory, but as the technology is advancing all the time Weibel and his colleagues assumed that solutions to the problems they encountered will be found eventually, and therefore they simulated the data capture process by using the TeX document formatting system to create machine-readable records that could be used to produce copies of the title pages looking like facsimiles of the originals, and thus they were able to concentrate on the tasks that would be involved in processing the data after the optical scanning stage.

Before anything could be done with the data it was necessary to extract it from the TeX file. This was done using a parser which wrote the space-delimited character strings, called tokens, and their attributes (i.e. page location coordinates, type style and type size) to a token file which served as the input to the main system written in PROLOG. In addition to the tokens and their attributes, statistics describing the page as a whole (e.g. specifying positions of margins) were also recorded in PROLOG's internal database. Next, the individual tokens were amalgamated into functionally meaningful units, which might be expected to correspond to different bibliographic fields, by adding them to a data structure until changes in font or size were encountered, or white space exceeded a certain specified value.

As in previous work on title page interpretation, the rules used are based on three different kinds of condition: layout, the simple occurrence of particular words, e.g. articles, conjunctions and prepositions, and the actual meaning of certain words or phrases, e.g. 'edited by'. Another way of characterizing the rules is to distinguish between those that do and those that do not depend on previous rules for their application. A typical example of the former type is the rule that a compound token is a statement of responsibility if it precedes an affiliation phrase (such as the name of a university). Obviously this would depend on the prior execution of a rule for affiliation phrases, and consequently the rules were arranged in precedence classes to control their order of application. Another requirement is that account should be taken of differences in the reliability of the rules, and therefore to indicate the strength of the resulting inference a confidence factor was assigned to each rule. Initially this was done on the basis of the researchers' judgement, but the values were modified where necessary in the light of experience with the system. Normally the ratings were in the range 1–10, but if there was no doubt about the conclusion the value used was 100. The rule interpreter processes each compound token against every rule, and if the condition is satisfied the inference and its confidence rating are recorded. Thus, after all the rules have been tested each of the compound tokens has associated with it a list of confidence factors, possibly for different verdicts. These are then simply added and the verdict with the highest sum determines the bibliographic field to which the compound is assigned.

A random sample of the title pages of recent monographs was divided into two, and the first half was used as a training sample for refining the rules and confidence factors. The system was then tested on the other half. Over 80% of the bibliographic fields present were correctly identified but the easiest were ones which are not normally used as access points, namely the publisher, place and date of publication, and the edition. The most difficult were other title information (identified successfully in 63% of cases), statement of responsibility (70% success) and title (76% success), the last two of which would normally be used for access. However, one of the common errors was including other title information with the title, and that would not affect retrieval.

On the whole, considering that the system was simply a prototype with just 16 rules, its performance was encouraging. The authors suggested that it could be improved by making greater use of syntactic analysis, by checking authority files of personal and corporate names, and by reducing or enlarging images to bring them within the range of current OCR devices. However, to attain performance levels comparable to those of human experts, four problems would have to be overcome:

1. The need somehow to incorporate a deeper understanding of the task of cataloguing, as two title pages may have very similar layouts and yet have completely different bibliographic interpretations.
2. The extreme irregularity of some layouts. The authors gave an example of a title spread over two pages and the letters of the individual words were not aligned either horizontally or vertically.
3. Some special fonts used for artistic purposes might not be readable by OCR devices.
4. The complexity and ambiguity of AACR2 rules and their dependence on knowledge of the real world.

For these reasons the authors conclude that the development of an unattended cataloguing robot is unlikely in the foreseeable future, but nevertheless an automatic system might still be useful since a human cataloguer could quickly inspect documents and set aside those needing special attention, leaving the bulk to be processed by the machine. They also expressed the hope that studies in automated cataloguing would contribute towards future revisions of cataloguing rules.

Nearly all the work done so far has been of an experimental nature, but an expert system which it is hoped will be used routinely is currently under development by a software house in Germany (Rauth and Schnellbach, 1987). The planned system will be a successor to a prototype for cataloguing journal articles, known as AUTOCAT, that was designed at the Technical University of Darmstadt. Two kinds of knowledge are used in AUTOCAT: the first concerns the structure of journals and their records while the second relates to the process of creating records. A hierarchy of frames is used to represent the structural knowledge, and it includes a general specification of the components of a typical journal, followed by more detailed specifications of each of these components, e.g.:

A journal consists of a table of contents, articles...

An article consists of a heading and a text.

A heading consists of the title and the author's name.

An author's name consists of forename(s) and a surname.

The contents of a text may be described by an abstract, descriptors, and a class number.

.

.

.

Although different articles will have different titles and will normally be by different authors, some information, such as the journal title, volume number, will be the same for all articles in the same volume, while all those in the same issue will have the same issue number and date. Furthermore the layout and typography of the contents pages of the different issues are unlikely to vary. Consequently, when cataloguing journal articles a lot can be known about the bibliographical and physical characteristics of the items in advance – a situation markedly different from that prevailing when monographs are catalogued. AUTOCAT's structural knowledge was obtained by studying the characteristics of 330 journals containing articles on nuclear physics. In addition, the system's knowledge base includes heuristics for recognizing bibliographic fields and rules for producing entries in accordance with the INIS (International Nuclear Information System) code. The recognition heuristics are arranged in a hierarchy of modules, each of which acts as an expert for some particular field, as shown in Figure 5.6. The modules in the upper levels control the activities of those below them.

AUTOCAT was written in PROLOG and a Kurzweil Data Entry Machine was used as the principal means of data input. Its successor, AUTOCAT 2, is intended to be a commercial product that will accept data from electronic publishing systems as well as OCR equipment, and will have an improved interface so that the user will find it easier to modify the knowledge base, e.g. when adding structural information about new journals. It has been suggested that ideally the new system should be developed so that it could also cope with other document types, such as dissertations, and different cataloguing codes, e.g. not only INIS but also RAK, the German equivalent of AACR2, thus making it more of a general-purpose expert cataloguing system.

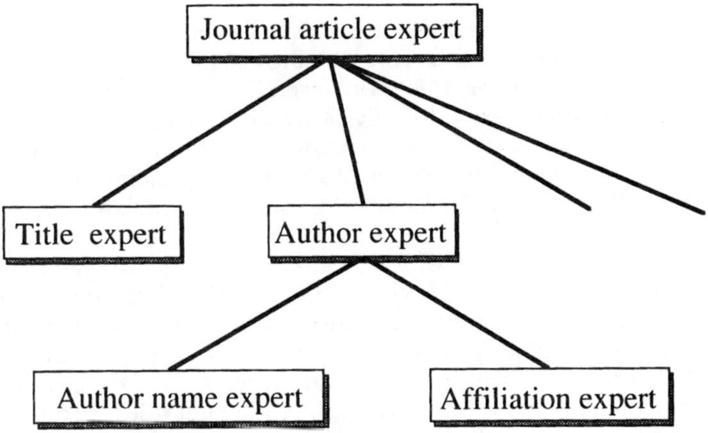

Figure 5.6 *Hierarchy of recognition modules in AUTOCAT*

5 Conclusion

During the 1980s three different approaches to the creation of an expert cataloguing system were tried. The system may be a tool providing advice when wanted – a sort of partner interacting with the cataloguer to create a record – or it may be a machine operating in a largely autonomous fashion (Davies, 1986b). Of these alternatives the first would appear to be the simplest and therefore the most promising in the short run. Where expertise is rare, as in cataloguing maps, specialized systems could be very useful, especially if, like MAPPER, they really do incorporate genuine expert knowledge and not just the relevant AACR2 rules. Other areas in which specialized advisory systems might be desirable include audiovisual materials and computer software. General purpose advisory systems based simply on the code, such as Strathclyde's CATALYST, might also be of some use in working environments if they were integrated with normal cataloguing software, but otherwise their value would probably be confined largely to students of cataloguing. No doubt students would initially be quite intrigued by any such tool, but there are limitations to the usefulness of ordinary expert systems in educational settings. An intelligent tutoring system for cataloguing would require a model of the individual user's knowledge, or the lack of it, and that would have to be based on a detailed study of the thought processes and mistakes of novices. In the field of subject cataloguing as opposed to descriptive cataloguing this topic has received some attention. A prototype tutor for teaching students how to apply Library of Congress subject headings has been developed at the University of Pittsburgh, and the designers have considered the feasibility of continuing the project in order to produce a full-scale intelligent tutoring system (Katz, Schmandt and Metzler, 1989). However, in practical day-to-day cataloguing the aim of providing advice would be to assist rather than to educate the user, and therefore a module using text animation would be a worthwhile addition to any conventional system and a big improvement over the help facilities commonly available in such systems.

In principle, a system which creates records after interacting with the cataloguer to acquire both the bibliographic data and the information needed for determining which rules apply should be technically feasible, but judging by the experience of Hjerppe and Olander (1989) and Jeng's (1991b) study of rule applicability, the task of converting the provisions of AACR2 into production rules or some other appropriate means of representing knowledge would be far from straightforward. Furthermore, unless the resulting system was significantly faster than conventional ones it might not be cost-effective or acceptable to experienced users. However, existing systems could be enhanced by the adoption of some of the ideas proposed in connection with work in this field. It has been argued that the distinction between expert and conventional systems will become blurred, since for practical purposes in industry and commerce, knowledge-based modules incorporated in ordinary data processing systems would be more useful than standalone expert systems (Basden, 1983).

In so far as the assignment of MARC codes requires expertise (Epstein, 1987) steps in that direction have been taken by the designers of some library automation systems, including DOBIS/LIBIS (Brophy *et al.*, 1990) and URICA (Jones and Rea, 1989). Some rules for the selection of access points, such as the one requiring added entries under the names of the second and third authors, would also be easy to execute automatically but most would be difficult to apply without preliminary interaction with the cataloguer. In contrast, there would be considerable scope for guiding the input of data in accordance with the instructions concerning the structure of records in part 1 of AACR2. Some conventional systems, including those in which MARC code assignment is automatic, do prompt the user to enter particular fields, but much more could be achieved if the prompts were tailored closely to the type of item being catalogued, (e.g. an ordinary monograph, proceedings of a conference, a serial, map etc.) thus making use of some of the properties of frames. To go further and attempt to produce an economically feasible expert record production system rather than an enhanced conventional one would be a major undertaking, and although pilot projects would be useful for getting information about the efficiency of different designs and ways in which they could be improved, it would probably be better to revise existing cataloguing codes before attempting to implement any such system for practical use. Indeed it may be better to take a fresh look not only at cataloguing rules but also at the form and functions of catalogues, as Hjerppe (1986) has been doing.

The case for extensive revisions of cataloguing codes would be even greater if it were desired to implement fully or largely automatic systems, since then it would be necessary to get rid of rules involving conditions whose existence could only be determined by the exercise of human judgement, otherwise the use of such systems would have to be confined to relatively simple cases. With fully automatic systems technical feasibility would be more of a problem, but economic feasibility would be less so. This is because an automatic system would achieve much greater savings in human labour and would probably also be much faster than one which interacts with the cataloguer. Even if the capital costs turned out to be too high for many libraries, just a few such systems installed in national and other major research libraries could have a profound and widespread impact by eliminating backlogs of work and thereby improving hit rates in bibliographic networks and reducing the amount of original cataloguing that needed to be done in other libraries. Much of the data necessary for cataloguing new publications will be potentially available in electronic form as a result of the growing use of computers by authors and publishers, and the problems of recognizing and manipulating this data will be eased if the Standard Generalized Markup Language gains widespread acceptance.

Bibliographic data has always been available from publishers and booksellers, who could hardly hope to do business without it, and will be increasingly available in electronic form even when the full text of the publications is not. Although the data may not always be full enough for cataloguing purposes, it is normally sufficient for checking whether or not a library has the item(s) concerned before ordering, and in integrated library automation systems the acquisitions records can be used at the cataloguing stage, saving time and effort. Checking a single item in the catalogue would not take long, but as orders are often batched it would be desirable if this process could be automated too. At the University of Bradford an expert system was developed for improving quality control in catalogues by detecting duplicate records and merging them in a way that created upgraded versions (Ayres, Huggill and Yannakoudakis, 1988). Similar techniques for detecting matches could be used for checking publishers' or booksellers' records against the catalogue at the ordering stage and would also be desirable for preventing the creation of duplicate records by any expert system used for retrospective cataloguing.

Automatic cataloguing of material that is not available in electronic form will become feasible when OCR devices of greater sophistication and reliability are developed and more work is done on elucidating and testing heuristics for interpreting title pages. However, even if the cataloguing code were revised to eliminate rules requiring judgement, human cataloguers would still be needed to deal with books having very unusual or complicated title pages. It would probably not be very difficult to produce a system that could cope satisfactorily with the majority of cases, but no doubt the law of diminishing returns would apply and successive increments in capability would require proportionately far greater increases in the complexity of the knowledge base. Perhaps before that point is reached it would be worth trying a connectionist approach to title-page interpretation, since if it proved successful, the system would be capable to a certain extent of learning to cope with the more frequently encountered problems as its mistakes were corrected by the user.

The precise level of performance achieved by an automatic cataloguing system might matter less than the ease of distinguishing between items it could cope with and those which needed to be dealt with by a human cataloguer. If increasing the proportion that could be coped with automatically meant that the user found it much more difficult to decide which items should be catalogued manually, then the benefits of the improved performance of the machine might be lost. One way around this difficulty might be to try and develop a system that would be capable of recognizing items which would probably create difficulties for it, e.g. those with strange typography or unusual title page layouts.

In assessing performance, the nature of the mistakes made would need careful study. Would they be largely confined to the description or would they affect information retrieval? If the latter, would that be because the form of the access points was incorrect, or because headings which should not be access points were chosen, or because some access points were missed altogether? How easy would the mistakes be to detect and put right? If the errors were largely a matter of omitting additions to certain headings, or failing to select some relatively unimportant access points, then they might not matter much, particularly if the records affected could be upgraded as a matter of routine, as would be the case if a national agency such as the British National Bibliography or the Library of Congress were to use an expert system to produce for immediate use records which were later inspected, and if necessary amended and transmitted to the holders of the original versions.

Therefore, whether a given level of performance was satisfactory or not would depend partly on the division of labour between human and machine, and between the local library and national or other major sources of bibliographic data. The actual level achieved would depend not only on the technology but also on the nature of the cataloguing rules used, particularly the requirement for 'world knowledge' over and above the information that could be gained by inspecting title pages and searching authority files. Many of the writers who have considered the relevance of expert systems to cataloguing have suggested that existing codes need extensive revision if full advantage is to be taken of the technology. Revision along traditional lines would not be enough, as was shown by Sandberg-Fox's (1972) study which found very little difference in the ease of simulating rules from the Anglo-American and the older ALA codes. A catalogue stored on a computer is a database and might be expected to conform to the principles of database design, but Fidel and Crandall (1988) concluded that AACR2 conflicts with those principles. Therefore the case for extensive revision is good.

Simplifying cataloguing codes would facilitate the automatic application of their rules, thus tending to make the cataloguing process less expensive; but would users suffer as a result? According to de Jager (1985) the difficulty readers have in making proper use of the catalogue is a consequence of their ignorance of the rules and principles upon which it is based, but has little to do with the precise provisions of those rules, and therefore revising AACR2 would by itself neither hinder nor help the readers. Other kinds of knowledge are also required if the catalogue is to be an effective instrument of communication, as shown in Figure 5.7, but the amount of 'world knowledge', in this case subject knowledge, normally incorporated in bibliographic records is small. De Jager suggested that the catalogue's syndetic structure (which is dependent upon authority files and cross-references) should be regarded as a network in which the individual bibliographic records are treated as frames to which explanatory information about the subjects of the items is attached. Then the inadequacy of the user's knowledge of cataloguing principles will recede in importance and become less of a problem.

Various other proposals for augmenting the catalogue have been put forward from time to time (Cavanagh 1985; Kilgour, 1985; Hjerppe, 1986) which, if implemented, would make it a much more powerful tool. Although the fundamental principles of author/title cataloguing – that access should be provided to known items and related items, should be collocated – will still remain valid, the means by which they are put into effect may change (Davies, 1986c). The old consensus or paradigm that has held sway since the time of Cutter (1904) is breaking down (Davies, 1987). As far back as the early 1960s it was suggested that new cataloguing rules might be needed as a result of developments in electronic data processing (Gull, 1961). So far however, the main effect on codes has been an indirect

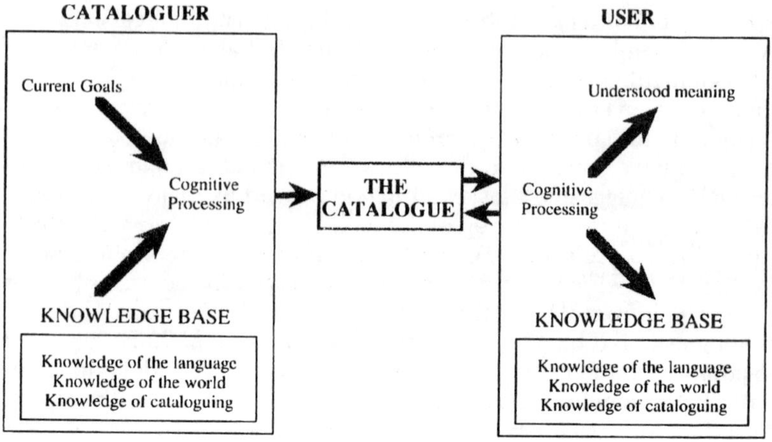

Figure 5.7 *Communication in the catalogue*

one (Malinconico , 1980). Automated authority files, which unfortunately were still rare when AACR2 was introduced, make it easier to alter headings, thereby reducing the amount of work caused by changes in rules, and consequently the compilers of the code were somewhat bolder than they might have been otherwise. As Meador and Wittig (1988) observed, if the introduction of electronic data processing in libraries was a factor in reducing resistance to change, then the advent of a new technology demanding flawless logic is likely to lead to pressure to rid the code of its inconsistencies. It would probably be premature to undertake a fundamental revision of the code before a new consensus shows signs of emerging concerning the role, content and structure of the catalogue and the process by which it is created and maintained, but by the beginning of the 21st century the implications of current advances in artificial intelligence and computer technology might be clear enough for us to form a fresh vision of what we wish to achieve.

6 References

Atherton, P. (1965) [Comments]. In *Proceedings of the Second Conference on Machine-Readable Catalog Copy* (Library of Congress, 1965), p. 14. Washington DC: Library of Congress

Avram, H.D. (1972) *RECON pilot project* Washington DC: Library of Congress

Ayres, F.H., Huggill, J.A.W. and Yannakoudakis, E.J. (1988) The Universal Standard Bibliographic Code (USBC): its use for cleaning, merging and controlling large databases. *Program 22*, 1988, 117-132

Basden, A. (1983) On the application of expert systems. *International Journal of Man–Machine Studies*, **19**, 461-472

Beetle, C. (1949) (ed) *ALA Cataloguing Rules for Author and Title entries* 2nd edn. Chicago: ALA

Black, W.J., Hargreaves, P. and Mayes, P.B. (1985) HEADS: a cataloguing advisory system. In *Advances in intelligent retrieval: Informatics 8* (Oxford, 1985) pp. 227-239. London: Aslib

Brophy, P. *et al.* (1990) *DOBLIS/LIBIS: a guide for librarians and systems managers.* Aldershot: Gower

Burger, R.H. (1984) Artificial intelligence and authority control. *Library Resources & Technical Services*, **28**, 337-345

Cavanagh, J.M.A. (1985) A proposed distributed optical catalog: a new basis for library automation. In *Proceedings of the 1985 Videodisc, Optical Disk and CD-ROM Conference and Exposition* (Philadelphia, 1985) pp. 36-42. Westport: Meckler

Cutter, C.A. (1904) *Rules for a directory catalog* 4th edn. Washington DC: US Government Printing Office

Davies, R. (1986a) Cataloguing as a domain for an expert system. In *Intelligent information systems: progress and prospects*, ed R. Davies, pp. 54-77. Chichester: Ellis Horwood

Davies, R. (1986b) The computer: a tool, machine or partner? *MARC Users Group Newsletter*, **86**, 36-45

Davies, R. (1986c) Expert systems and cataloguing: new wine in old bottles? In *Expert systems in libraries*, ed F. Gibb, pp. 67-82. London: Taylor Graham

Davies, R. (1987) Outlines of the emerging paradigm in cataloguing. *Information Processing & Management*, **23**, 89-98

Davies, R. and James, B. (1984) Towards an expert system for cataloguing: some experiments based on AACR2. *Program*, **18**, 283-297

de Jager, K. (1985) The library catalogue – an artificial intelligence perspective. *South African Journal of Library and Information Science*, **53**, 83-88

Epstein, H. (1987) An expert system for novice MARC catalogers. *Wilson Library Bulletin*, **62**, 33-36

Ercegovac, Z. (1986) Artificial intelligence and cataloging reasoning: promises and pitfalls. In *Proceedings of the 7th National Online Meeting*, (New York, 1986), eds. M.E. Williams and T.H. Hogan, pp. 109-117. Medford: Learned Information

Ercegovac, Z. (1990a) *Research on knowledge-based descriptive cataloging of considerable importance cartographic publications: an experimental advice-giving system, MAPPER (cataloging, HYPERCARD).* PhD Thesis, UCLA, Los Angeles

Ercegovac, Z. (1990b) Proposed definitional conditions as a basis to study the concept of map author. *Cataloging & Classification Quarterly*, **10**, 19-50

Eyre, J. (1986) Which experts, what systems – who cares? *MARC Users' Group Newsletter*, **86**, 1-9

Fidel, R. and Crandall, M. (1988) The AACR2 as a design schema for bibliographic databases. *Library Quarterly*, **58**, 123-142.

Gibb, F. and Sharif, C. (1988) CATALYST: an expert assistant for cataloguing. *Program*, **22**, 62-71

Gorman, M. and Winkler, P. (1978) eds. *Anglo-American Cataloguing Rules*, 2nd edn. London: Library Association

Gull, C.D. (1961) How will electronic information systems affect cataloging rules? *Library Resources & Technical Services*, **5**, 135-139

Hjerppe, R. (1986) HYPERCATalog and three meta-schemata for database views. In *Online Public Access to Library Files: 2nd National Conference* (Bath, 1986), ed. J. Kinsella, pp. 101-110. Oxford: Elsevier

Hjerppe, R. and Olander, B. (1985) *Artificial intelligence and cataloging: building expert systems for simple choice of access points for entries; results and revelations.* Linköping: Linköping University, Department of Computer Science (Report LiU-LIBLAB-R-1985:1)

Hjerppe, R. and Olander, B. (1989) Cataloging and expert systems: AACR2 as a knowledge base. *Journal of the American Society for Information Science*, **40**, 27-44

James, B. (1983) *Expert systems for library cataloguing functions.* MPhil Thesis, University of Exeter, Exeter, UK

Jeng, L.H. (1986) An expert system for determining title proper in descriptive cataloging: a conceptual model. *Cataloging & Indexing Quarterly*, **7**, 55-70

Jeng, L.H. (1987) *The title page as the source of information for bibliographic description: an analysis of its visual and linguistic characteristics.* PhD Thesis, University of Texas at Austin, Austin, USA

Jeng, L.H. (1988) The language of a title page. In *Proceedings of the 51st ASIS Annual Meeting* (Atlanta, 1988) pp. 31-35. Medford: Learned Information

Jeng, L.H. (1991a) Knowledge representation of the visual image of a title page. *Journal of the American Society for Information Science*, **42**, 99-109

Jeng, L.H. (1991b) The structure of knowledge base for cataloging rules. *Information Processing & Management*, **27**, 97-110

Jones, K.E. and Rea, G.A. (1989) *URICA: a guide for librarians and systems managers*. Aldershot: Gower

Katz, S., Schmadt, L. and Metzler, D. (1989) *A prototype tutoring system for subject cataloging*. Pittsburgh: University of Pittsburgh School of Library and Information Science (Report No. LIS022/IS89005)

Kilgour, F.C. (1969) Computerization: the advent of humanization in the college library. *Library Trends*, **18**, 29-36

Kilgour, F.C. (1985) *Beyond Bibliography: 3rd British Library Annual Research Lecture*. London: British Library

Malinconico, S.M. (1980) AACR2 and automation. In *The making of a code: the issues underlying AACR2*, ed. D.H. Clack, pp. 25-40. Chicago: American Library Association

Meador, R. and Wittig, G.R. (1988) Expert systems for automatic cataloging based on AACR2: a survey of research. *Information Technology and Libraries*, **7**, 166-171

Rauth, U. and Schnellbach, C. (1987) Das AUTOCAT-Konzept der wissenbasierten Formalerfassung von Zeitschriftenaufsätzen. In *Deutscher Dokumentartag 1987: von der Information zum Wissen, vom Wissen zur Information* (Bad Durkheim, 1987), ed. H. Strohl-Goebel, pp. 303-318. Weinheim: VCH Verlagsgesellschaft

Sandberg-Fox, A.M. (1972) *The amenability of a cataloging process to simulation by automatic techniques*. PhD Thesis, University of Illinois at Urbana-Champaign, Urbana-Champaign, USA

Sandberg-Fox, A.M. (1990) Selection of main entry: a conceptual model. In *Expert Systems in Libraries*, ed. R. Aluri and D.E. Riggs, pp. 135-154. Norwood: Ablex

Schwartz, H. (1986) Expert systems and the future of cataloguing: a possible approach. *LIBER Bulletin*, **26**, 23-50

Shaw, M. *et al.* (1980) *Using AACR2: a step-by-step algorithmic approach to part 2 of the Anglo-American cataloguing rules*. London: Library Association

Svenonius, E. and Molto, M. (1990) Automatic derivation of name access points in cataloging. *Journal of the American Society for Information Science*, **41**, 254-263

Svenonius, E., Baughman, B. and Molto, M. (1986) Title page sanctity? The distribution of access points in a sample of English language monographs. *Cataloging & Classification Quarterly*, **6**, 3-21

Verona, E. (1971) (ed) *Statement of principles adopted at the International Conference on Cataloguing Principles* (Paris, 1961). Definitive edn. London: IFLA

Vizine-Goetz, D., Weibel, S. and Oskins, W. (1990) Automating descriptive cataloging. In *Expert systems in libraries*, ed. R. Aluri and D.E. Riggs, pp. 123-134. Norwood: Ablex

Weibel, S., Oskins, M. and Vizine-Goetz, D. (1987) Automated title-page cataloging. In *Proceedings of the 50th ASIS Annual Meeting* (Boston, 1987), ed. C.C. Chen, pp. 234-240. Medford: Learned Information

Weibel, S., Oskins, M. and Vizine-Goetz, D. (1989) Automated title-page cataloging: a feasibility study. *Information Processing & Management*, **25**, 187-203

Wellisch, H.H. (1980) The cybernetics of bibliographic control: towards a theory of document retrieval systems. In *Theory and Application of Information Research: Proceedings of the Second International Research Forum on Information Science* (Copenhagen, 1977), ed. O. Harbo and L. Kajberg, pp. 82-100. London: Mansell

Wittgenstein, L. (1958) *Philosophical Investigations.* Translated by G.E.M. Anscombe. Oxford: Blackwell

Yaghmai, N.S. and Maxine, J.A. (1984) Expert systems: a tutorial. *Journal of the American Society for Information Science*, **35**, 297-305

Chapter 6

Expert systems and online information retrieval

Gwyneth Tseng

1 Introduction

Over the last decade or so prodigious efforts have been made to design software which mediates between the searcher and remote online information retrieval systems in order to simplify searching. Different approaches have been taken: the use of expert systems is one of them. This chapter examines in a general way the functionality of these intermediary systems, and gives selected examples which illustrate how expert systems have been used in their development.

Online information retrieval systems are interpreted here in the general context of remote-access commercial services such as DIALOG, BRS and DataStar. Artificial intelligence (AI) and expert systems, however, have been applied more widely in information retrieval: to the design of interfaces for highly structured database management systems, for example. Elsewhere, intelligent information retrieval (IIR) systems architectures have been prototyped to explore new and better ways to store, describe and retrieve documents. Many such prototypes incorporate their own test collection of documents, rather than acting as a front end to commercial services, and use a range of different AI techniques. Some of this work is mentioned here because it impinges on issues which should concern the designer of expert intermediary systems for online information retrieval.

Some relevant research also overlaps with other fields of library and information science. Use of expert systems for OPAC searching; for reference and referral work; for document representation and indexing; and particularly, natural language processing. These are covered in other chapters, and not explored in detail here. For a more extensive treatment of the subject, the reader is referred to Alberico and Micco (1990).

2 Online information retrieval

Today's public access online retrieval services operate on a commercial basis and are accessed remotely via telecommunications networks. Each service, and there are many of them, hosts a selection of databases containing huge quantities of information which can be selectively searched to retrieve small, and hopefully, useful and relevant extracts. Databases may contain either bibliographic, other textual, or numeric data records, but in all cases they are searched using text retrieval software. Words and phrases entered by the searcher are matched as character strings against those in a particular database, and records containing the search terms are retrieved and may be printed or downloaded to the user's terminal. Search terms may be combined using Boolean and positional connectors to specify a suitable occurrence relationship between the terms in matching records, and complex search formulations can be built up in this way (see, for example, Hartley *et al.*, 1990).

While online retrieval systems have revolutionized information searching since the early 1970s, they are still by no means straightforward to use. Traditionally they are searched by a trained intermediary who is well versed in some of the huge array of services and databases available, knows the login procedures and command languages, can search quickly to minimize charges for connection time, and can devise a suitable search strategy to optimize the retrieval results for the client. However, even the trained intermediary, operating in a specialist subject domain, can be overwhelmed by the range of different hosts, networks and databases now available, each with their individual retrieval software, technical protocols and charging mechanisms.

Nor is deciding what search terms to use a trivial task. Language used in the information store is rich and varied in its vocabulary, its syntax and orthography, and intrinsically unsuited to the exact character-string matching techniques used in most text retrieval software. If the words and phrases chosen as search terms are not there in the texts to be searched, then nothing will be found even if suitable material exists in the database. Controlled vocabulary indexing systems help ameliorate this problem, but they have their downside: the searcher must also understand the indexing scheme and how best to apply it.

Whereas a highly structured DBMS might reasonably be expected to locate the record for the oldest employee in a personnel file, there is no way a traditional text retrieval system could be asked simply to locate a guidebook for the most picturesque country in Europe. Herein lies a further problem with standard text retrieval systems: 'picturesque' is a subjective term which means different things to different people. Some will enjoy rugged mountain scenery, others, rolling countryside or sandy beaches. The query must be specified more precisely, in terms which will match the vocabulary in the database, and a competent intermediary will help a client to do this. It is, however, because the enquirer's knowledge of the subject is incomplete that the retrieval system is being consulted. In such situations it may not be possible to formulate an accurate query at the first attempt. Browsing and interaction with the database may be more appropriate, with intermediate findings at best helping the user to modify and improve his search, at worst serving to overload him with irrelevant items. Hence, the outcome of a search, and its overall cost, are very variable and can depend to a great extent on the skill of the searcher.

Little wonder then, that considerable effort has been expended to develop interfaces which make online searching easier, more profitable and less time-consuming. The aim has been to design software which will take over some or all of the tasks which have traditionally devolved to the human intermediary. Whilst this might improve direct access to online services by the client or 'end user', the work of the intermediary might also be streamlined. To the end user, an expert intermediary system could offer the attractions of privacy, convenience, an unfailing memory and round-the-clock availability; it could also circumvent any misunderstanding of the search topic between client and human intermediary. To the busy librarian, computer-mediated end-user searching might save time spent on simple enquiries and might seem an attractive alternative to providing lengthy end-user training programmes.

3 Front ends, intermediary systems and expert systems

A variety of terminology is used in the literature to describe the software which assists the online searcher: front end; interface; intelligent intermediary system; expert searcher system; and other variations on these themes. In the majority of cases, and necessarily when applied to remote access online retrieval services, such systems are complementary to, and not a replacement for, the host's retrieval software. They may be located on a particular host's computer; on a dial-up gateway or VAN which may link through to a number of different hosts; on the searcher's PC or institutional mainframe; or on some hybrid system (see for example Detemple, 1989). They all share a common intention – to provide an easy-to-use, transparent interface to one or more hosts. Efthimiadis (1989) recently published a bibliography of articles which describe both commercial and prototype systems. A recent article in Library Micromation News (Anon, 1990) reviews five PC-based products: Tome Searcher (expert-system based); IT – Information Transfer (partially expert-system based); sidetalk; current contents connection; and Pro-Search. Burton (1989) describes a UNIX-based transparent gateway to both online services and in-house databases.

The earliest efforts were to automate the routine, procedural parts of the search process, and have been very successful, with a large number of front ends now on the market. Most offer:

- control over data communications
- automatic dialling and logon to a range of hosts at a keystroke
- automatic logoff
- selective downloading of search results to local storage on the user's PC

More sophisticated front ends may also offer:

- a menu or other simple interface to enter terms and formulate a Boolean search
- a transparent gateway to several hosts and easy switching between them
- translation of the search to the target command language
- uploading of a preprepared search at a keystroke
- merging and post-processing of downloaded results
- assistance with database selection

Williams (1986) gives a more detailed taxonomy of these functions.

Although all the functions listed above can be, and usually are, automated using conventional programming techniques, and without recourse to any form of artificial intelligence, we are now beginning to see the successful application of expert systems to some of them. Lirov and Lirov (1990), for example, have proposed an expert system for the creation of subject bibliographies from downloaded references. Their system, known as REX (Reference EXpert system) is written in PROLOG and encodes known relationships between descriptor terms in the references as rules which govern the order and formatting of the bibliography.

Ideally, an *intelligent* front end or intermediary system should incorporate all the procedural tasks of conventional front-end software, as well as emulating some of the intellectual and cognitive skills of the human intermediary. Several different approaches have been taken, but expert systems and natural language processing are the two branches of artificial intelligence that have proved to be the most fertile so far. Walton (1988) nicely sums up the potential of expert systems:

> 'Like a human intermediary, an expert system is able to interact with the client, ascertaining the nature of his problem and asking pertinent questions to fill the gaps in the information needed. It can suggest a solution to the problem, or advise on a particular course of action from the data contained in its own knowledge base. It can also explain its line of reasoning and justify its response.'

To achieve this, the expert intermediary system must possess two key components: a knowledge base and an inference engine. In broad terms, the knowledge base should include retrieval knowledge (of command languages, database structures and search techniques, for example); subject domain knowledge, such as thesaural knowledge, to help the user formulate a question to the retrieval system; and a knowledge of users. The inference engine applies the knowledge to emulate the problem-solving techniques of the human intermediary.

Most expert intermediary systems developed so far fall into two broad categories: those for searching remote online databases and those for use with local collections of documents. Of the first type, one of the earliest was CONIT, which was developed for searching the NLM Elhill version of Medline, SDC Orbit and DIALOG (Marcus and Reintjes, 1981). CONIT provided a general-purpose standard interface for all three hosts which incorporated extensive help facilities. Later versions were able to rank databases in order of likely relevance to the search topic, and to give limited advice on how to broaden or narrow a search (Marcus, 1985). Whilst it did contain a knowledge of search commands and how to apply them, CONIT did not incorporate any subject domain knowledge to help the searcher formulate queries. More recently, expert intermediary systems with extensive subject knowledge bases have been designed to support searching in specific databases or subject areas. Notable examples include CANSEARCH and MenUSE for searching Medline (Pollitt, 1987, 1988a) and Tome Searcher, originally for searching INSPEC but then developed for other databases (Haynes, 1988). One example of the many projects concerned with searching local test collections is that described by Gauch and Smith (1989) which was developed to search full-text documents across a generality of subjects. Their system consists of a number of components including text retrieval software and an expert system. Like CONIT, this expert system does not contain domain knowledge, but it does contain retrieval knowledge – of search strategies and text analysis procedures – which is used to formulate and reformulate Boolean queries, and to analyse retrieved passages of text in order to rank them according to likely relevance to the user.

Although many expert intermediary systems have been reported in the literature, very few have them have gone beyond the prototype stage. Nevertheless, these prototypes clearly demonstrate the potential of expert systems. Functionally, there is quite a lot of difference between them. Some act as advisers when help is requested by the user; others monitor the search and intervene when mistakes are detected; yet others assume control over the whole search process. Many provide a comprehensive interface which mediates the whole search from start to finish, although expert systems techniques may only be deployed in some of the steps. A few systems simply provide offline decision support. Many of the more successful expert intermediary systems are database- or subject-specific, although some tackle general retrieval problems which are domain-independent.

The distributed expert-based intermediary system (DEBIS) aims to build a network of expert systems, each tackling independent subproblems, but all contributing to a common goal and exchanging information to achieve their individual subgoals. This type of architecture is suggested by the MONSTRAT model developed by researchers at the City University, London, and the Free University of Berlin (Belkin, Seeger and Wersig, 1983; Brooks, Daniels and Belkin 1985, 1986). Here, ten distinct intermediary functions are described in detail. Whilst MONSTRAT remains a theoretical model, other research has led to the development of prototype and skeletal DEBIS. Notable projects include I^3R (Croft and Thompson, 1987), CODER (Fox, 1987; Fox and France, 1987) and IOTA (Chiaramella and Defude, 1987). These use test collections of documents and have not so far been developed for remote database access, but they do point the way to very sophisticated modelling of retrieval processes, and have contributed greatly to research in the field.

4 Expertise in online searching

Let us look next at those parts of the search process which call on the knowledge, judgement and intuition of the intermediary, and which have been shown to hold real potential for expert systems development. Seen at a very broad level these are:

- communication with the client to establish, as clearly as possible, a statement of the information need
- selection of suitable sources of information
- planning and formulation of a search strategy
- execution of the search, including strategy modification to refine results

- interpretion of the search results and explanation to the client

Sweeping categorizations such as this have been attempted by very many commentators. They can be a useful starting point for a model of the search process but can also disguise the range and complexity of activities which are involved at each stage. Yet these activities must be articulated if an expert system is to emulate the behaviour of a human intermediary. Creating the knowledge base and inference engine can be an enormous task, which should start with a detailed analysis of the work of experienced searchers. In practice, only a few development projects have attempted to elicit intermediaries' expertise by direct observation and interview. Fortunately, there is now a substantial body of empirical research and investigative work on how experts actually conduct searches. The interested reader could not be better advised than to refer to a research report by Belkin and Vickery (1985) which examines interaction in information systems in detail and reviews research in all but the second of the aforementioned areas.

The intention in the following sections is to examine the first four broad stages in the search process, indicating background research into the underlying mechanisms and giving some examples to illustrate the use of expert systems techniques to emulate human expertise. Interpretation and feedback to the client are not separately discussed; a major feature of any expert system should be that it can explain its own decisions and line of reasoning at any stage.

4.1 Establishing the information need: user modelling and problem description

A user's initial description of his information requirement is often vague and incomplete, and the process of reaching a more precise specification suitable for an online retrieval system is then one of negotiation between client and intermediary. The eventual success of an online search crucially depends on the intermediary's correct interpretation of the nature of the information need. Meadow and Cochrane (1981) were two of the first authors to consider this question in depth in relation to online searching. During a presearch interview, the human intermediary clarifies the information need and search objectives in order to produce a clear description of the problem, which can subsequently be translated into a search strategy. An intelligent front end should conduct a dialogue with the user to do the same.

Belkin, Seeger and Wersig (1983) developed this theme further and indeed they argue that there are situations where there is 'no specific "information need", but there are people in problematic situations where ... different kinds of information provision may be helpful'.

Extending the ideas behind the MONSTRAT model to a detailed set of functions of an intelligent interface for information retrieval, Brooks, Daniels and Belkin (1985) identify three which are particularly pertinent to the elucidation of the search topic:

Function		Description
1.	Problem state	Determine position of user in problem treatment process, e.g. formulating problem, problem well specified, etc.
2.	User model	Generate description of user type, goals, beliefs, knowledge, etc, e.g. graduate student, thesis, etc.
3.	Problem description	Generate description of problem type, topic, structure, environment, etc.

The first of these functions is considered alongside the third in the ensuing discussion.

4.1.1 USER MODELLING

Brooks, Daniel and Belkin (1985) studied the communication between human intermediaries and their clients by recording presearch interviews. The transcripts reveal that the subjects spent much of the interview eliciting details about the user, rather than discussing the information problem directly. These include information about the user's subject background and research interests, what department they work in and at what level, what they already know about the search topic and what has been written on it, any known useful documents, prior knowledge of information retrieval and so forth. This understanding of the characteristics, background, communication style and experience of the user helps the intermediary to attune their questioning to suit particular clients and to interpret and assess the reliability of the user's statements. It can also contribute to the eventual search formulation. In an academic environment, for example, the type and level of information needed by an undergraduate student is likely to be different from that needed by his academic tutor, even if their subject statements are similar.

Brooks further argues for the separation of the problem description and user modelling functions when represented in a knowledge base, although clearly there must be interaction between the two. In most library situations, different users' problem definitions will be highly variable, whereas it may be possible to devise a standard set of frames, for example, which can be used to record general characteristics of users. Over time, a more complete profile of a particular user might be built up as more searches are undertaken – which databases they have used before, for example. The general intention is to then use this knowledge to make inferences which help to formulate new queries. The user model might also influence the type of feedback and explanation provided by the intermediary software, though little research appears to have been directed at this issue so far.

Many expert intermediary systems – including all the distributed expert-based intermediary systems mentioned before – do now incorporate some form of user modelling. Brajnik, Guida and Tasso (1987) discuss research in the field, and describe the user modelling submodule of the IR-NLI II DEBIS. Here, after an 'interview' with a new user to ascertain basic information such as educational background and professional experience, a 'model builder' extracts a basic model from a set of stereotypes, which it gradually extends as more searches are carried out for the same person. The model is used to direct the dialogue of the presearch interview, to avoid repetitious questioning, to interpret terms which have different meanings in different disciplines, and to help interpret the current problem description by drawing on existing knowledge of the user.

Other intelligent systems which incorporate some form of user modelling include GRUNDY (Rich, 1983), the PLEXUS referral system (Vickery and Brooks, 1987) and the front end to patent databases described by Ardis (1990). Modelling criteria typically include the user's subject background, academic level and professional experience; what they already know of the current search topic; whether they have consulted information systems before, for what problems, with what goals and with what success; and whether they are aware of relevant search tools such as thesauri or classification schemes.

Very sophisticated modelling techniques indeed would be needed to handle a heterogeneous user population, and some of the more successful expert intermediary systems have been subject- and/or situation-specific.

4.1.2 PROBLEM DESCRIPTION

Identification of what Brooks, Daniels and Belkin (1985) describe as the 'problem state' is an important precursor to defining the search problem. A user at an early stage of formulating a problem is likely to produce an incomplete description of it, and deeper probing by the intermediary system may be needed. In order to establish the problem description, the intelligent intermediary system must not only rely on the user's original request statement but must also seek clarification of the topic and of unfamiliar or ambiguous terminology.

A wide variety of approaches has been taken in the development of systems capable of questioning the user to refine the search topic. Several rely on the existence of a domain-specific knowledge base, which may incorporate a dictionary, thesaurus, subject classification, a more sophisticated semantic network, or some synthesis of all of these. These approaches are more applicable to integrated retrieval systems than to systems for searching remote online databases, although thesaural knowledge has been built into some expert intermediary systems. For example, the CIRCE system described by Aragon-Ramirez and Paice (1985), locates thesaurus terms which are related to terms in the user's original query, and then questions the user to establish the relevance of these.

An important issue is whether the examination of the topic has been taken as far as it can. In the case of the human mediated search this is highly dependent on the skill and judgement of the intermediary. The PLEXUS prototype – a referral system for answering questions on horticulture – (Vickery and Brooks, 1987) basically establishes a threshold for the proportion of terms in the query which must be recognized in the system's internal dictionary. Other intelligent retrieval systems take an equally pragmatic approach relevant to their own domain. This is, however, an issue which warrants far more investigation.

As well as exploring the search topic, an intermediary system should seek to establish why the information is needed; whether high recall and/or high relevance are called for; how many items are expected; and what levels of technical detail are required. In other words, a complete picture of what the user anticipates and expects from the search. These parameters will affect the choice of strategy later on, and are incorporated into many working models.

4.2 Selection of the information source

Part of the skill of the information professional is in assessing the suitability of different types of information resource for particular problems – hardcopy, online, CD-ROM and so forth. No expert intermediary systems known to this author take such a totally holistic view of source selection. Simply in the realm of commercial online services, there are hundreds of hosts and thousands of databases worldwide. The knowledge base for a multidisciplinary selector capable of fine discrimination between sources would be awesome indeed.

Most automated database selection aids in the public domain do not use AI techniques. Cross-file indexes have long been offered by a number of hosts – DIALOG's DIALINDEX and DataStar's CROSS, for example. These indexes report on the total number of postings for a simple search across a subset of the databases offered by the particular host.

Other database selectors use increasingly specific subject menus to help the user to home in on a suitable database. The approach has proved practicable on a number of online host and gateway services – DIALOG's Business Connection (Lambert, 1989) and the EASYNET gateway (Balas, 1989) are good examples. However, it may be difficult for a user to choose from a menu of subjects. At the broadest level, for example, would a search on the technology of medical lasers come under medicine, engineering, or science and technology?

Most research on expert systems for online information retrieval has been concerned with the search process itself and development prototypes have concentrated on a single database or type of database – such as full-text – where questions of database selection are not at issue. Nevertheless, as information sources continue to proliferate and as users become more demanding in their searching, increasingly discerning criteria will be needed to discriminate between sources and expert systems may be able to provide these.

Offline PC-based expert systems to advise on database and host selection have been developed in prototype by Trautman and von Flittner (1989), by Newham (Newham, 1987; Morris, Tseng and Newham, 1988) and by Pugh (1989). Each of these ranks its database recommendations according to search requirements which are elicited by direct questioning of the user. Trautman and von Flittner's system includes information on all databases offered by 16 of 'the world's most popular hosts'. The knowledge base was essentially constructed from published directories of databases. These are notoriously lacking in detail and so the knowledge base was supplemented with information from published database reviews.

Both Newham and Pugh constrained their prototypes to far tighter domains – company and marketing information, respectively. Large numbers of databases are available in both fields, each with their own very specific strengths and weaknesses in content and coverage. Experts with considerable experience of searching within these domains were interviewed to establish precisely what criteria they use to select hosts and databases. The experts also provided detailed information on the content and utility of particular databases, and this was incorporated in the expert system knowledge base. Neither system has yet been formally evaluated, although informal testing by expert intermediaries has so far been encouraging and the work is now continuing.

Database selection has also been incorporated into more comprehensive expert intermediary systems such as EURISKO (Barthes and Glize, 1988), IANI (Berg Hansen and Rottboll Andersen, 1988) and

SAFIR (Reiter, 1989). All these systems restrict their advice to a limited number of databases and hosts.

Well designed expert database selectors and advisers may be capable of fine discrimination between sources for a particular query. Like more conventional types of directory though, they are difficult to keep up-to-date because the external knowledge they use is constantly changing. The more detailed and discriminating (and therefore, useful) the knowledge base, the more demanding the problem, especially in volatile subject areas. Despite this conundrum, expert systems do hold considerable potential for providing better decision support for database selection than most currently available alternatives, and the field is ripe for further research and development.

4.3 Planning and formulation of the search

Having satisfactorily described the problem and chosen a source, the intermediary's next task is to formulate the search for input to the chosen retrieval system. Broadly this involves:

- selection of an appropriate search strategy
- selection of search terms to represent the subject of the search
- construction of syntactically correct commands in the target language of the chosen host service

4.3.1 STRATEGY SELECTION

Bates (1987) defines a search strategy as 'a plan or approach to an online search ... [which] operates above specific term choice and command use'. Hawkins and Wagers (1982) described several different types of strategies, one of which, the 'building blocks' approach, is the most obviously suited to the Boolean operators offered by text retrieval languages. Here, synonymous or quasi-synonymous terms are combined under separate concept headings (a logical OR relationship) and the resulting concept blocks combined (logical AND) to build a compound subject query. Several intelligent front ends just offer the building blocks strategy without giving any further choice. For example, CONIT (Marcus, 1986) was designed to assist users to identify the separate concepts in their search and then to formulate a Boolean expression.

Other expert systems have been used to suggest or to select appropriate strategies from an available range. A good example is the IR-NLI model proposed by Guida and Tasso (1983), which permits users to state their query in natural language and assists them with the construction of a search strategy. During the presearch interview, users are asked to allocate a score to each concept block, based on its perceived degree of relevance to the search. The selection of strategy type is then made by high-level rules such as:

IF (postings count of all concepts is high) AND
(generality level of all concepts is similar)
THEN select building blocks approach

Lower level rules, also using information gleaned during the pres-earch interview, can further refine the selection. For example:

IF (building blocks) AND (high recall)
THEN search free text

Pejtersen (1987) relates user modelling criteria to different types of search strategy, whilst, like IR-NLI, the EURISKO expert system (Barthes and Glize 1988) also uses a rule-based approach to select a strategy from a limited number described in its knowledge base.

4.3.2 TERM SELECTION

An intelligent intermediary system should be able to:

- identify suitable search terms in the user's request
- advise on, or eliminate any unsuitable search terms
- suggest additional or alternative search terms
- advise on whether to search any particular term across all fields of the database record (free text), or to impose restrictions such as search as controlled vocabulary descriptor, company name etc.

Whilst most intermediary systems incorporate term selection, comparatively few have used expert systems to do so. The more popular AI techniques are natural language processing (to analyse the user's query) and semantic modelling of the subject domain (to enrich the query terms). In essence, a database thesaurus or classification scheme is a semantic model of the subject area. Paice (1986), however, argues that most published thesauri make inadequate domain-specific knowledge bases for a good intermediary system. Most alternatives rely on creating an extended semantic network which will, for example, handle query terms that cannot be found in the thesaurus or which provide an extended description of the meaning and usage of terms. Examples include CoalSORT (Monarch and Carbonell, 1987), CODER (Fox, 1987) and SCISOR (Rau, 1987). CoalSORT is a prototype intelligent interface to an in-house bibliographic database on coal liquefaction. Here, a frame-based semantic network of terms was derived by consulting subject experts. Each frame holds information such as the meaning of the term, its generic name, and examples of its use. Indexers and searchers browse the network using windows and menus to identify appropriate terms and documents.

Of course, semantic networks marry the intermediary system to a particular subject domain or database. Moreover, the semantic network can be expensive to build and store. Bruandet (1989) outlines the automatic construction of a knowledge base from document texts using production rules to integrate new terms into the domain knowledge. Her approach has had little success so far across a generality of texts, but may show potential in restricted subject areas.

Sormunen and Alkula (1988) regard the semantic network as too complex to build for public access online retrieval systems, and instead favour the interactive thesaurus browser. This latter approach has been quite successfully implemented by Pollitt (1988a) whose MenUSE system incorporates, in essence, an interactive browser for the MeSH thesaurus, itself a search tool for the Medline database. Part of the success of Pollitt's system undoubtedly rests on the sophisticated semantic relationships between thesaurus terms which are an integral feature of MeSH itself.

Although not strictly an expert system, CIRCE, described by Aragon-Ramirez and Paice (1985) copes with both exact and inexact matching between the user's search terms and the target thesaurus. In common with a number of other systems, it relies on dialogue with the user to disambiguate candidate search terms with multiple meanings. Other approaches to mapping search terms to document content in intelligent retrieval systems have been based on word frequencies, statistical associations and fuzzy matching.

Fidel (1986, 1987) takes the argument one step further back, and considers the choice between using free text and controlled vocabulary search terms, or some combination of the two. This choice can profoundly affect search results. Based on an observational study of human intermediaries, Fidel has derived a decision tree to help choose between controlled and free text 'search keys' depending on whether a particular term is a 'single meaning' or a 'common' term. Whilst considerably more research is needed as to how such entities could be recognized, the model could be a good starting point for the construction of a set of selection rules for use in an expert system. The example of IR-NLI given previously illustrates one working prototype that does consider the choice between controlled and free terms.

4.3.3 SEARCH STATEMENT FORMULATION

Once a search strategy and search terms have been selected, it may appear to be a routine matter to translate these into search statements for a particular retrieval system. Indeed, many intelligent front ends do take a simple algorithmic approach using a building blocks strategy, simply inserting a search command and correct Boolean operators. However, all command languages offer considerable flexibility in the construction of search statements, even once a strategy has been formulated, and this has a considerable impact on search results. For example, different positional connectors can be used to specify that two search terms must be adjacent in matching records, or within the same descriptor term, sentence or paragraph. Procedures for entering classification numbers can be complex and quite beyond the time and patience of busy end users to assimilate.

Good examples of expert systems which tackle these issues are MenUSE (Pollitt, 1988b) and its predecessors, CANSEARCH and GENSEARCH. In these, stored knowledge is essentially of two types: knowledge of the subject domain, based on MeSH thesaurus terms and knowledge of the sophisticated techniques which control the use of MeSH for indexing and retrieval. Indexing conventions are expressed as a set of rules, coded as PROLOG statements, which infer the most appropriate search formulation for the selected search terms. CANSEARCH has been tested in field trials, and whilst it is outperformed by human intermediaries, it does help clinicians to construct good search statements with very little prior training. This is a very positive contribution of expert systems research to the practical problems of end-user searching in an important, but complex, database.

4.4 Search strategy modification

Online searching is an interactive process whereby intermediate results can be used to refine the search terms and strategy in order to optimize the final output. Many different tactics are available to the searcher to do this, and again we rely on the work of Bates (1979a, 1979b) for an early taxonomy of them. Other commentators such as Fidel (1985) and Harter and Rogers Peters (1985) have also described a very large number of variously called heuristics, tactics, 'rules-of-thumb', or 'tricks of the trade', to help improve an online search. Perhaps an expert system could help to choose between them?

Heuristics, by their nature, do not have strict rules governing their use; they are tentative guidelines which may be more or less appropriate in different situations. Careful choice and balancing of different tactics can be a subtle business: broadening a search term to achieve better recall may cause an unacceptable drop in precision, which might then be compensated for in some other way. A model of this process would be complex indeed, even assuming that problem definition remains static. In practice, the intermediate results of an online search can change the user's perception of the retrieval system or can help to clarify a previously vague problem description. Hence the original topic specification, expected output, search goals and constraints can all change as the search progresses.

A major weakness of non-intelligent front ends and some intermediary systems is that they provide little or no guidance on how to improve a less than successful search. First generation intermediary systems tended to offer only general advice (such as 'narrow your search by using more specific search terms'), or to offer a very limited selection of alternative tactics.

Despite the considerable complexity, the idea of an expert system to suggest highly focused search tactics is an attractive one. As late as 1988, Hawkins suggested that this was an aspect of intelligence that was still virtually untouched in intermediary systems. Essentially, even though search tactics have been extensively described in the literature, very little is really known about how and to what effect human intermediaries really do use them. Despite the fact that there is still a lot to be understood about how different tactics interact with each other, and how effective they really are in particular circumstances, most recent expert intermediary systems do make some attempt to use them to help improve search output.

Strategy modification should be linked both to the original problem description and to an evaluation of intermediate postings: the searcher must recognize that the initial strategy is inadequate to a greater or lesser extent, and have some perception of what is wrong with the results. Virtually all existing expert systems approaches ascertain search performance feedback simply in terms of the number of items retrieved against a target number (too many, too few, none at all) and in some cases, their perceived relevance or usefulness. The more sophisticated offer further analysis of search results and problem-specific advice from an extensive knowledge base of tactics and common errors.

OAK, developed for the US Department of Energy DOE/RECON and BASIS online services (Meadow *et al.*, 1989), is a good example. OAK has a number of components, including OAKASSIST, which helps in formulating and entering a search, and OAKDEC, which gives specific advice on search reformulation (Meadow, 1988). OAKDEC uses criteria such as set size, user assessment of the use and usefulness of particular records, and number of records reviewed by the user to reach a recommendation. It also collects data on user behaviour and attitudes to its own recommendations.

MOSS, a prototype expert system designed by Walton (Walton 1988; Morris, Tseng and Walton, 1989) can recommend from a large number of search tactics, applicable across a range of business databases. The system is offline, and was developed to explore a detailed model of search tactics and the circumstances of their use. A question answering system guides the user to a precise specification of the search problem, and then particular tactics are suggested and explained. For example, the advice might be to drop the lowest posted concept from a search, with guidance on how to identify it.

IDEA, an Intelligent Database Enquiry Assistant (Houghton, Rich and Bass, 1987) is similar, although here question-specific as well as general advice can be given. The knowledge base incorporates a subject thesaurus, so that general advice such as 'use broader search terms', can be supported by specific suggestions. IDEA includes a 'user question handler' for 'why', 'what' and 'how' questions such as 'how do I narrow a search?'.

A domain-independent approach is adopted in a prototype for searching full-text databases described by Gauch and Smith, 1989. Here, the expert system itself evaluates the search results and decides whether to reformulate the query, based on the original target number of items, the actual number retrieved and the tactics tried so far. The system is restricted to choosing between just three tactics to broaden or narrow the search: use of broader or narrower terms; tightening or loosening word proximity requirements; and swapping Boolean operators. Once an appropriate number of items are retrieved, they are ranked by probable interest to the user based on statistical and contextual text analysis.

Elsewhere, strategy modification has been built into domain, database- and/or situation-specific intermediary systems which can target the search problem in hand. For example, if the expert system holds domain knowledge, then attempts can be made to assess the ambiguity or generality of particular search terms. In PLEXUS, modification can be achieved by removing, adding or replacing particular search terms (Vickery *et al.*, 1987). Criteria for identifying candidate terms are user assessment; number of postings (the more heavily posted terms are considered to be less discriminating); and criteria based on semantic categories.

Other significant examples of expert systems which tackle strategy modification include CONIT (Marcus, 1986) and EURISKO (Barthes and Glize, 1988).

5 Human–computer dialogue

Many designers of intelligent front-end systems take the view that the ideal interface is one which allows the user to enter a query in unconstrained natural language, and even to respond to specific questions, for example at the user modelling and problem definitions stages, in the same manner. In terms of current technologies, this usually involves keyboard input.

Unconstrained natural language input is not, however, a prerequisite for an intelligent front end, and can have some disadvantages for those who are not comfortable using a keyboard. Indeed, as development tools, few expert systems shells offer a natural language facility to the expert systems designer.

As early as 1983, Belkin, Seeger and Wersig suggested that different types of dialogue may be appropriate for different types of users in varying problem states. Certainly, whatever vocabulary is used, it should be suited to the user's knowledge of both the subject and of IR jargon. Besides natural language, other approaches include menus, limited vocabulary input, closed questions, choice of dialogue for experienced and novice searchers, and graphical interfaces.

CANSEARCH, for example, uses menus with touch-sensitive screens to browse and select MeSH thesaurus terms. Pollitt (1988b) argues that unlike natural language, menus 'avoid the problems created by potentially ambiguous user statements on the subject matter of their search'. Monarch and Carbonell (1987) describe different types of browsers which, they suggest, give the user a far clearer picture of the scope and organization of the database than a natural language interface can do.

Another interesting approach is the use of graphical interfaces such as those described by Thiel and Hammwoehner (1987) for searching full-text documents on the topic of office automation, and by McMath, Tamaru and Rada (1989) for thesaurus browsing.

Systems that do incorporate natural language query analysis are supported by some form of large, comprehensive retrieval lexicon and/or semantic network. Most begin by using simple techniques such as stop lists and stemming algorithms to identify important word stems and phrases. The query text may then be further analysed syntactically and/or semantically and the results used to generate new search terms or to question the user further.

Natural language interfaces have achieved some success, particularly where the domain knowledge required to support them can be contained or kept simple. There are several examples of natural language interfaces to intelligent retrieval systems: CODER (Fox and France, 1987), IOTA (Chiaramella and Defude, 1987), and IR-NLI (Guida and Tasso, 1983) are all good examples.

Fewer systems provide a natural language interface to a commercial retrieval system, but some examples do exist: CITE which was developed several years ago at the National Library of Medicine (Doszkocs, 1983); EURISKO which accepts single-sentence queries for around 30 databases (Barthes and Glize, 1988) and Tome Searcher (Haynes, 1988). Although these point the way forward, we are still very far from having robust and open-ended natural language interfaces for all but a few commercial online databases.

6 The integrated expert system front end

Many intelligent front ends do deal with every aspect of the search process, providing the user with assistance from the point of sitting down at the terminal, to logging off with a printout or file of results. In fact it is not always easy to ascertain whether or not AI techniques have been adopted in some commercial products, as vendors shy away from the hype that once surrounded some so-called expert intermediary systems that contained very low-level, if any, real expertise. Where they are used at all, expert systems techniques tend to be used in some, but not all of the stages in the search. Some more fully integrated expert system front ends to remote online databases do exist, in prototype or as operational systems. Some of the most promising, which are still under active development, and which have not been described earlier, are outlined below.

6.1 The EURISKO system (Barthes, Frontin and Glize, 1987; Barthes and Glize, 1988)

EURISKO is a PC-based system, developed at Paul Sabatier University in France, which guides the user through a search. Its knowledge base contains information about documents, search strategies, database structures and contents. A query, expressed as a natural language sentence (in French), is parsed and the user is asked to supply truncation points for significant terms. English terms can be added if necessary. A database is selected from a subset of about 30 offered by the Télésystèmes Questel and Cedocar hosts. A suitable strategy is formulated, presented to the user for checking, and then sent automatically to the host. Strategy types were defined in consultation with expert intermediaries. Depending on the user's assessment of the relevance of the output, modification techniques are recommended. Ongoing work on EURISKO is concentrating on the reformulation of strategies.

6.2 IANI (Anon, 1989; Berg Hansen and Rottboll Andersen, 1988)

IANI provides intelligent access to a number of Nordic hosts, and a conventionally programmed interface to other international hosts including DIALOG, STN and ESA. The PC-based software offers all the essential features of a front end – automatic logon, communications, uniform command language, uploading and downloading, merging, sorting and editing results. AI techniques, in the form of an object-oriented rule-based system, are used to help the user to select hosts and databases and to formulate search strategies. It is envisaged that the software will be ported to a UNIX environment, so that interfaces to local as well as remote databases can be built.

6.3 Tome Searcher (Vickery 1988; Haynes 1988)

Tome Searcher evolved from the PLEXUS system described by Vickery and Brooks (1987). It was first launched commercially by Tome Associates as a PC-based product, designed for searching the INSPEC file on ESA-IRS and on DIALOG. In Tome Searcher, a natural language processor allows the user complete freedom in formulating the query statement, but the user is also prompted to enter details such as date range and target output size. The system holds a thesaurus subset and a dictionary, which includes postings data from the remote database. These are used to advise on strategies which are likely to be too broad or too narrow, and to suggest additional or alternative search terms. Strategy formulation and modification routines are included, as well as a command language interface. Once the user is satisfied with the strategy, the system automatically logs on to the host, performs the search, downloads the results and logs off. Interfaces to other databases on ESA, STN Orbit and DIALOG have been developed, as well as a selection aid, Tome Selector. Commercial sales of these products have been modest and they have now been withdrawn from the open market. Instead, the company is tailoring them for use in specialist information environments, and is also cooperating with the EURISKO team to develop a new, multilingual intelligent interface to four European hosts (IMIS).

6.4 An expert system for online patent searching (ARDIS 1990)

Some libraries have applied expert systems very effectively to 'real-world' retrieval problems which are locally constrained, though the time and effort involved should never be underestimated. One example, reported to be in heavy use by the public at the McKinney Engineering Library at the University of Texas, has been described by Susan Ardis (1990). This provides a transparent interface to patent files on DIALOG and the US Patent and Trademark office's database, CASSIS. Search experts on the library staff contributed to the domain and retrieval knowledge in the knowledge base. Patent searching was chosen because there was a demand from end users who find both the hardcopy and online sources difficult to understand. A highly structured, closed menu system prompts users to specify their search goals and topic, as well as their previous experience of the patenting process, of patent searching and of appropriate indexing schemes. The user has a choice of searching in assisted or unassisted mode, and in the former case the system itself transparently chooses the database, logs on and performs the search, and prints results.

7 Prospects for the future

Several aspects of the online search process would seem to lend themselves to an expert systems approach and this has spawned a considerable amount of valuable research and development in the field during the 1980s. Whilst much encouraging work has been, and still is being, achieved in the design and development of expert intermediary systems, particularly prototypes, a watershed has been reached. Early enthusiasm has been tempered by a better understanding of the issues that must be addressed if expert systems are to continue to contribute to the development of better interfaces to online retrieval systems.

Not least amongst these, the aim and purpose of an intermediary system must be clear. There is still widespread confusion over whether the expert interface should be designed for end users, for existing intermediaries, or for both. Paice (1986) makes the point that in other domains – medical diagnosis for example – expert systems act as decision support tools for the expert, not the layman. Interfaces will not be successful unless they address this question clearly.

One of the major contributions of expert systems research has been in helping to describe in detail the tasks involved in online information retrieval, and the knowledge required to support them. In order, however, to develop a sound model of the search process, a still better understanding of the decision-making processes that go to make a successful online search is needed. To what extent do variations in searcher style and behaviour significantly affect the outcome of a search? Can there be a successful way of pooling expertise and reaching a consensus – and is a consensus really necessary?

Some commentators doubt the suitability of information retrieval as a domain for expert systems research. Brooks (1987) points out that the knowledge domain is too extensive and wide-ranging, with little agreement amongst experts about how to tackle a particular search problem. Certainly the prospects are remote for a universal expert system interface to a large number of hosts and databases, which is also suitable for use by a heterogenous user population. Expectations for such an interface are now recognized as being over-ambitious, but this should not lead to disillusionment. Where objectives have been more modest, systems with considerable promise have been developed. The need for better – more user-friendly and more intelligent – interfaces to online retrieval systems is in no doubt, and their design and development will continue apace for some time to come. Expert systems are not the only technique that will contribute to this effort, but in the design laboratory at least, they have shown that they can make an important contribution.

To date, the majority of expert systems projects have led to the development of research prototypes, or to local systems for particular organizations. Very few have subsequently appeared in the wider public domain, and then with little commercial success. The reasons for this are not hard to find. Vast strides in improving the usability of online systems have been made by conventional front ends, which may be built far more cheaply than expert systems which use large knowledge bases and sophisticated inference engines. The more impressive expert systems projects have been limited and focused in their objectives, with well specified and constrained functionality. Such systems have still to prove their commercial viability. Perhaps, with investment and backing from the information industry itself, they yet might.

References

Alberico, R. and Micco, M. (1990) *Expert systems for reference and information retrieval.* London: Meckler Corporation

Anon (1989) Single search language. *Information World Review*, **43**, 14

Anon (1990) User-friendly front-end software for online searchers. *Library Micromation News*, **23**, 12-14

Aragon-Ramirez, V. and Paice, C.D. (1985) Design of a system for the online elucidation of natural language search statements. In *Advances in intelligent retrieval: Informatics 8*, pp. 163-190. London: Aslib

Ardis, S.B. (1990) Online patent searching: guided by an expert system. *Online*, **14**, (2), 56-61

Balas, J. (1989) Through the gateway with EasyNet. *Computers in Libraries*, **9**, (10), pp. 22-24, 26

Barthes, C., Frontin, J. and Glize, P. (1987) EURISKO: an artificial intelligence tool for automatic online retrieval. In *Online Information 87: Proceedings of the 11th International Online Information Meeting* (London, 1987), pp. 431-442. Oxford: Learned Information Ltd

Barthes, C. and Glize, P. (1988) A case study of planning in information retrieval. *Expert Systems for Information Management*, **1**, (1), 50-65

Bates, M.J. (1979a) Information search tactics. *Journal of the American Society for Information Science*, **30**, (4), 205-214

Bates, M.J. (1979b) Idea tactics. *Journal of the American Society for Information Science*, **30**, (5), 280-289

Bates, M.J. (1987) How to use information search tactics online. *Online*, **11**, (3), 47-54

Belkin, N.J., Seeger, T. and Wersig, G. (1983) Distributed expert problem treatment as a model for information systems analysis and design. *Journal of Information Science*, **5**, (5), 153-167

Belkin, N.J. and Vickery, A. (1985) *Interaction in information systems: a review of research from document retrieval to knowledge-based systems.* Library and Information Research Report 35. Boston Spa: British Library

Berg Hansen, I.B. and Rottboll Andersen, T.R.R. (1988) IANI – intelligent access to Nordic information. In *Online Information 88: Proceedings of the 12th International Online Information Meeting* (London, 1988), pp. 705-713. Oxford: Learned Information Ltd

Borgman, C.L. (1989) All users of information systems are not created equal; an exploration into individual differences. *Information Processing and Management*, **25**, (3), 237-251

Brajnik, G., Guida, G. and Tasso, C. (1987) User modeling in intelligent information retrieval. *Information Processing and Management*, **23**, (4), 305-320

Brooks, H.M. (1987) Expert systems and intelligent information retrieval. *Information Processing and Management*, **23**, (4), 367-382

Brooks, H.M., Daniels, P.J. and Belkin, N.J. (1985) Problem descriptions and user models: developing an intelligent interface for document retrieval systems. In *Advances in intelligent retrieval: Informatics 8*, pp. 191-214. London: Aslib

Brooks, H.M., Daniels, P.J. and Belkin, N.J. (1986) Research on information interaction and intelligent information provision mechanisms. *Journal of Information Science*, **12**, (1/2), 37-44

Bruandet, M.F. (1989) Outline of a knowledge-base model for an intelligent information retrieval system. *Information Processing and Management*, **25**, (1), 89-115

Burton, H.D. (1989) The Livermore intelligent gateway: an integrated information processing environment. *Information Processing and Management*, **25**, (5), 509-514

Chiaramella, Y. and Defude, B. (1987) A prototype of an intelligent system for information retrieval: IOTA. *Information Processing and Management*, **23**, (4), 285-303

Croft, W.B. and Thompson, R.H. (1987) I^3R: a new approach to the design of document retrieval systems. *Journal of the American Society for Information Science*, **38**, (6), 389-404

Detemple, W. (1989) Future enhancements for full-text databases. *Online Review*, **13**, (2), 155-160

Doszkocs, T.E. (1983) From research to application: the CITE natural language information retrieval system. In *Research and development in information retrieval*, ed. G. Salton and H.J. Schneider, pp. 38-50. New York: Springer Verlag

Efthimiadis, E.N. (1989) *Online searching aids: a subject bibliography on front ends, gateways...* British Library Information Guide 11. Boston Spa: British Library Board

Fidel, R. (1985) Moves in online searching. *Online Review*, **9**, (1), 61-74

Fidel, R. (1986) Towards expert systems for the selection of search keys. *Journal of the American Society for Information Science*, **37**, (1), 37-44

Fidel, R. (1987) Controlled vocabulary and free textsearching: searchers' selection of search keys. In *ASIS '87: Proceedings of the 50th ASIS Annual Meeting* (Boston, 1987), **24**, pp. 71-73. Medford, NJ: Learned Information

Fox, E.A. (1987) Developement of the CODER system: a testbed for artificial intelligence methods in information retrieval. *Information Processing and Management*, **23**, (4), 341-366

Fox, E.A. and France, R.K. (1987) Architecture of an expert system for composite document analysis, representation and retrieval. *International Journal of Approximate Reasoning*, **1**, (2), 151-175

Gauch, S. and Smith, J.B. (1989) An expert system for searching full-text. *Information Processing and Management*, **25**, (3), 253-263

Guida, G. and Tasso, C. (1983) An expert intermediary system for interactive document retrieval. *Automatica*, **19**, (6), 759-766

Harter, S.P. and Rogers Peters, A. (1985) Heuristics for online information retrieval: a typology and preliminary listing. *Online Review*, **9**, (5), 407-424

Hartley, R.J. *et al.* (1990) *Online searching: principles and practice.* Sevenoaks: Bowker-Saur

Hawkins, D.T. (1988) Applications of artificial intelligence and expert systems for online searching. *Online*, **12**, (1), 29-43

Hawkins, D.T. and Wagers, R. (1982) Online bibliographic search strategy development. *Online*, **6**, (3), 12-19

Haynes, D. (1989) Tome-Searcher: intelligent interface for searching and retrieving information. *Computers and Libraries*, **2**, (1), 2-3

Houghton, T., Rich, C. and Bass, A. (1987) Front-end software to on-line database searching: IDEA (Intelligent Database Enquiry Assistant) Presented at a Conference on Knowledge Based Systems, 1987 and available from the authors, BT Development and Procurement, BT Laboratories, Martlesham Heath, Ipswich, Suffolk, IP5 7RE, UK.

Lambert, C. (1989) DIALOG Business Connection: the end-user solution? In *Online Information 89: Proceedings of the 13th International Online Information Meeting* (London, 1989), pp. 161-168. Oxford: Learned Information Ltd

Lirov, Y. and Lirov, V. (1990) Online search + logic programming = subject bibliography: an expert systems approach to bibliographic processing. *Online Review*, **14**, (1), 3-12

McMath, C.F., Tamaru, R.S. and Rada, R. (1989) A graphical thesaurus-based information retrieval system. *International Journal of Man–Machine Studies*, **31**, (2), 121-147

Marcus, R.S. (1985) Development and testing of expert systems for retrieval assistance. In *Proceedings of the 48th ASIS Annual Meeting* (Las Vegas, 1985), **22**, pp. 289-292. New York: Knowledge Industry Publications

Marcus, R.S. (1986) Design questions in the development of expert systems for retrieval assistance. In *Proceedings of the 49th ASIS Annual Meeting* (Chicago, 1986), **23**, pp. 185-189. Medford, NJ: Learned Information

Marcus, R.S. and Reintjes, J.F. (1981) A translating computer interface for end-user operation of heterogeneous retrieval systems. Part I: design. Part II: evaluations. *Journal of the American Society for Information Science*, **32**, (4), 287-317

Meadow, C.T., (1988) OAKDEC, a program for studying the effects on users of a procedural expert system for database searching. *Information Processing and Management*, **24**, (4), 449-457

Meadow, C.T. *et al.* (1989) Online access to knowledge: systems design. *Journal of the American Society for Information Science*, **40**, (2), 86-98

Meadow, C.T. and Cochrane, P. (1981) *Basics of online searching.* New York: Wiley

Monarch, I. and Carbonell, J. (1987) CoalSORT: a knowledge-based interface. *IEEE Expert*, Spring 1987, 39-53

Morris, A., Tseng, G.M. and Newham, G. (1988) The selection of online databases and hosts: an expert systems approach. In *Online Information 88: Proceedings of the 12th International Online Information Meeting* (London, 1989), pp. 139-148. Oxford: Learned Information Ltd

Morris, A., Tseng, G.M. and Newham, G. (1989) MOSS: a prototype expert system for modifying online search strategies. In *Online Information 89: Proceedings of the 13th International Online Information Meeting* (London, 1989), pp. 415-434. Oxford: Learned Information Ltd

Newham G.H.W. (1987) *An expert system for online business database selection.* MSc dissertation, Loughborough University of Technology, UK

Paice, C. (1986) Expert system for information retrieval? *Aslib Proceeding*, **38**, (10), 343-353

Pejtersen, A.M. (1987) Design of intelligent retrieval systems for libraries based on models of users' search strategies. *Proceedings of the 1986 IEEE International Conference on Systems, Man and Cybernetics* (Atlanta, Georgia, 1986), **2**, pp. 1082-1087. New York: IEEE

Pollitt, A.S. (1987) CANSEARCH: an expert systems approach to document retrieval. *Information Processing and Management*, **23**, (2), 119-138

Pollitt, A.S. (1988a) A common query interface using MenUSE – a menu-based user search engine. In *Online Information 88: Proceedings of the 12th International Online Information Meeting* (London, 1988), pp. 445-458. Oxford: Learned Information Ltd

Pollitt, A.S. (1989b) MenUSE for medicine: end-user browsing and searching of MEDLINE via the MeSH thesaurus. *International Forum on Information and Documentation*, **13**, (4), 11-17

Pugh, H. (1989) *An expert system for selecting online marketing databases.* MSc dissertation, Loughborough University of Technology, UK

Rau, L.F. (1987) Knowledge organization and access in a conceptual information system. *Information Processing and Management*, **23**, (4), 269-283

Reiter, M. (1989) Improving online information retrieval with an intelligent front-end system. In *Online Information 89: Proceedings of the 13th International Online Information Meeting* (London, 1989), pp. 597-604. Oxford: Learned Information

Rich, E. (1983) Users are individuals: individualizing user models *International Journal of Man–Machine Studies*, **18**, 199-214

Sormunen, E. and Alkula, R. (1988) A prototype for a knowledge-based intermediary system. In *Online Information 88: Proceedings of the 12th International Online International Meeting* (London, 1988), pp. 291-300. Oxford: Learned Information Ltd

Thiel, U. and Hammwoehner, R. (1987) Graphical interaction with a full-text oriented information system: the retrieval component of the end-user interface TOPOGRAPHIC. In *Application of Micro-Computers in Information Documentation and Libraries. Proceedings of the Second International Conference* (Baden Baden, 1986), eds. K.D. Lehmann and H. Strohl-Goebel, pp. 343-444. Amsterdam: North Holland

Trautman, R. and von Flittner, S. (1989) An expert system for microcomputers to aid selection of online databases. *Reference Librarian*, **23**, 207-238

Vickery, A. (1988) The experience of building expert search systems. In *Online Information 88: Proceedings of the 12th International Online Information Meeting* (London, 1988), pp. 301-314. Oxford: Learned Information Ltd

Vickery, A. and Brooks, H.M. (1987) PLEXUS – the expert system for referral. *Information Processing and Management*, **23**, (2), 99-117

Vickery, A. *et al.* (1987) A reference and referral system using expert system techniques. *Journal of Documentation*, **43**, (1), 1-23

Walton, K.P. (1988) *An expert system feasibility study of online business search strategies.* MSc dissertation, Loughborough University of Technology, UK

Williams, M. (1986) Transparent information systems through gateways, front ends, intermediaries and interfaces. *Journal of the American Society for Information Science*, **37**, (4), 204-214

Chapter 7

The future of expert systems and artificial intelligence technologies in libraries and information centres

Ralph Alberico

1 Knowledge media

This chapter will attempt to predict the impact of expert systems and artificial intelligence on libraries over the next ten years. Five areas will be considered: knowledge media, knowledge industries, knowledge institutions, modes of discourse and implications. The predictions here are conservative, with a basis of already existing technology. That having been said, it is necessary to point out that in the next few years there will almost certainly be unforeseen technological advances which will represent fundamental departures from current technology. Consequently, by the year 2000 things that have not even been thought of in 1990 will probably be a familiar part of the technological landscape. For example, we may already be seeing the beginning of a paradigm shift in artificial intelligence research towards a renewed emphasis on connectionist approaches. It is also conceivable that we will have biologically engineered computers by the year 2000 (Drexler, 1987). Any predictions based on today's technology should therefore be taken with a grain of salt. It is quite likely that the next generation will bear little resemblance to current technology.

One of the most prescient forecasts of what libraries would be like by the year 2000 was published 25 years ago. Of all the predictions which have been published, *Libraries of the future* (Licklider, 1965) is the most on target and directly relevant to artificial intelligence. *Libraries of the future* represents an ambitious attempt to pose technological solutions to the problems of libraries. Project Intrex, an early experimental attempt by the Massachusetts Institute of Technology (MIT) to develop an electronic library, incorporated many of the ideas expressed in *Libraries of the future*. Many of the concepts underlying the project and the book had their origin in the then fledgling field of artificial intelligence, which was just taking wing at MIT. Among the participants in the project were several pioneers in artificial intelligence, including such notables as John McCarthy, Richard Bolt, Daniel Bobrow and Marvin Minsky.

Libraries of the future is essentially a book about knowledge representation, natural language processing and interactive computing. It is one of the first books on applied artificial intelligence. In it Licklider proposed a new schema to replace that of the physical library, a schema which would not centre on physical books but on knowledge itself. Licklider called this new schema a 'procognitive system', meaning 'for knowledge'.

The procognitive systems described by Licklider were not designed to focus on physical documents but on the 'facts, concepts, principles and ideas that lie beyond the visible and tangible aspects of documents'. Like the artificial intelligence programs of today, procognitive systems are not concerned with data but with knowledge. The key criterion for determining whether a work of the mind should be incorporated in the system was whether it contained 'transformable information'. In other words, could the text or image on the page of the physical book somehow be transformed to knowledge which could be used with a computer?

> 'The criterion question for the delimitation was: "Can it be rephrased without significant loss?" Thus we delimited the scope to include only "transformable information". Works of art are clearly beyond that scope, for they suffer even from reproduction. Works of literature are beyond it also, though not as far. Within the scope lie secondary parts of art and literature, most of history, medicine, and law, and almost all of science, technology, and the records of business and government.' (Licklider, 1965)

Licklider did not have the advantage of being able to extrapolate from the current hardware and software base, and Project Intrex could not be easily implemented with the technology of its day. Nevertheless, his is still a provocative account of a possible future in which knowledge media supplement information media and knowledge systems replace information systems. Especially important is the idea of transformation. The ability to transform information is as important to today's expert systems as it was to the procognitive systems discussed in *Libraries of the future*.

Nowadays it is easier to see how expert systems might emerge as a new knowledge medium, serving functions not served by existing print and electronic media. Initially, expert systems will focus on recording esoteric knowledge which is now shared among small groups of human experts and which has not previously been recorded in any format. The future of expert systems in libraries will follow the evolution of expert systems as knowledge media. Expert systems, which are now clever, occasionally useful computer programs, will eventually assume an important role as a format for recording the working knowledge of human experts. Information media vary in suitability for carrying different types of messages, and expert systems are no exception. One of the major uses of expert systems will be to reconcile the differences among other information media, but the following two basic problems are likely to remain:

1. Knowledge is growing exponentially. The classic 'information explosion' is being compounded by the introduction of new computer-based media, and the merging of existing media. Not only will there be much more recorded knowledge, there will be new formats and forums for storing and communicating knowledge.

2. Knowledge is heterogeneous. There is no such thing as a uniform structure for representing knowledge. Knowledge is not data. It is fuzzy, abstract, and bound up with language, and consequently any thesauri, classification schemes, record structures or formalisms for representing knowledge are limited.

Before turning to expert systems, let us briefly examine the evolution of other information and knowledge media. Media will be examined in terms of representational power, ease of distribution, and level of interactivity.

1.1 Representation, distribution and interaction

The story begins with the use of symbols to represent things. Among the first representation formalisms were pictograms – images which bore a one-to-one correspondence with things in the physical world. Pictograms are not the best way to represent the realm of human discourse, since there are many concepts which cannot easily be expressed in pictorial form. There are parlour games which are similar to charades but which require the person providing the clues to draw pictures instead of miming, and anyone who has played those games knows how difficult it is to represent certain ideas as pictures.

After pictograms came ideograms – images used to represent ideas, not just things. Like today's computer icons, ideograms are efficient, making it possible to represent complex concepts as single condensed images. On the negative side, like icons, ideograms are easily subject to misinterpretation.

One of the most fundamental advances in the human ability to use symbols came around 2000–1000 BC, when the alphabet is thought to have originated. After its introduction the alphabet was spread by Phoenician merchants throughout the ancient world (Johnson, 1973). Instead of images, or ideas, symbols were linked to sounds. The key to representing spoken language had been found, so that any idea which could be expressed with the spoken word became transformable to the written word. Symbols achieved a new representational power.

Printing, the next big leap, was important not because of its representational power but because of its potential for distribution. The printed book is a mass medium: the book extended the representational power of writing to the populace. Printing made ideas portable. More recently we have seen electronic media, which in many ways can be distributed more efficiently than printed works.

Of the big three electronic media – telephony, television, and radio – telephony seems to have had the greatest impact on our working lives. With few exceptions, radio and television are not found in the workplace – they are still considered entertainment. The telephone, on the other hand, has become ubiquitous. Why? Maybe it is because the telephone is one of the most interactive of electronic media.

Lately we have seen computers used as interactive media. Initially computers were viewed as giant calculators, but they are now seen in more dynamic terms. The benefit of using an online computer system comes from the dialogue with the machine. The telephone provides the ability to transform the sound of a distant voice to the sound of a speaker held at one's ear. An interactive computer provides an even greater ability to transform and manipulate information. Eventually it will be possible to carry on a dialogue with a formal representation of another person's experience in some narrow area.

Media which were once separate in our minds are now all part of a confusing hybrid. Images, sounds, written words, pictures, and television can all be carried on the same information network. Representation methods, distribution mechanisms and interactivity are becoming more closely bound together. Expert systems provide the potential to represent and distribute knowledge in an interactive medium, and also to help us navigate other forms of knowledge media. Let us now turn to expert systems as knowledge media and consider the implications for libraries.

1.2 Expert systems as knowledge media

Stefik (1986) considers the expert system not only as a vehicle for solving problems but as a medium for preserving and communicating human knowledge. Expert systems are capable of both storing and applying knowledge, and coupled with network communications capabilities and display technologies, they will form the core of a medium for collaborative problem solving. Collins and colleagues view the interactivity of expert systems as essential to their role as media for knowledge transfer. The 'tacit knowledge' required to make sense of the knowledge encoded in an expert system is supplied by the user of the system as he or she interacts with it (Collins, Green and Draper, 1985).

Early artificial intelligence research focused on reasoning capabilities, but efforts to simulate human reasoning with a machine met with only limited success. Eventually attention shifted towards the representation of large amounts of specific knowledge. Artificial intelligence researchers found that greater success could be achieved by concentrating on specific knowledge from narrow domains rather than on general approaches to problem solving. While it was not possible to duplicate human reasoning ability, it was possible to transform human decision making in specialized fields of endeavour to computerized knowledge bases.

So far, the strength of artificial intelligence research has been its representational power, not its reasoning capability. The impact of this technology on libraries will be in two areas:

1. The integration of knowledge-based systems with existing information technologies.
2. The steady introduction of new formats for storing and communicating knowledge.

Let us now compare expert systems with traditional books. The act of reading a book is a one-sided affair. Meaning is supplied by the reader – the book merely stores information. Searching an online database is a little different, but the underlying process is essentially the same: meaning is supplied by the searcher. Only that which is specifically requested is provided; the online system has no way of identifying relevant material which is available but which does not meet the requirements of the searcher's Boolean query. Unlike a book, which is essentially a passive medium, an expert system is a dynamic medium. Meaning is determined by the nature of the interaction between an expert system's knowledge base and a person. A knowledge base will be more unpredictable than a database; much of the knowledge is fuzzy or uncertain, and the knowledge base will often reflect that uncertainty. Building a query to a typical online database is like using the index in a book. Using a knowledge base is more like a conversation which can change its direction as participants interact with one another.

Expert systems are said to have a modality. Among the commonly identified modalities of expert systems are diagnosis, planning, design, monitoring, and tutoring. For example, the MYCIN system is a diagnostic system in the field of infectious disease, while the related GUIDON system is designed to function in a tutorial modality (Clancey, 1987). Intelligent tutoring systems are highly interactive, with the goal of building an image of a learner's state of knowledge, identifying gaps in his knowledge of a domain, and developing strategies to 'teach' the student. Library expert systems will function in a number of modalities – diagnosing information needs, planning search strategies, and classifying materials are a few examples. However, the majority of expert systems implemented by libraries will almost certainly function in a primarily tutorial modality, teaching researchers about information sources and how they are used.

1.3 Knowledge engineering

Steady progress is being made in increasing the representational power of computers, but we have not yet seen anything which approaches the representational breakthrough of the alphabet. Nor have we seen a breakthrough in our ability to distribute knowledge bases that is analogous to the breakthrough printing gave us in our ability to distribute the written word. And it is still a difficult task to get human experts to express what it is they know. Knowledge engineering, the process of building expert systems, has a long way to go.

Two of the main components of knowledge engineering are knowledge acquisition and knowledge representation (see Chapter 1). Before expert systems can be successfully implemented on a large scale, major problems of knowledge engineering must be overcome in each area. The vast majority of the existing corpus of knowledge has never been recorded. Most of the world's knowledge base is locked up in the heads of men and women. There is a great difference between the idealized knowledge demanded by the system of formal publication, and the things that go on in people's heads as they solve problems.

1.4 Knowledge acquisition

Knowledge acquisition is widely acknowledged to be the great bottleneck of expert system development. One of the major obstacles to knowledge acquisition is the tendency of human experts to compile knowledge, i.e. to compress all the steps required to solve a complex problem into a single mental construct. It is difficult to decompose the knowledge of human experts, breaking down an approach to problem solving into the separate steps required by the computer. Another problem is the problem of articulation. People find it difficult to say how it is that they know even the simplest things. Finally, there is the logistical problem. Knowledge acquisition is typically a labour-intensive process, requiring many hours of contact between domain experts and knowledge engineers.

The future will bring more experimentation with machine-assisted knowledge acquisition. Michie (1986) proposes a knowledge refinery whose purpose is to streamline the process of knowledge engineering. According to Michie, expert systems can be used:

- 'to get knowledge into the machine
- to test it
- to debug it
- to fill gaps
- to extend it
- to modify it

and finally,

> to put the knowledge back into human hands in an improved form'.

The primary method recommended by Michie is machine induction, a process by which rules are derived from examples. Efficient algorithms have been developed for generating rules from sets of examples, analogies, and cases supplied by human experts. An induction system, if given examples of sufficient number and quality, could learn how experts solve problems.

Another approach to automated knowledge acquisition is to use the computer to engage the domain expert in a dialogue in which rules are suggested, evaluated and modified if necessary. The famous MYCIN system had a complementary knowledge acquisition system called TIERESIAS, which allowed the diagnosticians using MYCIN to examine and modify the system's knowledge about diagnosing diseases and recommending courses of therapy (Buchanan and Shortliffe, 1984). The future will bring an increased emphasis on both techniques, with hybrid knowledge engineering systems which will collect examples by means of a dialogue, and induce rules from them.

The repertory grid technique for analysing the constructs and belief systems of human experts also holds promise as an automated knowledge acquisition tool (Shaw and Gaines 1987; Boose, 1985). We are also likely to see more graphically oriented knowledge acquisition systems which help human experts draw knowledge maps of their domains. Hypermedia knowledge acquisition systems will allow humans to build knowledge bases by building connections between different pieces of the literature.

An even more intriguing possibility is to derive knowledge directly from electronic and printed texts. In the medical field especially there have been a number of attempts to derive knowledge from published texts and available databases. Among the more notable examples is the Hepatitis Knowledge Base (Bernstein, Siegel and Goldstein, 1980) which was derived from review articles on hepatitis diseases and developed cooperatively by a panel of human experts. The current labour-intensive method of fitting the knowledge carried by documents into largely hierarchical knowledge structures will increasingly be supplemented by machine acquisition of textual knowledge.

Researchers are working on programs which extract meaning from text, and a number of linguistic and statistical techniques have been developed. The knowledge-acquisition bottleneck may be partially overcome by automated transformation of databases into knowledge bases. The first large-scale efforts to transform source texts into expert systems have involved technical and procedures manuals, and eventually the effort will extend to most of the categories of works identified by Licklider.

One possible scenario for automating the knowledge acquisition process centres on the following technological advances:

1. Fast, accurate, inexpensive OCR (Optical Character Recognition) to convert source texts to machine-readable form.

2. Hybrid natural language processing/expert systems which use domain knowledge bases and linguistic approaches to extract meaning from documents; such systems will use contextual knowledge to determine the meaning of texts.

3. A method for correlating and structuring the knowledge in order to understand the relationships between different parts of a text and between different texts.

4. Methods for making inferences from knowledge drawn from multiple sources and consensus-building techniques.

5. User interfaces which allow human experts to review, evaluate and certify the knowledge bases generated from text.

1.5 Knowledge representation

Knowledge representation also has its problems, but there are solutions on the horizon. First let us look at the problems. One is the 'brittleness' of knowledge used by most expert systems. Expert systems, unlike human beings, have difficulty, in realizing when they are approaching the boundaries of their knowledge. They are only competent in narrow domains. As it nears its limits, the typical expert system does not degrade gracefully. The knowledge in the system is represented in simple terms and an expert system cannot draw upon the rich world knowledge upon which a human can draw. Expert system knowledge bases are usually built of surface knowledge, not deep knowledge.

Knowledge representation formalisms tend to be inflexible, and much knowledge cannot be represented as rules, frames, or logical predicates – the three most commonly used techniques. None of them alone is adequate for representing all the different ways in which people solve problems. Commonsense knowledge has proved to be an especially intractable problem. It is also difficult to maintain dynamic representations, that is, to keep track of a changing state of knowledge. With large knowledge bases, resolving conflicts between different pieces of knowledge is necessary to avoid what is known as a combinatorial explosion.

One solution to the difficulties of representing deep knowledge is model-based reasoning, which relies upon deep causal models rather than simple rules-of-thumb. Hybrid representation schemes are also starting to be seen. Different types of knowledge lend themselves to different types of representation formalisms, and the next generation of ES development software will permit the easy interweaving of different schemata. Hybrid systems will use rules to represent certain types of procedural knowledge, and frames, semantic networks and logical predicates to represent declarative knowledge.

Progress is also being made in the ability to reconcile conflicts over which piece of knowledge to draw upon to solve a problem. Domain-specific knowledge will remain important, but there will be growing interest in meta-knowledge, which will be required in large systems to determine which chunks of an expert system knowledge base should be activated as the solution to a problem develops.

Blackboard systems are a way of reducing the brittleness of expert systems by allowing knowledge bases to communicate with one another, using a common mechanism known as a blackboard. The HEARSAY speech understanding system (Erman, Hayes-Roth and Reddy, 1980) was the first to use the blackboard architecture. The blackboard is an area of working memory used to represent the emerging image of a problem as it is being solved. Separate expert system modules contribute to the solution and use the blackboard to share information. As conflicts are resolved between separate modules, partial solutions are erased from the blackboard and new possibilities are written in. At any point in time the blackboard can contain the strategic plan for solving a problem, pertinent facts, and an agenda of specific tactics. Each expert system module is able to contribute to the solution by drawing upon its own knowledge and relating it to the state of the problem represented on the blackboard.

Distributed artificial intelligence will become increasingly important. Object-oriented programming has emerged as a new paradigm. Knowledge structures called objects share messages with one another, and the data and instructions for transforming objects are bound up together. When an object is defined, it is told how to respond to different types of messages and how to exchange messages with other objects. In the future this technique will be expanded to represent many different types of knowledge. Higher levels of abstraction will be possible for representing the information objects handled in libraries.

1.6 Connectionism

Some of the earliest efforts to develop artificial intelligence focused on representing knowledge by modelling human neural activity. This neural approach quickly gave way to efforts to model the cognitive process. After a long dormant period, there has recently been renewed interest in the neural approach, which is also known as connectionism (Waltz and Feldman, 1988). Connectionism is based on the human nervous system, in which each neuron can receive a number of simultaneous inputs, the combined intensity of which determines whether that neuron will 'fire', passing impulses to neighbouring neurons in an interconnected network. Connectionism is concerned with patterns of activation rather than formal models; as it is computationally demanding and does not work well with traditional computer architectures, it was abandoned in favour of the formal representation schemes which are widely used today.

Neural networks aim to mimic the physiological activity of the brain, with the firing of the network determined by the pattern and intensity of the inputs to its nodes. Neural networks, like brains, operate on several parallel levels simultaneously. It is the pattern of activation among individual processors which is significant. Neural networks are unlikely to be accepted for advice giving, tutoring and consultation because of their opacity.

Parallel approaches and neural networks will be increasingly applied to machine learning. Networks will analyse the activation of processors triggered as an information system is presented with retrieval problems, and will be able to reorganize themselves for better performance. As information systems become sensitive to the needs of users, relevance feedback will assume new importance. Neural networks will be able to recognize pertinent materials by comparing them with ingrained patterns derived from items which are known to be of interest.

We shall also see neural networks used in converting printed documents to machine-readable files by recognizing type fonts. When someone has worked out how to apply neural networks to bibliometrics, these networks may end up being most useful for problems of indexing, classification and cataloguing. Words extracted from documents will be compared with one another, and documents illustrating similar patterns of content words will be automatically classed together. Much research will focus on determining which parts of a document are most useful for expressing its meaning. Later will come an emphasis on deriving meaning from multiple sources.

One of the reasons for the renewed emphasis on connectionist approaches is the growing potential of parallel processing. Traditional computers solve problems one step at a time, with each subproblem handled in sequence by a single processor. Parallel computers incorporate multiple processors working in concert with one another to solve separate subproblems simultaneously. Problems are solved in parallel, non-sequentially. Parallel processing has great potential for information retrieval tasks, particularly where large unstructured databases are involved. In parallel information retrieval systems, each processor is responsible for keeping track of its own set of documents. A parallel system is able to search different sets of documents simultaneously, greatly reducing the processing time required for complex queries. There are already a number of experiments under way in this area, and parallel processing is likely to assume even greater importance in the future (Stanfill and Kahle, 1986). Parallel processing is also more efficient than sequential processing, reducing downtime by redirecting workflow to the processors most prepared to handle the task being addressed.

The concept of sharing problem solving tasks among multiple processors does not have to be limited to the processors in a single computer. Other experiments have demonstrated the potential for distributing tasks among interconnected, but physically remote, computers. Operating systems of the future will be designed to accommodate high levels of interaction among different types of computers. Databases and knowledge bases will be made available in distributed environments and shared by different machines.

One strong possibility for the future is the distributed online expert system. Distributed expert systems will support collaborative problem solving using similar methods to those employed by blackboard systems. Cooperating minicomputers have already been used to solve problems which supercomputers have been unable to solve, demonstrating that there are advantages to a distributed approach.

Edited books and journals contain collections of knowledge derived from multiple sources. Nevertheless, once those formats are published those multiple sources of knowledge become part of a single physical entity. The compilation of separate knowledge sources is handled not by the reader, but by the editor and publisher. Distributed knowledge bases, on the other hand, will make it easier to compile knowledge bases derived from multiple sources. In the future we will see more community knowledge bases derived from, and maintained by, communities of knowledge sources.

There will also be interacting knowledge bases, with expert systems able to communicate with one another and to exchange knowledge to solve problems. Each expert system on a knowledge network will draw upon its own store of data and knowledge to add to the common pool of knowledge. Each node in the knowledge network will have access to the knowledge spread across the entire network.

Knowledge systems are already serving as front ends, assisting people who must interact with large databases. In the future we will see knowledge systems which can use information from databases as a basis for decision making. Expert systems will also be able to use databases for updating, modifying and maintaining knowledge bases. Using formal representation methods, we will teach knowledge bases about the contents of databases. Using connectionism, knowledge bases will learn by obtaining data from external sources. Intelligent agents will solve problems collectively by forming societies and communicating with one another (Minsky 1986).

Connectionism offers real advantages over more formal approaches, but has disadvantages as well. Among the advantages of connectionist systems are that:

1. Knowledge can be derived from the real world; connectionist systems can learn from experience.

2. Connectionist systems are more robust; they are more likely to degrade gracefully as they approach their limits.

3. Connectionist systems are less labour-intensive; the tedious intellectual work of acquiring and encoding knowledge is handled by the machine as it learns from experience or examples.

4. Connectionism implemented on parallel computers is more efficient because the separate steps required to solve problems can be handled in tandem.

Connectionist systems also have disadvantages:

1. Connectionist systems are opaque; the decision-making process cannot be decomposed, the multiple inputs leading to a decision cannot be measured and analysed. Only the sum of inputs is available; trace and explanation facilities are not possible.

2. Unlike heuristic programs which are based on logic, connectionist programs are based on pattern matching. It is

not possible to examine the assertions leading to a particular course of action. Formal proofs are not possible.

The advantages of connectionism offset the disadvantages of logic-based systems and vice versa. Future systems will employ a combination of the knowledge-based approach used by traditional expert systems and the brute force approach of connectionist systems. Expert systems of the future will combine the ability to take advantage of greater processing power offered by parallel computers with formalized knowledge about problem domains.

2 Knowledge industries

Though artificial intelligence has a history of over 30 years, a marketplace for knowledge media is just beginning to emerge. There will soon be a critical mass of high performance hardware and network delivery capabilities which will, for the first time, make it feasible to distribute knowledge bases to those requiring access to symbolically encoded knowledge. Database growth will foster knowledge base growth; the two formats will feed on one another. In fact, knowledge bases will be needed to effectively search the growing percentage of large, unstructured databases. In libraries, knowledge-based approaches to assisting researchers will become the norm.

Market analysts agree that artificial intelligence is the fastest growing segment of the computer industry. A study by the US Congressional Office of Technology Assessment (Information Technology R&D, 1985) cites market forecasts which predict that research and development, which in 1983 accounted for 50% of activity, will shrink to 5% by 1993 and that artificial intelligence sales will rise from $66 million to $8.5 billion per year during the same period. Investment in artificial intelligence technology will increase significantly, while at the same time moving from the R&D sector to the commercial sector.

The downward migration of artificial intelligence has already begun. LISP machines or expensive workstations are no longer required to mount memory-hungry artificial intelligence applications. Activity is beginning to shift from R&D laboratories to the commercial sector, and from an emphasis on hardware to software and services.

Major initiatives like the Japanese Fifth Generation Project, the British Alvey Programme, the European ESPRIT project, and the proposed US High Performance Computing initiative will bear commercial fruit in the 1990s. Standards for knowledge representation will arise from these major government efforts. The Japanese have already settled on the language PROLOG as their development vehicle.

Shell software is designed to facilitate the development of expert systems by providing a framework upon which to build. While there are few commercially available expert systems, there is already a substantial market for shell software – an indication of widespread experimentation. Before we see widely available knowledge bases, we shall see knowledge-based front ends to existing databases. A number of promising research projects are already under way; Smith (1987) and Fox (1987) review the current state of the art.

Knowledge engineers are gearing up for the production of commercial knowledge bases, but most work is still in the experimental phase. It is uncertain whether current database publishers will become knowledge base publishers. Most likely the knowledge base industry will evolve in a similar way to the database industry, with government agencies, national libraries, professional societies, research universities, and existing commercial vendors all being important players. Knowledge-base development by libraries may begin with special libraries, which will collect and codify knowledge within their areas of specialization.

Two issues will arise when commercial systems become widely available:

1. The establishment of standards for knowledge representation. It will be necessary to determine the best ways to represent different kinds of knowledge in different kinds of domains in such a way that knowledge bases can be shared. There will be pressure for standards of knowledge representation.

2. Distribution of knowledge bases. Closely related to the issue of standards is the issue of how knowledge bases should be distributed. Some knowledge bases will be distributed along with databases on optical media. We might see core journal collections on CD-ROM accompanied by knowledge navigation software which incorporates domain and subject knowledge. Other knowledge bases will be distributed separately, but will require constant maintenance and open connections to sources of electronic data. This is already happening in medicine, one of the most active areas of research on knowledge-based front ends. The Medline system of the US National Library of Medicine is likely to be the first online database to require a knowledge-based front end. Like databases, knowledge bases will be distributed over high-capacity networks, in addition to being mounted on individual workstations.

Knowledge acquisition and representation are complex, time-consuming, labour-intensive activities, involving both a knowledge engineer and domain experts. Good knowledge bases will be expensive. Knowledge-base distributors, knowledge engineers, and domain experts will each play a role in the knowledge-base industry. Charging for knowledge-base services will become an issue and the fee structure is liable to be confusing. In cases where a knowledge base was derived from multiple source texts, it will be exceedingly difficult to determine who deserves credit and royalties, and also to validate such knowledge.

2.1 Development tools and environments

At present, expert system shells provide knowledge structures, inference mechanisms and user interfaces for expert systems (see Chapter 1). Expanding markets for advisory systems will spur development of more sophisticated shell software. Expert systems development will move into the realm of the domain expert as shells reduce the development time needed to create an expert system, and once standards have been developed, shells will become the norm for development projects. Shells will come with skeletal knowledge bases, so that eventually it will be difficult to differentiate between a knowledge base and a shell. We may expect shells for information retrieval systems to come with built-in domain knowledge derived from thesauri and standard reference sources in the domain.

Emphasis on development environments will make system modularity important. Expert systems must be designed to accommodate new knowledge easily, and the ability to port knowledge and inference procedures from one system to another will be crucial. The future expert system market will allow people to piece knowledge-based systems together from separate components, much as it is now possible to build a stereo or personal computer system from separate components. More flexible hybrid representation schemes will be possible; there are already a number of development environments and shells which combine rules and frames. Shells will also reflect the object-oriented programming paradigm, and support graphical user interfaces and high levels of connectivity.

The recently introduced X-Window display systems will provide an ideal hardware medium for next-generation shells. It will be possible to look at different types of information being delivered over sprawling networks to multiple windows on the screen. Imagine being able to use one corner of the screen for an interactive video conference with colleagues spread about the globe. In another corner of the screen is a retrieval system which allows conference participants to browse through large collections of information, using vocal commands if desired, to display items of interest. It will also be possible to call up videos that participants want one another to see. It will not matter where information is coming from: if the shell is aware of its existence, and it is available on the network, just about anything can be summoned to the screen.

Shells and networks will some day speed the assimilation of artificial intelligence technology by placing it in the hands of everyday people, but this has not happened yet. Commercial artificial intelligence technology is not a consumer market, and expert systems are not commodity items. Knowledge engineering is still required for large projects and large projects, beyond the ken of any single person, are still the bailiwick of institutions. Existing institutions, primarily government and the universities, have served as the proving ground for artificial intelligence. As we have seen, the library as an institution has had a long affiliation with artificial intelligence. The next section will examine the impact of artificial intelligence and expert systems on the library as a knowledge institution.

3 Knowledge institutions

We shall see the library flourish not as a building, but as a concept. Designing libraries which 'know' their own contents has been a major concern of artificial intelligence research since the beginning, and remains of interest (Feigenbaum, 1989). Much of the current impetus for the adoption of artificial intelligence technologies has come from government agencies and national libraries which have been heavily involved in the following areas:

- development of prototype systems
- development of knowledge representation schemes
- experimentation with knowledge-based indexing, abstracting, and classification
- experimentation with specialized development environments for specific domains of knowledge

Medical information is the focus of the largest concerted effort, and breakthroughs are likely to come first in medical informatics. In the US the National Library of Medicine has been the major impetus for research and development. Other national libraries in the US, including the National Agricultural Library, have begun to experiment with expert system development. As knowledge-based systems become more acceptable in the library community, libraries will begin to purchase and maintain interactive knowledge bases for their clients.

Government projects will push forward the frontiers of artificial intelligence research in libraries, but government projects will not serve as the vehicle by which artificial intelligence is introduced to individual libraries. Initially, artificial intelligence will be introduced to individual libraries in the form of small advisory systems.

Small PC-based systems will proliferate widely, in most cases preceding commercially available systems.

The availability of easy-to-use, inexpensive (albeit limited) shell software will lead to a great deal of experimentation with small systems. Many libraries are already experimenting with so-called 'toy' projects. As librarians become more familiar with artificial intelligence by experimenting with small-scale projects, their level of sophistication will increase. High-end microcomputers and powerful shells will also help to encourage experimentation by libraries.

Artificial intelligence will come bundled with OPACs, online services and communications networks. It is the commercial knowledge base industry, rather than local development efforts, which is likely to benefit most from government research and development initiatives. Before examining the commercialization of artificial intelligence technology in libraries, let us look at the future of home-grown artificial intelligence in libraries.

Library-developed expert systems will address problems in a number of areas. Most will focus on narrow domains with an emphasis on local concerns. Information and referral systems will be among the first expert systems to be developed by libraries. Clients will use such systems to find out about community events and services, with systems offering advice on topics such as nutrition, gardening, home health care, and looking for a job. Directory information will be accessible from many routes. There will be interactive calendars and locally useful ready-reference knowledge bases.

Tutorial systems will also be the focal point of development activity. User education will be the objective of many small systems. The idea is to help clients use resources within narrow domains by recommending specific sources, and providing instruction within the context of specific clients' specific information problems. Tutorial systems will make it possible to deliver instruction when it is needed and where it is needed. Expert systems will assume an important role in library instruction and clearing houses will allow libraries to share tutorial systems with one another. Tutorial systems may one day replace library workbooks and other forms of in-house documentation for user assistance.

Many libraries will develop intelligent pathfinders, designed to meet needs not addressed by more global information systems. It will become cheaper to distribute the kind of information contained in library user aids electronically than it will be to distribute it in printed form. Advisory systems will also be easier to modify and revise than traditional printed user aids. Electronic pathfinders will be updated frequently as experts on library staffs refine them to focus on narrow subject domains or particular formats such as manuscript collections or maps.

The next generation of user guides will:

- incorporate knowledge of clients' needs
- make possible increased exploitation of local resources
- help automate access to the functions and services of printed reference sources
- capture knowledge of local collections and services held by long-term employees (many of whom will be retiring)
- provide guides to the literature of specialized disciplines
- integrate different types of reference tools and provide direct 'hooks' to sources of electronic data
- allow researchers to filter out unwanted information

In cataloguing, individual libraries will encode small subsets of the AACR2 cataloguing rules while also attempting to capture the knowledge of experts for use by less experienced employees. Once again the emphasis will be on narrow subject areas and on cataloguing specialized formats such as computer databases, musical scores, and maps. Expert systems linked to subject heading lists and classification schedules will assist cataloguers in decision making. Expert systems are also ideally suited to handle tricky problems of authority control with accuracy and consistency.

3.1 Commercial artificial intelligence in libraries

The first wave of commercial knowledge bases will be electronic reference works and CD-ROM databases accompanied by knowledge-based search software. Vendors of online databases will also offer navigation capabilities based on knowledge of the structure and contents of databases. Online database vendors will have a more difficult time than CD-ROM vendors in adapting their search software to knowledge-based approaches. CD-ROM vendors will have the advantage of being able to design knowledge structures based on new paradigms, instead of having to work with existing data structures which were developed for search software with a qualitatively different approach. CD-ROM vendors will also be able to bind data more easily with the programs for manipulating them.

Eventually database producers will also get into the act by restructuring the data they sell to accommodate new generations of search software. Front ends will incorporate new methods in addition to the traditional Boolean search approach. There will be more front ends which rely upon semantic knowledge to help researchers formulate queries. Emphasis will shift from building Boolean queries to approaching the search on a conceptual level. Searchers will work with concepts rather than terms. The current, generation of experimental knowledge-based front ends (Brajnik, Guida and Tasso, 1986; Marcus, 1983; Pollitt, 1987; Croft and Thompson, 1987; Smith *et al.*, 1989) will evolve into commercial systems supported by database producers and online vendors. Tome Searcher and IANI are examples of this trend in the European online market.

Vendors of integrated library systems will begin to incorporate artificial intelligence technology in their products. Processing in integrated library systems will become more distributed. Intelligent workstations will take over many of the tasks now handled by minicomputers, and intelligent networks will take over tasks now accomplished with mainframes. Both OPACs and bibliographic utilities will require powerful workstations as terminals, with software at the terminal end of the connection employing locally developed user profiles and search heuristics to provide intelligent assistance.

Online vendors and utilities will also provide more open architectures, allowing greater levels of customization, making it possible for libraries to modify integrated library systems and develop their own knowledge-based front ends. Emphasis will be on improved user interfaces; there will be many intelligent browsing systems to take advantage of powerful workstation terminals with windowing and high-resolution graphics capabilities. Existing classification, vocabulary control and indexing schemes will be adapted for use with expert systems.

The thing we now call an OPAC (Online Public Access Catalogue) will become a server on a knowledge, information and communications network. The OPAC server will be able to maintain dynamic images of its users, analysing their interaction with the various knowledge and databases available from the net. Each workstation will configure itself to meet the needs of the people it serves. OPACs will analyse user inputs and suggest alternative subject terms. Users will be able to select their own display formats. Intelligent browsers will present researchers with options suggested by an image of their research needs. Systems will be able to diagnose problems, recognizing inefficient search strategies and seeking to remedy them. Advice and instruction will be offered when it seems they are needed. Queries can be built cooperatively, taking advantage of the server's knowledge of database structures and thesauri. There is already a sound experimental basis in the areas of user profiling, error diagnostics, and knowledge-based query construction.

Information utilities and cooperative networks such as OCLC (Online Computer Library Center) are actively supporting artificial intelligence research on a number of fronts. Cooperative networks are liable to play a major role in the assimilation of artificial intelligence technology in libraries. For example, by requiring powerful workstations as terminals, networks are forcing many libraries to acquire hardware platforms on which expert systems can be mounted.

One of the more ambitious efforts now under way is Project Mercury, a cooperative venture between a bibliographic utility (OCLC), a university (Carnegie Mellon University), a hardware manufacturer (Digital Equipment Corporation) and a professional society (the American Association for Artificial Intelligence) (Evans *et al.*, 1989). One of the goals of Project Mercury is to develop an intelligent interface which will help researchers search local library and computer resources, and which will, when necessary, establish connections to external electronic resources. Researchers need not be concerned with the physical location of information because information in the system is stored logically rather than physically. The intelligent interface will assist researchers at the conceptual level, focusing on search refinement rather than on retrieval of documents.

Another area in which networks, bibliographic utilities and national libraries are expected to play a major role is in the development of interfaces between knowledge-based systems and existing information systems. There is already a substantial information infrastructure in place and it would not make much sense to abandon totally all of the work which has already been done. Developing methods to integrate new technologies with old will therefore become a major concern.

Current classification schemes and vocabularies such as MeSH, LCSH, and UDC will serve as part of the infrastructure for connecting databases to knowledge bases. New schemes will also emerge. Let us hope that new schemes will include built-in links to existing schemes and standards.

The vast majority of the existing store of graphic records is still available only as print on paper. In some fields (science and technology for example) it will be desirable to convert existing records to machine-readable form and to fit the information they contain into knowledge structures such as logical predicates. In other areas, it will neither be desirable nor economically feasible, and in those fields it will make more sense to apply expert systems to the problems of identifying and retrieving existing information formats.

Stonebraker and Hearst (1988) consider the methods for integrating expert system and database technologies. The dominant approach so far has been loose coupling. Loose coupling involves using an expert system shell to establish links between a rule base and a database. Tight coupling, on the other hand, involves building rules directly into the database management system. Systems designed to take advantage of existing databases and data structures such as the MARC record will most likely employ loose coupling. New generations of databases will be able to incorporate knowledge of database contents from the beginning, employing tight coupling and resulting in improved performance and greater efficiency. In the future knowledge-based search, assistance will be built into databases when they are designed.

Eventually there will be dialled-access expert systems which can communicate with one another to help researchers locate information. Online databases will be supplemented by online knowledge bases, the output of which will vary tremendously, depending upon the interaction with the inquirer. Some systems will be able to answer specific questions within specific areas of expertise; others will be display-oriented with the ability to display different pieces of a knowledge base in response to a researcher's line of inquiry.

3.2 Library investment in AI technology

There will be a shakeout period during which the acquisition and maintenance of knowledge bases, and access to them, will compete with traditional media for library funds, while knowledge producers, consumers, distributors and institutions will seek to accommodate one another. There will be many attempts to assess the social, scientific and economic value of knowledge-based systems. The early market for interactive knowledge bases is likely to be quite confusing as pricing schemes are established.

To be able to offer knowledge bases to their clients, libraries will have to purchase workstations with the memory and display capabilities required by artificial intelligence software. Services to support knowledge base use must also be developed, and library budgets will have to accommodate the expense of providing access to knowledge bases. Some institutions may well have to clarify their role in knowledge base development and maintenance projects. Project Mercury provides evidence that the foundation for large-scale cooperative projects is already being laid.

OCR and other forms of digital recording will make possible the transformation of some collections into more interactive formats, and many libraries will apply artificial intelligence technology to existing collections while offering value-added services. Measuring and paying for these services will become important issues. Even those libraries which do not produce knowledge bases will play a role in the knowledge base industry as major consumers. One role that the library as an institution can play is as a switching centre and node on the knowledge networks of the future. Another role will be to serve as an education centre, developing tools and tutorial systems to assist clients in using the network.

Libraries will continue to maintain local resources and some libraries will become major knowledge-base producers. Librarians will assume the responsibility for helping clients develop interfaces and profiles. Libraries will also assume much of the responsibility for tracking royalties and transferring funds to information providers. Services such as high-resolution printing and large-scale downloading are most likely to be handled at the institutional level rather than by individuals.

3.3 A scenario

One scenario for the future involves the library serving both its own clientele and as a node on a knowledge network, each institution maintaining its own unique collection of data and knowledge bases but each also providing access to collections and services available through interconnected networks. Local knowledge bases will be designed to help clients exploit locally available core resources, and also to facilitate network access and to help clients develop profiles, filters and personalized navigators. The modes of interaction offered by the system will be defined by its knowledge of the subject areas it covers.

Let us take the field of physics as an example. Why not begin with the INSPEC database which has over 50 searchable fields, many of which will accept numeric values for things like stellar mass, computer speed or electrical resistivity? We can expect vendors of such richly representative databases to develop knowledge-based front ends which take advantage of how information is used within the domain. We can also expect to see development tools for customization within specific domains such as materials science or particle physics. Such tools will take advantage of knowledge of both the conceptual structure of the domain and how the literature of the domain is organized. Development tools will help capture, organize and index knowledge from subfields of the primary domain.

A physicist carrying out research on the physical properties of some new material need not be concerned with whether information is coming from a periodicals database, a patent database or a numeric database of spectral data. The system will supply information based on its understanding of the problem at hand; the original format of the information supplied will be of only secondary interest.

There will be tools which can transform data which are available on the system. Citation analysis takes advantage of the system of intellectual provenance by which information is produced to identify relationships between documents. Other forms of analysis will take advantage of the values present in the database. Researchers will be able to draw associations between values in different parts of the database and between information stored in different databases. Someone might want to use the INSPEC database, for example, to correlate computer speed and electrical resistivity, since each concept is represented by numerical values in the database.

Future researchers will be able to ask questions of the form, 'Is there evidence of a relationship between X and Y, in the literature?', where X and Y are values monitored by available databases. In the future researchers should also be able to ask questions of the form, 'Can I use the data in X database to generate a three-dimensional, holographic simulation of Y process?', where X and Y are collections of data and processes the system knows about.

A physics knowledge base would include the following components:

1. Bibliographic databases, with front ends for specific subdisciplines and databases.
2. Development environments for different subdisciplines; for example, a materials science shell would differ from a shell built around astronomy.
3. A journal refereeing system capable of routeing submissions to those most qualified to review them, and incorporating consensus-building routines by which knowledge could be validated.
4. A citation network connecting all of the cited and citing papers in the system and including facilities for bibliometric analysis.
5. Large full-text databases corresponding to journal articles, books, and reports on research in progress.
6. Large image databases including such things as electron microscope photographs, images from space probes and satellites, magnetic resonance images, spectrographs, holographs, and star atlases.
7. High-speed telecommunications for exchange of scientific correspondence and delivery of the many types of information available on the system.
8. Handbooks for subdisciplines such as astronomy, earth science, particle physics and fluid dynamics, with each handbook encoded so as to be able to answer natural language questions by using the knowledge it contains.
9. Large numeric databases with analytic and simulation software capable of analysing and transforming large collections of data, such as the star catalogues which are available to astronomers or the data on more than 250 000 sources of infrared radiation detected by the IRAS survey.
10. Knowledge bases derived from segments of the literature,

such as review articles on bosons, or studies involving the use of Langmuir probes, or physical properties of superconductors.

11. Access to signal data in real time, for example, radiotelescope data or data from satellites and space probes.
12. Community access to data from experiments in progress, along with software to analyse the literature and suggest possible reviewers; researchers would use the system to define the communities who would have access to experimental data.
13. Access to specialized software, computer hardware and instrumentation on the network.

Knowledge networks will be built of bodies of knowledge centring on a single area of inquiry. Hierarchically organized, richly interconnected stores of specialized knowledge will provide working scientists with access to information drawn from diverse sources. One of the most difficult problems confronting the builders of knowledge networks will be ensuring security and privacy to network participants while also fostering open communication. Knowledge networks which do not allow a great deal of individual control by users are not likely to be well received.

4 Modes of discourse

The impact of expert systems and artificial intelligence technology on knowledge media, knowledge industries and knowledge institutions has been examined. Now let us turn to the user interface. Artificial intelligence technologies could have a dramatic impact on the ways in which people interact with recorded knowledge. Perhaps the most difficult thing to predict is the nature of the new modes of discourse which will arise. How does one interact with a knowledge network? Knowledge engineers will not only have to collect and encode knowledge, they will have to develop modes of discourse for communicating knowledge.

There are only two basic concerns involved with developing a mode of discourse between people and machines:

1. How does the person talk to the machine?
2. How does the machine talk to the person?

In a knowledge-based system, the way in which knowledge is presented will eventually become as important as the knowledge itself. And where multiple knowledge sources are involved, there will be a major emphasis on a seamless transition from one knowledge source to another. This will not be easy. It will take some time to determine which modes of discourse are possible. Networks will have to be designed with an idea of the kinds of questions people are likely to ask. Another concern is how to determine which services and data are available and to whom.

Part of the discourse with intelligent advisory programs will be determined by the nature of hardware, just as speech is determined by the structure of the larynx. Processing capabilities will increase markedly in the next decade, with 16 megabytes of RAM being the norm for desktop workstations. There will be increasing parallelism and optical computing, with transphasors beginning to replace transistors. Increased processing capability will enable more overheads to be dedicated to maintaining the user interface. Speech processing, which requires intensive computation, will become a real possibility.

As largely optical, digital storage capacities increase, the objects which used to be called 'documents' will be viewed less and less as physical objects, and more and more as intellectual artefacts. We already have pocket translators, which upon receiving a chip programmed with a language provide a simple, literal translation. In the future, database search modules will be embedded on chips, each chip providing vocabulary control and database navigation capabilities. There will be interchangeable onboard search assistants for different databases. Switching from Medline to INSPEC will one day be as easy as plugging in a new search module. Each module will contain the entire set of documentation and the entire vocabulary for its own database, and it will be possible to program each module with constraints and individual researchers' preferred ways of doing things.

We can expect display capabilities approaching those of the printed page, including motion as well. As display technology improves, much of the resistance to using interactive knowledge bases will disappear. The ability to transmit high-quality graphic images will also improve, enabling the desktop workstation to be used for high-fidelity video communication, which will in turn foster collaborative work groups.

In the future, large databases of all types will be bound up with knowledge about the concepts underlying the data, and networks will one day be the primary delivery media for knowledge bases. But databases will be so large that it will be impossible to 'see' an entire database at once. People will form models and images from the bits and pieces they see, and those images and models will form the basis for new modes of discourse. How will people interact with the network and with people at other nodes? And how will intelligent nodes interact with one another?

People communicate with language, both spoken and written. There has been research in both areas and it is likely to continue in both. There will also be attempts to invent visual languages for communicating with large stores of knowledge, following from earlier efforts using natural language approaches to understanding written documents.

The knowledge storage and retrieval systems of the future will undoubtedly combine expert system and natural language approaches. Expertise derived from humans will be most useful for identifying pertinent documents and helping people move through the documentary domain, but interpreting texts will require a natural language approach. Understanding the contents of documents will require deep linguistic knowledge.

Natural language processing has been applied to information-seeking problems at a number of levels. The earliest attempts took a syntactic approach, with the focus on building syntactically correct queries. More recent efforts have focused on semantics, concentrating on the meaning of a query and employing knowledge of thesauri in addition to knowledge about query languages. In the future attention will shift to pragmatics. An effort will be mounted to understand language as it is actually used – to derive meaning from context.

The expert system part of the interface will include knowledge derived from information specialists and domain experts. It will use meta-knowledge to determine the nature of the interaction. The natural language part of the interface will include a rich network of semantic, syntactic and pragmatic knowledge about the literature of the domain.

One factor influencing the machine's contribution to the dialogue will be its model of the user. One of the more influential applications of artificial intelligence to user modelling is the Grundy system developed by Elaine Rich (1979). Grundy engages its user in a dialogue, matches information obtained in the dialogue to stereotypes of different types of readers, and uses its model of the reader to recommend works of fiction. In the future there will be researchers' advisory systems which can be individualized to provide personal guides to domains of knowledge.

Adaptive interfaces place the user at the centre of things, adjusting the mode of interaction through an understanding of the problem and the user. Systems will anticipate the ways in which things can go wrong, and take corrective action. Take for example, EP-X (Smith *et al.*, 1989) a system for searching the environmental pollution documents indexed in *Chemical Abstracts*. EP-X presents its user with lists of available concept hierarchies based on knowledge of environmental pollution topics. It examines user behaviour, analysing patterns of inputs, and using its knowledge to infer goals and recommend strategies. EP-X displays all facets of the evolving search in separate windows, limiting what is presented to what makes sense in terms of the problem at hand. It seeks to reduce ambiguity by clarifying the meaning of terms which could be misinterpreted. Adaptive interfaces based on research such as that underlying the EP-X system will become the norm in the future. Systems will be responsive to the needs of researchers.

There will also be more question-answering systems. FRUMP (Schank and Abelson, 1977) was a natural language question-answering system based on a series of programs which were connected to the UPI wire service. FRUMP could answer questions based on the knowledge it received and the inferences it could draw from news stories available on the wire. Another famous program, LUNAR (Woods, 1977), used a database on lunar rocks to answer questions. LUNAR was able to answer questions relating to information which was not explicitly available in its database. The program was able to equate certain words with calculations it knew about, and could answer questions by performing those calculations on information which was available. Question-answering systems of the future will be able to transform the information raw material supplied by libraries to knowledge. It will be possible to infer new knowledge from existing knowledge and to use that new knowledge to answer questions.

Speech processing will become a more common way of issuing commands to computers. Large vocabularies with a range of 10 000 words, the ability to recognize the voice of more than one speaker, and the ability to recognize continuous speech in real time will all be available eventually. People will talk to machines. However, speech processing will be less useful for receiving information or advice from computers. Machines will talk to people, but only in limited task domains. The language used by computers to talk to people will be primarily a visual language, a language based on metaphor.

Expert systems, with their emphasis on explanation and trace facilities, have helped us to realize the importance of providing access to underlying structures and assumptions. Information systems of the future will be designed to allow easy viewing of information, especially those systems intended for work with large unstructured or partially structured databases. Systems which do not provide access to underlying structures and assumptions will not be readily accepted. The user will have complete control over what is displayed and how it is displayed. Multiple windows on the screen will display different views of a search in progress, pulling in pertinent information from wherever it is available. Future interfaces will suggest alternatives, clarify terms and display pieces of the thesaurus. An attempt will be made to discover each user's goals and to match those goals to chunks of recorded knowledge.

Hypermedia systems will flourish, and expert advisory systems will reap the benefits by allowing researchers to link pieces of knowledge together dynamically and by guiding users through knowledge trails and knowledge maps. Project HYPERCAT (Hjerppe, 1986) at Liköping University in Sweden represents an attempt to move away from the metaphor of the catalogue a – metaphor which has been retained by many electronic retrieval systems. The presentation of information about collections of recorded knowledge need not be limited by what can physically fit on a 3 x 5 card, nor should the presentation always follow a straight linear sequence.

Users of future information systems will be able to take advantage of hypertext guides which will lead them through the literature by identifying connections and relations. Free-from browsing will also be supported, and there will be mechanisms designed to encourage serendipitous discovery. Options which conform to a user image will be presented and searchers will select examples of the kinds of things they are interested in. Systems will maintain user images which can be activated for a specific search or maintained over time, changing as a researcher's interests change.

The word 'document' will assume new meaning as it becomes easier to build new knowledge artifices from parts of the available store. In those areas where information is transformable, large full-text files will serve as the source for new knowledge, with text, images, citations, simulations and videos all combined into what Edward Fox has called composite documents (Fox, 1987). Hardware standards such as DVI (Digital Video Interactive), and X-Windows will encourage the use of multimedia knowledge sources and graphic simulations.

There is a famous program called STEAMER which provides a good idea of where things are headed (Hollan, Hutchins and Weitzman, 1984). STEAMER is an intelligent tutoring system designed to train propulsion engineers for large navy ships. Training is carried out by presenting students with realistic simulated views of a shipboard propulsion plant in operation. Students can examine specific components of a ship's steam plant with different levels of detail. It is possible to view an abstract schematic or a detailed flow diagram of a specific subsystem.

It is also possible to see such things as the volume of liquid flowing through a pipe, and colour displays are used to represent different states that system components can assume. For example, if a pump is working it is displayed in green; if it is not working it is displayed in red. Students can also view instrument panels which would be available on a real steam plant, and control the operation of the simulated plant while viewing the results of their actions. Users of STEAMER learn about steam plants by operating in a virtual world which bears a close resemblance to the real world of a ship's propulsion system. Part of the expertise of a propulsion engineer is the ability to respond to the sound and feel of the propulsion plant, and one of the goals of STEAMER is to present students with a realistic simulation of this sound and feel.

Information systems of the future will increasingly use advanced display and simulation capabilities to present users with virtual realities. Fields and Negroponte (1977), Herot (1980) and Bolt (1985) describe spatial metaphors in information retrieval. Systems are being devised to allow people to locate information by 'flying through an information space'. A topic common to science fiction writers and futuristic interface designers, alike is the idea of sensory experience as interface (Gibson, 1984; Foley, 1987; Brand, 1987; Vinge, 1987). Already there is more use of colour, sound, motion, holographic imagery and simulations.

Instead of keyboards and monitors, people will use the head-mounted displays and 'datagloves' described by Foley (1987). Future input and output devices will make possible artificial realities. The views offered by future systems will change as the wearer of a display helmet moves her head. Actuators in datagloves will allow the simulation of touch, so that people will be able to 'feel' the objects in the scene presented in the display, and to manipulate them. Researchers will literally have the sense of 'moving from one area of inquiry to another'. It may one day be possible to simulate the experience of browsing through shelves, removing interesting books, and flipping through pages. Interacting with the store of recorded knowledge will become an increasingly sensory experience.

5 Implications

Information managers are going to be facing some tough questions soon. First will come the debate about allocation of resources, then about ownership of knowledge. Authors, publishers of knowledge-base source texts, knowledge engineers, domain experts and shell developers will all be able to claim credit in the production of a knowledge base. Reseachers themselves will become authors, as they use knowledge-based systems to compile new kinds of documents and to draw inferences from existing knowledge. Pool (1982) considers the impact of electronic information technologies the preservation of knowledge. What will become of the 'canonical work' in a dynamic information environment? The traditional roles of libraries as both preservers and communicators of knowledge may come into conflict with one another.

It is not too soon for libraries to think about capital investment in artificial intelligence technology and to study the implications of knowledge-base maintenance. Expert systems are unlikely to put librarians out of jobs, but they will change the nature of their work. Someone will have to maintain and evaluate the increasing number of large complex knowledge bases. Someone will also have to develop methods for integrating expert systems with the existing information infrastructure. The interviewing and classification skills of librarians will enable some to become knowledge engineers, a field for which qualified people will be in great demand.

Raj Reddy (Torrero, 1985) has said that in the future 'we will stockpile manufacturing capacity rather than finished goods'. Factories of the future will not stockpile things, they will store knowledge about how to make things. In a similar way libraries of the future will store access capacity the way we now store documents.

Instead of storing physical objects called books and journals, we will store rich networks of pointers to documents, and templates for delivering and displaying documents. Each 'document' yielded by the new system will be unique – the product of an inquiring human mind. Marvin Minsky has said (Feigenbaum, 1989) that books will 'talk to one another' in the library of the future. Arno Penzias (1989) describes a 'killer technology' as a technology which replaces an existing technology rather than supplementing it. Front-end knowledge-based navigation systems will almost certainly 'kill' traditional Boolean information retrieval systems, though Boolean capabilities will be retained by a new generation of heuristic browsing, fuzzy-match and knowledge-based systems. Boolean search will be useful in highly structured databases but not as useful for the large heterogeneous collections of information which will predominate in the future.

Nothing will kill the book as a concept, but new technology will create new types of books – new classes of intellectual artefacts, created with new methods of expression. Books will be created by integrating artificial intelligence and database technologies, and will also be generated from the transformation of information in knowledge bases. Research and scholarship will undergo fundamental changes as the human ability to record knowledge expands.

In conclusion, here are a few words of advice to librarians and information managers. Knowledge processing is here to stay and is worth knowing about. Continuing education is important. Make an effort to learn about artificial intelligence technologies: the best way to learn about something is by doing it. It is possible to use expert systems on a small scale, and inexpensive shells enable librarians to develop their own small systems, so that modest goals are appropriate. There is no need to try to clone a human being: that is not the idea behind any new medium.

Finally, cautious optimism is in order, but so also is healthy scepticism. It will take plenty of human knowledge to make informed decisions about expert systems.

References and recommended reading

Bernstein, L.M., Siegel, E.R. and Goldstein, C.M. (1980) The hepatitis knowledge base: a prototype information transfer system. *Annals of Internal Medicine*, **93**, (1), 165-222

Bolt, R.A. (1985) Conversing with computers. *Technology Review*, 35-43

Bond, A.H. and Gasser, L. (eds.) (1988) *Readings in distributed artificial intelligence*. San Mateo, CA: Morgan Kaufmann

Boose, J.H. (1985) A knowledge acquisition program for expert systems based on personal construct psychology. *International Journal of Man–Machine Studies*, **23**, 495-525

Branjnik, G. Guida, G., and Tasso, C. (1986) An expert interface for effective man–machine communication. In *Cooperative interfaces to information systems*, ed. L. Bolc and M. Jarke. pp. 259-308. New York: Springer-Verlag

Brand S. (1987) *The media lab: inventing the future at MIT*. New York: Viking

Buchanan, B.G. and Shortliffe, E.H. (1984) *Rule-based expert systems: the MYCIN experiments of the Stanford Heuristic Programming Project*. Reading, MA: Addison-Wesley

Carroll, J.M. and McKendree, J. (1987) Interface design issues for advice-giving expert systems. *Communications of the ACM*, **30**, (1), 14-31

Clancey, W.J. (1987) *Knowledge-based tutoring: the GUIDON program*. Cambridge, MA: MIT Press

Collins, H.M, Green, R.H. and Draper, R.C. (1985) Where's the expertise?: Expert systems as a medium of knowledge transfer. In *Expert Systems 85. Proceedings of the 5th Technical Conference of the British Computer Society*. pp. 323-334. Cambridge: Cambridge University Press

Conklin, J. (1987) Hypertext: an introduction and survey. *Computer*, (IEEE), **20**, (9), 17-41

Croft, W.B. and Thompson, R.H. (1987) I^3R: A new approach to the design of document retrieval systems. *Journal of the American Society for Information Science*, **38**, (6), 389-404

Drexler, E. (1987) *Engines of creation*. New York: Doubleday

Erman, L.D., Hayes-Roth, F. and Reddy, D.R. (1980) The HEARSAY II speech understanding system: integrating knowledge to resolve uncertainty. *Computing Surveys*, **12**, (2), 213-253

Evans, N.H. *et al.* (1989) *The vision of the electronic library: Project Mercury.* Mecury Technical Report Series, Number 1. Pittsburgh: Carnegie Mellon University

Feigenbaum, E.A. (1989). Toward the library of the future. *Long Range Planning*, **22**, 118-123. (i) p.122

Fields, C. and Negroponte, N. (1977) Using new clues to find data. In *Proceedings of the Third International Conference on Very Large Databases.* New York: IEEE, 156-158

Flores., F. *et al.* (1988) Computer systems and the design of organizational interaction. *ACM Transactions on Office Information Systems*, **6**, (2), 153-172

Foley, J.D. (1987) Interfaces for advanced computing. *Scientific American*, **257**, 127-135

Fox, E.A. (1987) Development of the CODER system: a testbed for artificial intelligence methods in information retrieval. *Information Processing and Management*, **23**, (4), 341-366

Frei, H.P. and Jauslin, J.F. (1984) Two-dimensional representation of information retrieval services. In *Representation and exchange of knowledge as a basis of information processes*, ed. H.J. Dietschmann, pp. 383-396. Elsevier: North-Holland

Frenkel, K.A. (1989) The next generation of interactive technologies. *Communications of the ACM*, **32**, (7), 872-881. [July 1989, special issue]

Gibson, W. (1984) *Neuromancer.* New York: Ace

Hayes-Roth, F., Waterman D.A. and Lenat, D.B. (1983) (eds.) *Building expert systems.* Reading, MA: Addison-Wesley

Herot, C.F. (1980) Spatial management of data. *ACM Transactions on Database Systems*, **5**, (4), 493-514

Hjerppe, R. (1986) Project HYPERCATalog: visions and preliminary conceptions of an extended and enhanced catalog. In *Intelligent information systems for the information society. IRFIS 6*, ed. B.C. Brookes, pp. 211-225. Elsevier: North-Holland

Hollan, J.D., Hutchins, E.L. and Weitzman, L. (1984) STEAMER: an intercative inspectable simulation-based training system. *AI Magazine*, **5**, (2), 15-27

Information Technology R&D: Critical Trends and Issues (1985) Washington, DC: US Congress. Office of Technology Assessment, OTA-CIT-268

Jacobson, C.E. and Witges, S.A. (eds.) (1986) *Proceedings of the Second Conference on Computer Interfaces and Intermediaries.* Alexandria, VA: Office of Information Systems and Technology, Defense Technical Information Centre. NTIS AD A174-000-0

Johnson, E.D. (1973) *Communication: an introduction to the history of writing, printing, books and libraries*, 4th edn. Metuchen, NJ: Scarecrow Press

Licklider, J.C.R. (1965). *Libraries of the future.* Cambridge, MA: MIT Press

Kinoshita, J. (1988). Neural networks at work. *Scientific American*, 134-135

McCarthy, J. (1984) Some expert systems need common sense. In *Computer culture: the scientific, intellectual, and social impact of the computer*, ed. H. Pagels, pp. 129-137. New York: New York Academy of Sciences

Marcus R.S. (1983) An experimental comparison of the effectiveness of computers and humans as search intermediaries. *Journal of the American Society for Information Science*, **34**, (6), 381-404

Michie, D. (1986) *On machine intelligence*, 2nd edn. p. 236. Chichester: Ellis Horwood

Minsky, M. (1986) *Society of mind.* New York: Simon and Schuster

Negroponte, N. (1975) *Soft architecture machines.* Cambridge, MA: MIT Press

Norman, D.A. and Draper, S.W. (eds.) (1986) *User-centered system design: new perspectives on human–computer interaction.* Hillsdale, NJ: Lawrence Erlbaum

OCLC Online Computer Library Centre. (1990) *Annual review of OCLC Research 1988-1989.* Dublin, Ohio: OCLC

Penzias, A.A. (1989) *Ideas and information: managing in a high-tech world.* New York: Norton

Pollitt, S. (1987) CANSEARCH: an expert systems approach to document retrieval. *Information Processing and Management*, **23**, (2), 119-138

Pool, I. de S. (1982) Culture of electronic print. *Daedalus*, **111**, 17-31

Quinlan, J.R. (1979) Discovering rules by induction from large collections of examples. In *Expert systems in the micro-electronic age*, ed. D. Michie, pp. 33-46. Edinburgh: Edinburgh University Press

Rada, R. and Martin, B.K. (1987) Augmenting thesauri for information systems. *ACM Transactions on Office Information Systems*, **5**(4), 378-392

Rennels, G. (1987) *Computational models of reasoning from the clinical literature.* Springer-Verlag Lecture Notes in Medical Informatics, no. 32. New York: Springer-Verlag

Rich, E. (1979) User modeling via stereotypes. *Cognitive Sciences*, **3**, 329-354

Ripley, G.D. (1989) DVI – a digital multimedia technology. *Communications of the ACM*, **32**, (7), 811-822

Schank, R.C. and Abelson, R.P. (1977) *Scripts, plans, goals and understanding: an inquiry into human knowledge structures.* Hillsdale, NJ: Lawerence Erlbaum

Sejnowski, T.J., Koch, C. and Churchland, P.S. (1988) Computational neuroscience. *Science*, **241**, 1299-1306

Shaw, M.L.G. and Gaines, B.R. (1987) An interactive knowledge-elicitation technique using personal construct technology. In *Knowledge acquisition for expert systems: an introductory framework*, ed. A.L. Kidd, pp. 109-136. New York: Plenum

Smith, L.C. (1987) Artificial intelligence and information retrieval. In *Annual review of information science and technology, 22*, ed. M.E. Williams, pp. 41-77. New York: American Society for Information Science/Elsevier

Smith, P.J. *et al.* (1989) Knowledge-based search tactics for an intelligent intermediary system. *ACM Transactions on Information Systems*, **7**, (3), 246-270

Stanfill, C. and Kahle, B. (1986) Parallel free-text search on the connection machine system. *Communications of the ACM*, **29**, (12), 1229-1239

Stefik, M. (1986) The next knowledge medium. *AI Magazine*, **7**, 34-46

Stefik, M. *et al.* (1987) WYSIWIS revised: early experiences with multiuser interfaces. *ACM Transactions on Office Information Systems*, **5**, (2), 147-167

Stonebraker, M. and Hearst, M. (1989) Future trends in expert database systems. In *Expert database systems. Proceedings from the Second international Conference*, ed. L. Kerschberg, pp. 3-20. Redwood City, CA: Benjamin Cummings

Torrero, E.A. (ed.) (1985) *Next generation computers.* New York: IEEE

Tou, F.N. *et al.* (1982) RABBIT: an intelligent database assistant. In *Proceedings of the American Association of Artificial Intelligence*, 1982, 314-318

Vinge, V. (1986) *Marooned in Realtime.* New York: Bluejay Books

Vinge, V. (1987) *True names and other dangers.* New York: Simon and Schuster

Waltz, D. and Feldman, J.A. (eds.) (1988) *Connectionist models and their implications: readings from cognitive science.* Norwood, NJ; Ablex

Wenger, E. (1987) *Artificial intelligence and tutoring systems: computational and cognitive approaches to the communication of knowledge.* Los Altos, CA: Morgan Kaufmann

Weyer, S.A. and Borning, A.H. (1985) A prototype electronic encyclopedia. *ACM Transactions on Office Information Systems*, **3**, (1), 63-88.

Winograd, T. and Flores, F. (1986) *Understanding computers and cognition: a new foundation for design*. Horwood, NJ: Ablex

Woods, W.A. (1977) Lunar rocks in natural English: explanations in a natural language question answering. In *Linguistic structures processing*, ed. A. Zampoli. Amsterdam: North Holland

Glossary of terms

Algorithm A step-by-step procedure that guarantees a correct outcome. Used in conventional programming.

Artificial Intelligence (AI) A computer-related discipline concerned with computer systems that can perform tasks and solve problems normally requiring human intelligence. Branches of AI include ESs, natural language processing, machine learning, robotics, translation and automatic computer programming.

Backward chaining A method of reasoning, in rule-based expert systems, in which solutions are found by trying to prove or disprove hypothesized conclusions.

Bidirectional search A method of searching which opportunistically combines forward and backward chaining.

Blackboard architecture An approach which offers the facility to record all intermediate results, decisions or strategies on to a central database, known as a blackboard. This architecture assists in the coordination and control of independent groups of rules or different ESs.

Breadth-first search A search strategy that examines all the rules or objects on the same level of the hierarchy before examining any of the rules or objects on the next lower level.

Certainty factor A number given by a user to indicate the certainty or confidence he or she has in a fact or relationship.

Confidence factor A number given by the expert system to express the level confidence in a conclusion.

Database The area in the expert system where the facts, advice and intermediate conclusions are stored. Often referred to as global database.

Deduction The reasoning process which leads from the general to the specific, using some system of logic.

Depth-first search A search strategy that proceeds down a single branch of the tree, examining one rule or object on each level of the hierarchy before moving to the next. If the search fails the next branch is examined.

Development environment A set of tools which may be used by developers programming in languages such as PROLOG and LISP. The tools will include debugging devices, developer interfaces and compilers.

Domain The application area under investigation.

Domain expert A person who is proficient at solving problems in a particular domain

Empirical knowledge Knowledge which is gained from experience.

End user The person who will use the expert system when it has been developed.

Expert system A sophisticated computer program that manipulates knowledge gleaned from experts to solve problems, draw conclusions and offer advice in a narrow field.

Expert-system shell An empty expert system into which a knowledge engineer can put codified knowledge and expertise.

Explanation The information offered to the end user to justify advice or a particular line of reasoning.

External interface The component of the expert system that links it to other programs such as databases, spreadsheets, data files etc.

Fact A statement that is universally accepted.

Forward chaining A method of reasoning, in rule-based expert systems, in which the data supplied activate rules which in turn work forward to activate other rules until sufficient matching for a solution can be found.

Frame A method of representing knowledge that associates objects or concepts with their attributes (called slots) and their values.

Global database The part of an expert system that provides a working memory for a particular consultation. It keeps track of the problem and the relevant previous history.

Heuristics The informal, little known 'rules-of-thumb' that experts acquire from experience of working in the application area.

Hierarchy An ordered network of concepts or objects in which some are subordinate to others.

Induction A method of reasoning by which a rule or general principle is inferred from a set of examples.

Inference The act of reaching a conclusion based on a set of logical rules.

Inference engine The part of the system that organizes and controls the steps taken to solve the problem.

Inheritance The ability of one object to inherit the characteristics of another. Inheritance is a feature of semantic networks.

Interface The component of the expert system which controls interaction between the system and the end user, developer or external programs.

Knowledge The facts and heuristics an expert system must have to behave intelligently.

Knowledge acquisition The process of extracting, structuring, refining and organizing knowledge and expertise from human experts and other sources, so that it can be used in a program.

Knowledge base The part of the system that contains the knowledge.

Knowledge-based system A program in which the domain knowledge is kept separate from the inference engine. The knowledge need not be obtained from an expert.

Knowledge engineer The person who designs and develops the expert system.

Knowledge engineering The discipline or process of building expert systems.

Knowledge representation The process of reorganizing, restructuring and formalizing the knowledge so that it can be represented as data structures in an expert system.

LISP One of the main AI programming languages used extensively in the USA.

Logic A formal method of describing knowledge using symbols.

Meta-knowledge Knowledge about knowledge.

Metarule A rule that describes how other rules should be used.

Natural language interfaces Interfaces that allow users to interact with the system using conventional language such as English. Only primitive natural language interfaces exist at present.

Object A physical entity, such as a house, or a conceptual entity, such as user-friendliness, which forms part of the knowledge base. Objects have attributes or characteristics which can have values.

Predicate calculus A knowledge representation technique that uses functions and predicates to describe relations between individual entities. A formal language of classical logic.

Problem solving A process which, given certain facts or conditions, involves investigating different strategies and alternative solutions before arriving at an answer.

Production rule A knowledge representation method that uses rules expressed as IF *condition* THEN *action*, or IF *condition* THEN *conclusion*.

Programming language A set of terms or symbols used according to very precise rules to write instructions, or programs, for computers.

PROLOG One of the main AI programming languages extensively used in Europe and Japan.

Protocol A record of an action, either physical or mental, made when accomplishing a task

Prototype A model constructed from the system specification.

Reasoning The process of making inferences or conclusions.

Representation The method by which knowledge is stored in the knowledge base.

Search The process of systematically examining and evaluating all alternative solutions to find the most acceptable.

Semantic nets or networks A knowledge representation method consisting of a network of nodes, standing for objects or concepts, and connecting arcs used to describe the relations between the nodes.

Shell See Expert-system shell.

Slot An attribute associated with an object, used in frames.

Symbol A string of characters or numbers that represent a real-world concept.

Transparency The ability of expert systems to offer explanations for the conclusions they reach or advice they offer, and to clarify, if necessary, why particular questions are being asked.

Uncertainty The term used in connection with incomplete data. Incomplete data can be supplied by both the user of the system and the original expert whose expertise and knowledge are encapsulated within the program.

User interface The part of an expert system that enables the user and system to communicate with one another.

Index